AF541784

TIMELINE
INDIA

TIMELINE INDIA

Rediscovery of the Chronology of a Ten Millennia Civilization

RAJNISH KARKI

RUPA

Published by
Rupa Publications India Pvt. Ltd 2025
7/16, Ansari Road, Daryaganj
New Delhi 110002

Sales centres:
Bengaluru Chennai
Hyderabad Jaipur Kathmandu
Kolkata Mumbai Prayagraj

P-ISBN: 978-93-6156-672-1
E-ISBN: 978-93-6156-192-4

First impression 2025

10 9 8 7 6 5 4 3 2 1

Printed in India

CONTENTS

PREFACE

The book in your hands is the culmination and fruition of a journey that began well over a decade ago. The anomalies of the dating of Chanakya's *Arthashastra* that I encountered during my research on the strategy of a nation-state set me forth on an enquiry. It couldn't have turned out to be more absorbing and meaningful—and bigger and wider in its expanse.

I soon found that the Indian chronology is anchored around Alexander's attack in 325 BCE and has not been updated for a century since 1920. The attack was of little consequence and its contemporaneity to Chandragupta Maurya was a flamboyant conjecture, unsubstantiated and spectacularly misplaced. A chronology is the string of events placed along an ordinal timeline, and if the anchor is inappropriate, the bulk of it becomes contentious and error-prone. This led to anything inconvenient being denied or ignored, and the hasty chopping, picking and choosing by the British, who outlined the Indian chronological construct and narrative thereupon, to suit their colonial intent and purposes.

For instance, hard archaeological evidence from Harappan sites dating back to the third millennium BCE and beyond was deemed exogenous to the Indian civilization. The colonial orientation continued, even after Independence, and the 1920 construct has stubbornly prevailed. On the other hand, Indian scholars, especially since the 1950s, have been able to align the Yuga system with the plethora of eras and calendars, and clean up the evidence from ancient texts for genealogical data and astronomical references. The latter, when deployed with the software available in the last couple of decades, yield precise and cross-verifiable dates. This burgeoning data from diverse sources, which is both hard and precise, needed to be incorporated.

My background in the natural and social sciences and my expertise in multidisciplinary research enabled me to bring to bear the full force and light of the scientific method on the construction of the Indian chronology. It is about the first instance of such research on the ancient period in any country of the world. The data after analysis and reconstruction resulted in definitive datings extending up to 7500 BCE and India having a civilizational continuity of ten millennia. It widened the enquiry about the origin and evolution of civilizations and their inter-relationships. All this has been put together to reach the general-interest reader too.

I have benefited from the work of a wide range of scholars from academia, from archaeology, astrophysics, Sanskrit and allied disciplines, in India and overseas. A few of them find mention as references in the text. This work continues and carries the legacy, going all the way to the eighteenth century.

Ranjan Joshi, a colleague and fine mind, has been with the idea of the book from its embryonic stages. I could rely on his sober and perspicacious advice at every step and turn. My wife, Manisha, and the now grown-up Ishaan and Trisha were a source of support, and often the first sparring partners for the exciting new things I seemed to find every day. Finally, Dibakar Ghosh and his team at Rupa have been focused, forceful and always reassuring.

1

INTRODUCTION

- Aren't we today a continuum and an outcome of the long march of time—billions of years of the universe and the earth, 350 million years of life on earth, the couple of hundred thousand years of the Homo sapiens and their quick takeover and domination of the earth, and then human civilization spanning a few thousand years?
- How do we understand the past? Isn't the right chronology of defining events along time the essential first step?
- Isn't looking back akin to looking ahead from the origin of civilizations?
- Who constructed the prevailing chronologies of India and other world civilizations, and when? Has it since been updated?
- Do we know much more and clearly, especially about India's deep past, to warrant a reconstruction?
- Shouldn't we employ the best of tools and methods now available to rediscover the chronology as a whole and its continuum?

Human being is the greatest accident of our universe. And civilization is its greatest outcome. Both would be almost inconceivable at any point in time during the billions of years in the past, as it would be anywhere else in the universe presently. Something like human civilization is inconceivable elsewhere, in the future too. It is our exceptional heritage. We need to have a good measure of civilizational evolution, to start with, through time and space on earth.

The questions above connect our exceptional human civilization and an understanding thereof to the major gaps and errors that currently exist. Much of these relate to the timelines of Indian civilization—when it originated, how it progressed and the way it is linked to other civilizations of the world, or the chronology of India's deep past. Errors in dating and formulating a sequence of events in the before the Common Era or the BCE period appear huge, considering what we now know clearly and have come to know, especially in the century gone by.

These have also made us aware of what we know that we don't know. This is an important step forward and with the range of research tools and methods now at hand, much of it will be known soon. It will open a new set of 'Knows' and 'Don't Knows', our knowledge base will expand and improve, and the gaps will shrink. Most of this new knowledge, however, will be of little use, unless we are able to organize the Indian chronology suitably with what we already know. And also, we need to define an enabling construct which facilitates the incorporation of new data as it emerges and the quest itself of acquiring new knowledge.

On the questions, the response is 'yes' to our being the product of billions of years of the march of time, and especially the arrival of human civilization a few thousand years before the Common Era. We understand the past by having a definitive chronology as the backbone of our understanding, and then cogently aligning all the relevant knowledge to give it a body and make it come alive. The chronology of India's deep past, apparently suffused with errors and gaps, forms a wobbly first step and impacts one's understanding. Yes, we should be able to go back all the way to the origin of human civilization in particular, and then come back to the present with aplomb and clarity for a robust understanding of our past.

The prevailing chronologies of civilizations in different parts of the world started being outlined by the Europeans in the nineteenth century. The British[1] put them together in the early decades of the twentieth century. This was particularly so for the chronology of India and their other colonies. They needed to get an understanding of various civilizations in order to set up the mechanisms and institutions for the governance of their worldwide empire, train the requisite manpower for its administration, and suitably reorient the colonized populace. The Indian chronology was laid out in two books by Vincent Smith[2] by 1920 CE, and these were taken as the authoritative and official history of India. The chronology has not been updated for a century, for India and for other civilizations as well. Some updates in the body of history have been made, but in the absence of the correct chronology, these changes have brought about more confusion and distortions.

The response to the last two questions is an unequivocal 'yes'. This is what we are endeavouring to do. The questions do lead us quickly to the objects and specifics of this book. Currently, the definitive chronology of India before the Common Era is based around an event.[3] Alexander's attack is the event under consideration, and it is dated back to 325 BCE, marking the end of a nearly two-year-old campaign here. The evidence from much older Harappan sites is not included as a part of Indian civilization and that from the Vedic corpus, for instance, is loosely defined over a millennia, *c.* 1500—500 BCE[4], but no specific events therein are dated. The first definitive date is the death of Buddha in 486 BCE, which was largely derived from the dynasties and genealogy of kings as well as the dynasties that ruled prior to Chandragupta Maurya, who was considered the contemporary of Alexander.

This is indeed a sparse and much-truncated base for the chronology of ancient India or the time before the Common Era. It is certainly inadequate to help build a robust and comprehensive understanding of Indian civilization and its deep past. Archaeologists often bemoan the paucity of hard evidence from India in comparison to other ancient civilizations, such as the Mesopotamian, Greek-Roman, Persian and Chinese civilizations.[5] They attribute it to the structures being largely wooden or temporary and that very few documents have since survived. But the paucity is more an illusion than it is real, as much of the evidence that exists has been ignored or has not been used suitably. They needed to dig and search harder, bring all that is available into consideration, devise appropriate tools and methods, and perhaps be open to possibilities of the extraordinary, the unexpected and the paradigm-shifting.

On the other hand, Indian civilization is one of the most fascinating in the history and evolution of the world. It stands out in its spread, richness and antiquity. It had more than its fair share of twists and turns, which leave a trail of unanswered questions—in what we seem to know or not, understand or not, and can put together or not. All this fuzziness accumulates and deposits into the present. Even the basics get contested and Indian civilizational history has become mired in controversies.

This is much more so for India than for any other country or region in the world. The infirmities of the unanswered extend into the public domain and descend into partisanship, prejudices and polemics. They have led to a conflicted, confused sense of Indian identity, from the individual to the national levels, and have also tended to form and accentuate fault lines, affecting the country's techno-economic progress and socio-cultural well-being. Nowhere are the gaps and differences more profound than in India's deep past or antiquity.

Many millennia have not been suitably accounted for and the dating of several defining events that have shaped India's distinctive civilizational ethos are still up in the air and not settled. This is where the practice of feeble and bad science in the inquiry and the methodology becomes evident. The discipline of history is a fine mix, in effect a conglomeration of the natural sciences—geology, biology and mathematics—and the social sciences' economics and anthropology, as well as several other applied disciplines. These make for an expanding and evolving base, from the centuries-old philology and archaeology to genetics and astronomy, which came into their own as ways of knowing the past due to advances in computing technologies in the last couple of decades.

These diverse disciplines are bound together by the scientific method, that is, the discipline, rigour and ethics of data validation and compilation, the analysis and findings, and the hypothesizing and theorizing. A multidisciplinary approach is essential for exploring the antiquity of India, as epigraphic or documented data becomes available only from around Ashoka's time. In order to explore beyond and into the deeper past, multidisciplinary scientific methods are needed, which is where we have been truly missing out in action.

As strange as it can be, this research into India's deep past has shied away from integrating knowledge across disciplines. The bulk of it has remained within the confines of individual disciplines. Each one holds hard and fast to its findings, but also tends to undermine and decry those of the others. Philologists led by William Jones and Max Müller were the first to plough into India's deep past by studying ancient texts, and they made the first set of theorizations in the late eighteenth and nineteenth centuries. But they have tended to ignore or underplay the archaeological findings available, especially from the early twentieth century. Thus, conclusions drawn by the two disciplines while exploring pre-history have remained unreconciled and have yet to be integrated for the further advancement of our knowledge of the past. The Harappa excavations, which date back to the third millennium BCE and beyond, were construed to be outside the purview of Indian civilization. And the philologists' initial theorizations on the languages of and the migrations into India, dated to 1500 BCE and later, continue to persist.

The philologists have tended to avoid refinements or corrections to their nineteenth-century theorizations through further research on the ancient texts themselves or by incorporating findings from other disciplines. Individual disciplines often resemble stand-alone camps, indulging in aggressive advocacy instead of informed and sober scholarship. This also extends to the newly emerged areas of astronomy and genetics-based studies, which are reluctant to recognize each other's findings while relying on similar computing technologies and advancements.

The practice of good science and a multidisciplinary method are essential to re-examine and discover Indian antiquity afresh. Though the need for a new approach can be traced to many decades and well up to the last century, for now there is urgency as well as opportunity. Debates on the basic facts and understanding of Indian antiquity are swirling around in the public domain and there is widespread confusion around the dating of pivotal events of our past, which need to be suitably addressed soon. Advances in data availability and validation, analytical tools and technologies, and multidisciplinary construct design, hypothesizing and theorizing, for example the application of replication and extension logic, make the endeavour for rediscovery an opportune one, too.

The multidisciplinary method builds upon the findings of various fields of scientific study. It is particularly appropriate here, as individual disciplines have tended to be stand-alone silos and often adversarial towards others. This methodology is not only equipped to consider and bring together all possible sources but also thrives in the richness and diversity across the natural, social and applied sciences. The findings of individual disciplines are the input for multidisciplinary research. The relevant data is carefully culled and then validated for internal consistency within a discipline. It is then cross-validated across disciplines. All the validated data is brought together to evolve a conceptual construct, which is elaborated into a few components or periods.

These individually cover a particular aspect, and together the whole phenomenon in a cohesive manner. The gaps and anomalies are hypothesized upon and tested through a deeper dive into the relevant data for repeatability and for the logical extension towards conclusions.

Such multidisciplinary work is an important step but will not be the end for something as fascinating as Indian antiquity. It will raise new questions for the individual disciplines, spurring further work and findings, and leading to new anomalies. The process of science and discovery will continue and keep advancing. The chronology of Indian antiquity or pre-history, which is the backbone of any definitive historical understanding and which is front and centre in all prevailing controversies and contradictions, is an obvious place to start and the launch pad for this rediscovery process.

A chronology is a string of mathematical facts that are unambiguous and consistent. It is also sequential and ordinal. Several historical events, conceivably over any length of time, can be reliably arranged along a sequence of time in a robust way. This provides clarity and solidity to what we know and what we don't, thereby directing further efforts suitably. The ordering of a chronology, in terms of scientifically calibrated years and smaller or larger units of time, aids in sharper testing and any corrections thereupon. On the other hand, there can only be confusion in the absence of a validated chronology, a situation that abounds currently, and therefore, this is a necessary first step forward.

The prevailing chronology of Indian antiquity comes across as muddled and truncated. In the 2021 edition of Romila Thapar's *Early India*,[6] which serves as the leading textbook in schools and colleges and a point of reference for research, the oldest (but not definitive) Indian dating to the level of a year is the ascension of Ajatashatru around 493 BCE. It is preceded by 1000 BCE as the point of 'availability of iron artefacts', which, however, is at least half a millennium later than the currently accepted archaeological data. This is preceded by just a line each, with no further break-up or details, on two exceedingly long periods: 500–1500 BCE for the 'composition and compilation of Vedic corpus' and 1700–2600 BCE for 'Harappan urbanization: Mature and Late Harappan'.

It lists another dozen dates or periods in half a page for the entire before the Common Era (BCE) period, with the next 1,300 years occupying a page and a half. Thapar's chronology is clearly incomplete and not updated. For instance, the Harappa periods have been redefined to include the 'Early Harappa' and 'Pre-Harappa' periods by archaeologists, subsequent to coming upon findings at sites such as Rakhigarhi, Kalibangan, Kot Dijian and Bhirrana since the 1950s. The 'mature' period is also revised to 3000 BCE and the timelines extend up to 7500 BCE for Pre-Harappa.

Thapar's chronology is no different, in effect, from that of Vincent Smith,[7] from well over a century ago. It truncated Indian history, fixing its origin at 600 BCE. His 1904 book and the 1915 one for school students became the standard and reference texts for history in India and elsewhere. These books are still considered authoritative. Most senior historians have done their learning, teaching and research around them, and then they went on to write their version of textbooks for students in post-independence India.

The archaeological discoveries at Harappa in the 1920s and the findings at other sites soon afterwards called for extending the timeline and reconciling the chronology. But it was not done, and the findings were treated as if they were external or exogenous to India and its history. It remains largely so till date, and thus appears as a stand-alone line, unconnected to any other event or system of dating in the chronology chart of India. Harappa and related sites now add up to an area that is larger than other ancient civilizations, the Mesopotamian, Egyptian and Chinese, taken together, and conceivably in terms of population too. Such a huge habitat located well within the Indian landmass will be intricately linked in its origin, progress and decline to the rest of Indian civilization. This lack of reconciliation and integration, including in the chronology, cannot simply be an act of laziness. This is indeed poor science, and in the lack of investigative efforts and scholarship, perhaps it is poor work ethics as well.

The handling of the 'Vedic' part is even clumsier. The study of Indian history through the modern, scientific method began with the translation and study of ancient texts in the mid-eighteenth century. Delineating the chronology, given the nature of the texts, was particularly challenging. There were calendars galore and they computed dates along a variety of eras or *Sakas*. But these were mostly based on sound astronomical principles and observations, and were accurate to the lunar-solar trajectories and that of several other constellations. Moreover, a category of texts, the Puranas, had compilations of the genealogies of rulers along the eras. These, especially the Vayu, Matsya, Vishnu and Bhavishya Puranas, had cross-verifiable data and became the primary resource for preparing the first-cut charts or drafts of Indian chronology.

There was feverish and extensive work all throughout the nineteenth century, and the chronology started taking shape in its second half. Alexander Cunningham, who travelled and lived in India for decades and founded the Archaeological Survey of India, wrote and circulated *Book of Indian Eras*[8] in 1859, which was finally published in 1883. Almost simultaneously, Max Müller, who studied and compiled various versions of ancient texts but never set foot in India, published *A History of Sanskrit Literature.*[9] Cunningham undertook an extensive exploration of the chronologies that had existed in India and their astronomical and mathematical bases, and validated 24 calendars and eras—with the most ancient being the Saptrishi era starting in 6777 BCE and the Kali era starting in 3102 BCE.

Max Müller reckoned the ancient Sanskrit literary corpus as rich and sophisticated, larger than the Greek and Latin ones combined, but did not take into account any of the by-then well-known findings on the Indian eras. He did not delve into and debate much about them either. He was aware of the data and the validity of the eras but was perhaps uncomfortable, having gone far down this road in the course of his work. Instead, he relied on William Jones's[10] contentious association of Sandrokottos with Chandragupta Maurya and Alexander's attack of 327–325 BCE to try outlining ancient Indian dates and forming a chronology. Ironically, he also recognized the Puranas and the genealogies therein, as well as other ancient texts, including Buddhist ones, as valid sources of historical data.

He tried to derive the dates for Buddha, and proposed 600–200 BCE as the period for the subsequent and related Sutra texts. He ascertained abruptly and arbitrarily, in just a couple of concluding pages, the period of the compilation as a uniform 200 years for each of the previous three sets of sequential texts, i.e. Brahmanas, 800–600 BCE; Mantra, 1000–800 BCE; and Chhanda or Rigvedic, 1200–1000 BCE. This, once published, found currency, owing to Müller's standing as a pre-eminent European Sanskrit scholar. The dates also fitted well with the colonial way of thinking and their political agenda. Interestingly, Max Müller rarely made a mention of or advocated this periodization, for instance in his celebrated 1882 series of lectures, *India: What Can It Teach Us?*[11]

Besides, this periodization, being inconceivably simplistic, tied everyone in knots while trying to fit in the Puranic genealogies. But they could not be rejected in the first place, as they served as the basis of all attempts to construct a chronology, all the way to William Jones and including Max Müller himself.

Vincent Smith, aiming to write authoritative textbooks on Indian history, therefore, decided to chop off everything prior to 600 BCE[12] and made the chronology commence from then onwards. His books became the accepted history of India and are largely recognized thus even now. Notably, Max Müller's periodization reappears in almost exactly the same way in Romila

Thapar's book. This is absolutely inexplicable, as it falls foul, at both the ends, of Vincent Smith and all that has been found in the last century.

About the only book exclusively focused on the topic, published during the same time in 1899, Mabel Duff's *The Chronology of Indian History*[13], starts from 3102 BCE. It ascertains the beginning of Kali Yuga or the Kali era from Friday, 18 February 3102 BCE. This is the conventional date, identified with the death of Krishna 36 years after the Mahabharata War of 3138 BCE. This occurs most frequently as the reference date in epigraphs and coins, which Mabel Duff extensively relied upon, in addition to the relevant works and collaborations with over half a dozen leading explorers of the Indian chronology who were based around London. She arranged the Indian data following the method and procedures that had been developed for Greek and Roman chronologies, marking out the dates that could not be fully ascertained.

Mabel Duff, however, anchored her version of the Indian chronology on the date of Alexander's attack. The emphasis perceptibly shifted to accounts of Greek origin, consequent plausibly to her method, and to those of the Chinese travellers in subsequent periods. This insidiously set forth another key infirmity in the writing of Indian history and its chronology, where undue emphasis and often the entirety of one's reliance were placed upon the data available from foreign visitors. They were not many, just around a dozen or so; not evenly spaced out to have any meaningful linkages or cross-references, and many a time full of contradictions. One can visualize a foreign traveller walking around, mostly alone, in the vast lands of India, facing language and several other constraints. These accounts can, at best, be weakly corroborative and certainly cannot be the primary source of data.

You would also note that the Indians are nowhere in picture. The chronology is being outlined and the history written exclusively by the British to suit their own interests and purposes. It was being done to cope with and rule India, a far bigger territory and population, and a civilization that was much more ancient and illustrious than what they were used to. The purpose of exploitation and extraction—incidentally, 'loot' was the first Indian word to enter the English vocabulary—was indeed overriding and pervasive.

This implied a need to dominate and to be perceived as superior, which could have influenced their conclusions, notwithstanding the scientific method, the sincerity and the dedicated efforts of these chroniclers. For example, Alexander's attack finds barely any mention in Indian texts, not only in the ancient ones but also those from the first millennium CE (Common Era) and later. It was a non-event or of little consequence to the shaping of Indian civilization, ethos and history, but was deemed appropriate as the anchor event and the date for outlining its chronology by European historians.

In comparison, the Mahabharata War and the beginning of the Kali era were, overwhelmingly, the most defining events of ancient India across its geography at that time, and subsequently even today. This is so for the bulk of religious texts that came about, and it also finds mention in many of the non-religious texts on the arts, theatre, literature and vocations. The Kali era appears pervasively in inscriptions, coins and the dates and references therein, all throughout and across regions. It is by far the more deserving and appropriate anchor for the Indian chronology and history.

A switch to the Mahabharata War as the anchor would also raise many new questions and anomalies in the existing chronology. However, there has been considerable advancement along multiple dimensions in the century gone by. The writing of Indian scholars, for example Kota Venkatachala,[14] who had faced hard-to-surmount challenges posed by modern education and the English language, started coming into its own from the early twentieth century. They could methodically reconcile the Puranic genealogies and align them to the Kali era by the 1950s, bringing to bear their superior knowledge of Sanskrit and better contextual understanding of the texts. They could go prior to the Mahabharata War too, and fairly authoritatively, till the beginning of the Saptrishi era in 6777 BCE.

The burgeoning archaeological data that is dated back to the eighth millennium BCE and the existence of human habitations in a significant portion of the Indian territory certainly render the Saptrishi and Kali eras plausible chronologically. Findings on the flow of the Gaggar-Hakra, the Indus and allied rivers, from geological and hydrological studies, present interesting possibilities on the origin, spread and collapse of the Harappan settlements. So do data on changes in ocean levels over millennia and their implications, and their relationship with ancient coastal settlements, which can be cross-referenced with textual data.

Moreover, astronomy simulation software is helping us track sky positions to as long ago as tens of thousands of years and down to the accuracy of hours, based, for instance, on the precession of equinoxes. These can be collated with astronomical references corresponding to a large number of events in ancient texts and precise dates can thus be arrived at. The ancient dating data from genetics is interesting, albeit, in the case of India, it is currently limited to just one Harappan sample, but the technique holds promise and some major inputs could come up in the next few years. Thus, the time is ripe for a fresh, original look at the Indian chronology. We are much better placed than we were a century ago when the chronology was first outlined and has largely stood still since.

This will be a rediscovery guided by the best of science and the multidisciplinary method. It will play out at two levels, at the level of the design or construct of the Indian chronology and at the level of details or the dating of specific events. We shall explore the alternative of the Mahabharata War as the right anchor, attempt a periodization of Indian antiquity thereupon as the overall construct and assess its efficacy. It could enable us to overcome the knots we have tied ourselves into because of accepting Alexander's attack as the anchor date for over a century, which has prevented us from updating the Indian chronology and has led to distortions and confusion.

A viable and effective construct ought to address the major anomalies and gaps that exist in our understanding of Indian history. Moreover, it should spur and direct further research and allow for suitable and timely updates. Some questions will inevitably remain in the rediscovered chronology. For these, the construct will provide testable hypotheses across disciplines to get to the correct and exact dating. That will progressively lead us towards the full and proper sequence of events and their precise datings, which a chronology always ought to be.

◆

In early 2008, my book on the strategic management of Indian companies, *Competing with the Best*,[15] was published. It tracked the evolution of a carefully chosen set of successful enterprises from the time of their founding, researching a typology and the viable and effective strategic constructs therein.

The book delved into company cases, socio-economic data and research findings of various functional areas of management and other related disciplines. It also drew upon my advisory work with the top echelons of medium and large corporations and the government for over a decade, and rounded up my teaching of strategic management since the early 1990s at IIM Ahmedabad and other leading institutions. The corporate strategy constructs were pioneering in many ways for a discipline hitherto dominated by American data and writings. The book did well and the publisher took it to a global stage in 2009.

Around that time, I shifted my operating base from Mumbai to New Delhi and considered exploring the strategy of the state.

Nation-states, akin to corporations, also have a strategy—in what they aspire for and how they go about it. The strategy is shaped by external as well as internal factors, which originate from its techno-economic and socio-political context and its trajectory of evolution. For this, I decided to take up two great works on statecraft in world history as case studies, Chanakya's *Arthashastra* and Machiavelli's *The Prince*.

The exploration started on a positive note, as I could compile very good translations of the two works and a lot of supporting material on their contexts and evolution. However, soon I encountered an anomaly in the case of the *Arthashastra* and its dating, and it persisted. The work made virtually no mention of a foreign attack. Nor the factors, the strategic moves and the success they achieved in driving the Greeks—who had occupied some territory after Alexander's attack—out of India. This did not truly fit in with the prevailing narrative where Chanakya, who groomed and guided Chandragupta Maurya and led him to accession as the ruler of Magadha, would be the architect of such a strategy.

Are the two events linked at all? Or are Chanakya, Chandragupta Maurya and the *Arthashastra* not linked to Alexander's attack at all, and they belong to two entirely different periods, conceivably separated by decades, centuries, or more? This was critical, since the chronology of the entirety of Indian antiquity was built around this association and the dating of Alexander's attack by scholars from the late nineteenth century onwards. Romila Thapar puts the attack and the accession four years apart from each other. We could not afford to have an iota of doubt in this regard.

The doubt put the skids on my research on the strategy of the state. It set me forth on a wide-ranging search in the field of world and Indian histories and chronologies. It has been an extraordinary journey for over a decade, but it did not leave me much wiser on this score. In early 2022, I wrote an article

'Re-Discovering Indian Chronology',[16] paving the way for this book.

There are two more research strands that have led my way. I was fortunate to have a grounding in business-economic history and the handling of empirical data as a historian. A couple of doctoral-level seminar courses at IIM Ahmedabad with Dwijendra Tripathi, where I was mostly the only student in 1990–91, imbued forever all my research with the historical perspective and rigour. He founded the discipline of business history, in parallel with Alfred D. Chandler at Harvard Business School, and also served as the General President of the Indian History Congress in 2002–03. Their method was emphatically inductive, with good documentation of the data itself being considered important enough. And the contours, hypotheses or theories, if they emerge consequently, though not necessarily, are indeed welcome.

The other strand is strategic management research, which is inherently multidisciplinary and has witnessed about the most sophisticated and effective application of the case method. The strategy of an entity is integrative and plays out over several horizons; thus, the research has to draw on findings from the several functional areas of management as well as economics, psychology, sociology and so forth. It has been unhesitatingly and boldly multidisciplinary, and thrived about the most in this aspect of it. This is important for our exploration of India's pre-history, where one needs to draw and integrate across multiple, diverse disciplines.

Exploring a case situation as stand-alone and as it exists, forsaking any theorization to start with, enables one to see the data afresh and dispassionately. This is helpful, as the Indian chronology is certainly cluttered with several partial, half-baked and outdated theories. We shall explore pivotal events first as stand-alone cases, such as the accession of Chandragupta Maurya and Ashoka and the death of Buddha, and put all the validated and relevant data together. The conclusions on the dating of specific events, whether definitive or probabilistic, can then be strung into a preliminary construct for further exploration and validation. Thus, the two strands—the historical perspective and the multidisciplinary and case research methodology—have come together somewhat fortuitously for this endeavour. They are appropriate and adequate for it too, perhaps uniquely.

This is a good juncture to define the time, space and boundary of our rediscovery of the Indian chronology clearly. The Second Battle of Tarain near Kurukshetra in 1192 CE, which took place between Mohammad Ghori and the Rajput Confederacy led by Prithviraj Chauhan, is a suitable upper limit. This marked the commencement of Islamic presence in mainland India and date-keeping in the Hijri era, which was already aligned with Western systems of dating and was subsequently reconciled with the Indian calendars too. Thus, there is little doubt on the dating of Indian events. There is consistency with other systems of dating across the known world after 1192 CE and the chronology is settled.

The lower limit is naturally the Holocene, around 9000 BCE, or from the end of the last Ice Age. This will be adequate and all-encompassing for dating the events of Indian chronology. Post-Holocene, civilization became feasible for the first time and began its long, uncertain formative process. Conditions became favourable for the Homo sapien hunter-gatherers to strike root and occupy places for longer periods and round the year. India and its varied sub-regions provided perhaps the most hospitable prospects to these groups. Agriculture was invented, animals domesticated, and the early contours of settled living started emerging. Lahurdeva in present-day eastern Uttar Pradesh and Mehrgarh in Baluchistan offer the earliest such data.[17]

With 9000 BCE and 1192 CE as the lower and upper limits in time respectively, the space termed as 'India' will mostly mean the Indian subcontinent or South Asia, and all the countries therein, including India, Pakistan, Bangladesh and Nepal. The present-day Sri Lanka was proximate geographically and culturally for most of the time and will be taken as such whenever appropriate. Moreover, the focus will remain wholly on the chronology. This is another sort of bound, and we shall get into the narrative and descriptive details only to the extent necessary for dating purposes.

The lay of the book chapters resembles an unfolding story of a riddle-like and fascinating phenomenon. First, we shall take a close and critical look at the Indian chronology as it stands currently, or the 'snapshot', and how this has been reached, or the 'movie'. It will be a scholarly appraisal, starting from the earliest attempts of William Jones, and of their data, analytical tools and techniques, and the conclusions they drew. This will give us a sense of their challenges and limitations and the importance of the breakthroughs made—and the specifics of wrong turns, anomalies, assumptions, approximations and gaps in the attempts both individually and collectively.

In the next two chapters, we shall scour the various disciplines for validated data related to chronology, which needs to be incorporated and reconciled. Archaeology and related findings from hydrology are the obvious places to start. Archaeo-astronomy and genetics are important emerging disciplines. There have been significant advances from the early twentieth century in the understanding of Puranic genealogies and dates and their alignment with the Gregorian calendar that became a standard since 1582 CE and the Julian calendar earlier. Similarly, in the last few decades, the Yuga system of recording time in India has been largely calibrated with Western and more prevalent methods of timekeeping. These findings across disciplines, after due validation, form a new data set that needs to be fitted into the chronology.

These three chapters will set the stage for a new or rediscovered construct of Indian chronology. Several multidisciplinary analytical tools and techniques come into play, from the triangulation of three or more data points to the validity and reliability of the construct. These are supported by a deeper dive into the most critical and controversy-prone datings, such as cases. The construct that anchors Indian chronology around the Mahabharata War leads to a comprehensive and discerning periodization of its antiquity—the 'Early Settling' period [*c.* 9000 BCE–6777 BCE], the 'Ramayana–Mahabharata' period [6777–3102 BCE], the 'Post-Mahabharata' period [3102–325 BCE] and the 'Gupta–Rajput' period [325 BCE–1192 CE].

These periods are organized around the defining events or ruling formation. The start and end years of the periods are accurate to the calendar year and represent a decisive shift in the contours of history, as they should. Our method of arriving at the construct and the periodization is, in effect, a dynamic 'assimilating–updating' framework for the chronology, to incorporate research and findings that will come up in the future. The framework can be deployed for other regions in the world, particularly for pre-history, as it enables one to move and integrate across many disciplines. This method is a far cry from and vastly superior to what prevailed since the early twentieth century, which tended to stunt research and summarily reject whatever didn't fit into a particular narrative as unreliable, mythical or exogenous, and thus remained nearly static.

We also look at the big picture of the rediscovered construct for its implications on India's later chronology, its history from the beginning and that of the world, and the linkages over millennia. The anomalies and questions that arise and the gaps that remain, with respect to the chronology, are enumerated.

Then, there will be a chapter each on the four periods. They detail out the sequence of major events of the respective periods in calendar years, or a range where there is a lack of a definitive conclusion or the event was spread over a long period. Events that are either very important or controversial in a period are explored as stand-alone cases too, prior to their integration into the chronological sequence. The emphasis, in particular, is on the continuity and change from the prior to the subsequent periods in history as well as the chronological questions and the gaps that remain.

Lastly, we shall reflect on the highlights of this endeavour for rediscovery and why it took so long to come about. The latter is due to a concatenation of multiple reasons. History was about the last of the social sciences to come fully on board as a scientific discipline around the 1960s. It had a much longer lineage than the others. Many versions of historical events and periods have tended to prevail simultaneously and they differed from each other widely, as each nation-state interpreted events to suit its own identity, pride and interests. Tampering with history has often been fair game for rulers, and a dispassionate, scientific exploration was very often resisted and delayed.

Moreover, in their interpretation and purposes, Indian history and chronology were overtly colonial from the beginning, and were by and from the outside. Post-Independence, the emphasis was on tailoring history for the purposes of nation-building, which led to another layer of deviation, and pushed further back the proper and fulsome application of the scientific method. The pressure to conform in school, college teaching and research, faculty appointment and career advancement made even the most obvious contours and overwhelming events of history hard to register, recognize and reconcile suitably.

This rediscovery of the Indian chronology could be the much-needed breaking out of the mould for the study of Indian history. It certainly opens a new vista into the understanding of Indian antiquity and may engender the renaissance of history and civilizational research and teaching in India.

2

WAYS AND MEANS OF INDIAN CHRONOLOGY

We take a closer look at the ways and means of the Indian chronology, as it has been till now. The road has been long, but often action has been sporadic. It begins in the late eighteenth century, sees a flurry during the late nineteenth and early twentieth centuries, only to become very quiet, curiously, during the last one hundred years.

The means, as noted in the previous chapter, have been typically located in one or the other discipline. Data is many a time happenstance and mostly guided by an explorer's interest and circumstances, rather than following the protocols of a scientific research design. The analysis is patchy and impressionistic and the conclusions are often abrupt and devoid of any attempt to reconcile them with the chronology findings that came earlier and from other disciplines. However, we need to draw on and work to the best of our abilities with what we have, as much as possible.

A 'chronological' or along-the-timeline assessment of key contributions from the late eighteenth century onwards brings a degree of method and continuity to the process. It helps explore the underlying linkages and build-up among the various contributions. This is a sort of 'movie' of the Indian chronology as it got outlined along the way, and it brings us to the 'snapshot' of what prevails currently. The movie-snapshot analysis is integrative and incisive, and it aims to determine where we stand—as a whole and on the specifics—and the ground that needs to be covered in order to understand a phenomenon fully.

THE MOVIE

William Jones (1746–94)[1] was truly the pioneer explorer of India's antiquity in the colonial era. He had a flair for languages, mastering Greek, Latin, Persian, Arabic and Hebrew while very young, and he translated a history of Nadir Shah from Persian to French when he was 24 years of age. Armed with an elite family background, good education, around a decade of legal practice and some dabbling in politics, he was appointed as the judge of the Supreme Court in Kolkata under the East India Company in 1783 CE.

This was when the companies' administration in India was getting formalized and streamlined. The appointment was a good perch for his search for an Indian code of ethics and jurisprudence, which could be put alongside the British common law for evolving a suitable framework for the courts here. He sought the help of scholars in Kolkata and around, and the search soon expanded and ranged wide into the ancient texts. Gaining proficiency in Sanskrit, he started compiling the manuscripts methodically and translating and writing about them. Within a year of his arrival, Jones gathered like-minded individuals and founded the Asiatic Society in Kolkata, albeit with no Indian members.

The society members were fascinated by the richness and diversity of Sanskrit literature, and it came to play a pivotal role in the exploration of Indian antiquity. Jones, who was its live wire, is personally identified with two significant observations. These are still influential and remain at the core of the framing of India's history and its chronology.

First, noticing a close resemblance among Sanskrit, Greek and Latin, he proposed that they had a common root and this could be a 'proto Indo-European' language. The root manifested itself in Persian, the Gothic and Celtic languages, and further into the other languages of Europe and India. Jones stated this in the '3rd Anniversary Discourse' of the Asiatic Society in 1786.[2] While many European scholars have also noted it, for over a century the observation spurred a proverbial scholarly industry—of trying to find the roots of the related languages, their derivatives and the linkages thereupon, and conjecturing about how these will have evolved and spread in Eurasia along the axes of time and space.

The proto Indo-European language has never been found or located. Yes, the resemblances exist, and there could be linguistic and thus civilizational linkages, but there is no hard and conclusive evidence on the direction of its flows or its time or chronology. Jones played on the frequent occurrence of the word 'Aryan' in Sanskrit, Persian and Germanic literature. He proposed the existence of an Aryan homeland somewhere in between Central Asia and the north of the Caspian Sea, from where one branch migrated northwest and the other came southeast and then split further in the directions of Iran and India.

The notion of a conquest was inexplicably added to the migration, perhaps because it rhymed with the times and the intent of British colonization. Jones was about the first to speculate on the 'Aryan Invasion'. It found fertile ground and gained currency as a 'theory' or 'AIT'. The accompanying timeline, which placed the invasion around 1500 BCE, was axiomatic and at the most, a convenient conjecture.

There was little basis to propose such a grand hypothesis, let alone terming it a theory. And no incontrovertible evidence, for instance, archaeological, epigraphic or even literary, has been found for nearly two and a half centuries. There have been migrations and their influences have travelled in various directions in Eurasia, but none of them were of the kind, in terms of the route or intent, that was speculated by Jones. This was clearly a wrong turn.

His second observation was to assert the identification of Xandrames—Sandrokottos—Sandrocryptus, Indian rulers mentioned in Greek writings, with Dhana Nanda, Chandragupta Maurya and Bindusara. This was based on a degree of phonetic similarity between 'Sandrokottos' and 'Chandragupta', whose rise was stated to coincide with Alexander's attack and consequent presence in India from 327 to 325 BCE.

This was another instance of aggressive conjecturing by Jones. There was no evidence thereof on the Indian side, as noted in the previous chapter, with Alexander's attack apparently being a non-event and finding no mention in ancient texts. Jones was well-versed in these and did not put forward any direct evidence from Indian sources. Instead, he talked of '...a discovery which accident threw in my way...'[3], of identifying 'Palibothra' that was visited and described by Megasthenes, with Patliputra, and quickly thereupon, Sandrokottos with Chandragupta Maurya. Both the identifications are largely speculative. They cannot be held out as scientifically valid, as they are neither empirical data nor a hypothesis based on incontestable logic. The latter needed to be tested for backward and forward implications anyway and this was never done.

We need to hold these identifications to the toughest scientific scrutiny, since they became influential in the construction of Indian antiquity. The entire chronology, in particular, has been based on the Alexander–Chandragupta Maurya contemporaneity. This is not a rock-solid base, but so speculative and wobbly, that it is actually hard to either prove or disprove scientifically. Moreover, there are contesting claimants to this phonetic similarity.

Another equally illustrious Chandragupta rose to the Magadha throne, after the Andhra-Satavahana dynasty's thirty-second and last ruler, Chandrasri, to establish the Gupta dynasty.[4] His son and successor was Samudragupta. The Greek references to 'Xandrames—Sandrokottos—Sandrocryptus' arguably have a greater phonetic similarity with the 'Chandrasri—Chandragupta—

Samudragupta' trio. It sequentially runs through the names of all three rulers. In comparison, Jones's equivalence between 'Xandrames—Dhana Nanda' and 'Sandrocryptus—Bindusara' is outlandish and phonetically invalid.

William Jones was indeed bright and prodigious in his output. He had the resourcefulness and the dedication to break ground for the exploration of Indian antiquity and texts. His flair for speaking and writing generated wide-ranging interest and attracted many others to explore further, thereby placing the study of ancient texts in the larger and public domain.

His two observations were remarkable at that time, in those early days and context. But unfortunately, they were amateurish and wrong turns, and do not respond to the test of scientific data and method fully. They have proven to be major distractions and even stumbling blocks in the understanding of Indian history, especially its chronology.

Alexander Cunningham (1814–93) brought the scientific method and rigour to the exploration of Indian antiquity through inscriptions and subsequently the Archaeological Survey of India, which he founded.[5] He arrived in India in 1833, initially to serve as an engineer in Kolkata, and for over three decades, took on a variety of roles, travels, surveys and excavations all over the country's vast geography.

An early influence and a close collaborator of his was James Princep (1799–1840), who deciphered Kharoshti and Brahmi in 1836 and thereupon the inscriptions on coins, copper plates, pillars and rocks. Cunningham helped identify all the Brahmi characters and thus opened an important window into India's past. The engravings on a large number of pillars and rocks strewn all over the country were found to be associated with Ashoka. Only two edicts carry some kind of reference to dates, but both are circular and inconclusive—for instance, the Gaya one dates the edict to the forty-second year after the death of Ashoka's father. Cunningham's significant contributions to the formation of the chronology included the excavation of the earliest remains at Bharhut stupa in northern Madhya Pradesh and dating them to the second century BCE. Another contribution of his was the compilation of the Indian eras and calendars.

He used the Kali era commencing in 3102 BCE as the anchor for his explorations.[6] And he tried to simplify and calibrate the solar and the lunisolar calendars in the *Kala Sankalita*[7] written by an earlier chronologist, John Warren, and the 'Useful Tables'[8] by James Princep, for calculating Indian dates. The Sanskrit title of John Warren's book is notable and the validity of the Kali era and calendars thereon is beyond any kind of question, doubt or reproach. Both solar and lunisolar calendars are based on the *Surya Siddhanta* and the rare conjunction of the five planets, the sun and the moon at the start of the Kali era. Cunningham further calibrated the Kali dating system to the Hijri, Seleukidan and Christian eras.[9]

The *Surya Siddhanta* is a defining text of Indian astronomy and mathematics. Attributed to Latadeva, a student of Aryabhatta, the earliest available version was compiled around fifth century CE. As is the case for most of these ancient texts, the *Surya Siddhanta* was also a living text for many centuries, with continuous updations and additions, and the oldest parts going back up to a millennium. It is renowned for several astronomical observations and the accurate estimates of the revolution period of the planets around the Sun.[10] The text authoritatively detailed the solar and lunisolar calendars beginning 3102 BCE, and served as the reference for subsequent Indian dating systems and later calendars, and it was also a reference for Cunningham.[11]

He ploughed into various Indian and foreign calendars, and brought to bear the burgeoning findings from coins and inscriptions on his attempt at the scientific dating of Indian events. For instance, Abu Rihan points at 319 CE as the end of the Gupta dynasty[12] and a copperplate inscription is dated to the 146th year of Skandagupta; thus, the dynasty could not have begun later than

173 CE. Since Skandagupta was its fifth ruler, and estimates of the duration of the dynasty's rule range from 150 to 250 years, the first ruler, Chandragupta, would have ascended to the Magadha throne anywhere between 75 BCE and 25 CE.

Cunningham noted in his 1883 *Book of Indian Eras* that the dates for the Gupta era or dynasty had still not been settled. One needs to find what significant new data or academic work of comparable analytical rigour makes Romila Thapar date the founder Chandragupta's ascension to 319–320 CE. This is three to four centuries later. If the dates for one of the most illustrious dynasties and its rulers of India vary so much, there is certainly cause to re-assess the whole of the Indian chronology root and branch.

He also dabbled in the Yuga system but could not go far. His conjecture that just one Kali Yuga spanned 432,000 years, being based on the precession of equinoxes that takes 26,024 plus 16/166 years to complete a cycle and the attempt of getting rid of fractions by multiplying 26,024 by 166 and adding 16, is remarkable.[13] But this estimate of the precession cycle was by Hipparchus. The corresponding Indian figures are 27,870 plus 150/155 years, according to Parasara, and 28,051 plus 146/154 years, according to Aryabhatta, as noted by Cunningham himself, and this does betray a sense of him being baffled by the Yuga system and resorting to putting apples and oranges together.

An important exploration of his was that of the Saptrishi era,[14] beginning in 6777 BCE. He estimated this era to be the oldest and the 'starting point of Indian chronology', sweeping aside the Yuga puzzle. He relied on the statements of Pliny, Solinus and Arrian, who noted that the Indians gave a list of 154 great kings who ruled for 6,451 years and three months when Alexander arrived in 326 BCE, and that added up to 6777 BCE. It was actually based on the 2,700 years cycle of Saptrishi or Ursa Major through the 27 Nakshatras or lunar houses. The year 1 BCE corresponded to the 4,077 elapsed, as per the location of Saptrishi, and adding another cycle of 2,700 years helped them pinpoint the beginning at 6777 BCE. There could plausibly have been more cycles earlier. Thus, Cunningham left the very 'starting point' of Indian chronology undecided! The question remained open, and towards greater antiquity, by way of the additional Saptrishi cycles or the Yuga chronologies.

Max Müller (1823–1900) is easily the most dedicated and prolific of the explorers of ancient India.[15] He brought to bear a scholarly method and depth to the exploration of Indian history, and is rightly reckoned as the founder of Indian and religious studies. Of German origin, he lived most of his life in the Oxford area and worked at the university there. His magnum opus was the 50-volume translation, *Sacred Books of the East.*[16] He truly admired Indian literature and thought, and with a phenomenal command of the Sanskrit language, did much to create awareness and respect for its antiquity—during and at the height of the British colonization project.

In essence a philologist, his contribution is huge and ranges over five decades. They are freely available too. We shall focus only on what is relevant to the Indian chronology. For this, the best and the most wholesome reference is his 1860 book, *A History of Sanskrit Literature*, and specifically, the introductory and the concluding pages. In these, Max Müller fully locked himself into the first observation of William Jones, without any questions or doubts, as if all of it were absolutely valid, and went further to build and propose an AIT.

This strangely involved the exclusion of every other source of data and exploration; for instance, the data produced by James Princep in the area of scripts and numismatics, and that by Cunningham on inscriptions, eras and calendars, and excavations. He begins, 'Fully seventy years have passed since William Jones...'[17] and refers to no other person, as if nothing else has happened, been found or mattered since then. The similarity among the Greek, Latin and Sanskrit languages is interesting, but at the most, it is a conjecture that is good enough and has to be backed by the material and on-the-ground evidence soon for it to have any sort of validity—or for its continuance as a hypothesis.

No material evidence of any sort has yet been found in support for the exceptionally long 250 years. The core 'proto Indo-European language' should have corresponded to a major civilization, strong enough to supposedly spawn the three great languages, and further, and should have left substantial archaeological evidence at its place of origin or homeland. This is the case for the decidedly much older, bigger settlements and at several places in Eurasia and beyond. Any migration, particularly one that came to dominate the global stage, will involve some conflict, battles, destruction and death. None of these have been found anywhere along the speculated northwest and southeast routes.

Max Müller was clearly wrong in taking up Jones's conjecture as late as the 1850s. Several explorers, such as Princep and Cunningham, had travelled widely while working in India in the intervening decades and had scoured through ancient texts, coins and inscriptions, but had found no direct or indirect indication of any sizeable migration or invasion. Müller's build-up to page 14 of the book: '... more difficult to prove that the Hindu was the last to leave this common home, that he saw his brothers all depart towards setting sun, and that then, turning towards the south and the east, he started alone in search of a new world...' could pass muster only as an act of literary and poetic imagination. Such major and protracted migrations are a matter of strong social and economic factors in the origin and host regions, and would certainly leave a trail of material evidences.

Compounding the error, he fully bought into Jones's speculation, the hint of a 1500 BCE timeline and the migration as an established chronological fact. He could marshal a few stray lines about battles from the Rig-Veda. Such battles were pretty frequent among various clans and the text has proven incredibly difficult to date. Reckoning these as evidence of an external invasion and the eventual victory of the Aryans, a race term that was conjectural then and discredited now, was aggressive and predisposed theorizing. The text itself was consigned to the invaders.

Not only that, Müller force-fitted his four-part sequential classification of the ancient Sanskrit texts into this timeline.[18] The Sutra, Brahamanas, Mantra and Chhanda classification is perceptive and sound, given his understanding of the literature, but the dating is problematic. One, they are based on Jones's highly contentious Alexander–Chandragupta Maurya contemporaneity theory and the derived dates for Buddha. Two, the attribution of exactly 200 years equally to each of the three earlier parts and dating the Chhanda part to 1200–1000 BCE is simplistic and has too much of Jones in it to gloss over.

He should have stayed away from the chronology and the theorizing on migration and invasion. Philology, as a discipline, is less suited for dating historical events. Müller may have been daunted by the colonizing project to dominate India and found refuge in William Jones, and tried to create whatever time-space and respect was possible for ancient Sanskrit literature. This sentiment comes through in the theme, content and tone of his 1883 series of lectures, *India: What Can It Teach Us?*, addressed to prospective civil servants. However, this is not science, and the chronology part of his work has to be set aside.

Vincent A. Smith (1843–1920), a member of the elite Indian Civil Services (ICS), tried to bring together and systematize all the findings on India's past.[19] The need for a single, authoritative chronicle and narrative was being felt at that time to inform those tasked with and involved in the running of the empire. India itself needed to be administered as a full-fledged Crown colony, including the organization of its system of education and teaching.

The first set of writings on India was based on secondary data and impressions, such as those of James Mill. They needed to be updated for the wealth of primary data and experiences that had accumulated since. A stocktaking and possible reconstruction of early Indian history was warranted towards the end of the nineteenth century. Moreover, the conjectures and hypotheses had been running in varied directions, often conflicting and causing confusion. Smith, who topped the 1871 batch of the ICS and served all the way to the top of the hierarchy in the United Provinces, wrote extensively on history during his tenure. He took early retirement after nearly three decades in India and settled down in Oxford town to write.

Smith, in his book on India's early history—first published in 1904 and then in 1906 as the second volume in an edited series—sought to align all the findings on India till date in a dispassionate fashion. He strove to realize the ideal expressed by Goethe, 'The historian's duty is to separate the true from the false, the certain from the uncertain, and the doubtful from that which cannot be accepted.'[20] This was much needed and overdue, but he erred on the side of caution. He reckoned the part of Indian history prior to 600 BCE as unknown or unverifiable, and thus dismissed it from contention altogether!

Thus, he proved himself to be no scholar or researcher. The latter, especially in history, never forsakes the ethics and quest for the unknown and is forever looking to go forth, holding on to every piece of data—even if rudimentary—as precious, and with whatever tools and pointers are at hand. Smith limited himself to writing early Indian history from 600 BCE, as if nothing existed earlier or could be conveniently ignored, and as if disposing of an assigned 'administrative task'.

He unquestionably accepts the Sandrokottos–Chandragupta Maurya identification, which was certainly not settled at that time and despite making a mention of Cunningham's *Book of Indian Eras*. Confining himself to the available inscriptions and the incidental references in Buddhist texts to the fifth and sixth centuries BCE, he decides upon 600–325 BCE as the earliest period of civilization in India.[21] But here too, he does not flinch from the pick-and-choose and relies on the Puranas as the most systematic record of the Indian historical tradition and dynastic lists. He notes that the Vayu, Matsya and Vishnu puranas are full and evidently based on good authority,[22] but cavalierly and conveniently, he does not take into account the fact that the dynastic lists extend many millennia in the past and are well beyond his 600 BCE limit.

Smith's other handicap, though inadvertent, was that he accepted the estimated start of the Gupta dynasty at 319–20 CE as a confirmed fact. He relied on the work of John Fleet,[23] which has been subsequently severely challenged, on re-reading the same inscriptions—for instance, the Kurtakoti and Shimoga copper plates of the Early Chalukyas—and others found later. A balanced consideration of all the available data and observations, for instance those procured by Cunningham and Müller, and which may have ranged and combined well with the inscriptional, would have kept him from going off track. Being broadly correct is better than being precisely wrong, and the building of a scientific theory calls for patience and studied application.

In addition to this, the book has two long chapters on Alexander's campaign, which are wholly based on Greek accounts and are totally one-sided. There are no references to the Indian side of the story. They are treated as enemies and fugitives all through.[24] The theme and tone is of someone taking pride in the glorious campaign of one's ancestors—a pretty long shot indeed for the British!

Smith's book cannot certainly make for an authoritative and dispassionate account of early Indian history. It may have served its thinly-veiled purpose during the colonial period. However, scholarly ethics, rigour and intent are an exacting test—where if you fail once, you fail forever—and Smith's work emphatically falls foul of this. This is indeed unfortunate for the discipline of history, as his subsequent book, *The Oxford School History of India* (1915),[25] became the standard teaching and reference text in the British Empire. One can imagine the distraction Smith's writings and perspective would cause for generations of impressionable Indian students. And the stumbles it may have caused to their later studies, interests and research work.

◆

The movie that is the Indian chronology, from its coming into being in the late eighteenth century to its maturing in the early twentieth century, is captured by these four descriptions. Remarkably, it is shaped by just a few contours of the understanding of history and a few big conclusions. These, whether right or wrong, determine its efficacy. Moreover, what is looked at and explored, and what data and conclusion gets chosen, is determined not only by what is available but also by who is searching for it and why. Ancient Sanskrit texts were most widely known to exist and could be accessed by the British soon after arriving in Kolkata and while sitting in the same city, and they were thus the first to be looked at.

The first step turned out to be unexpectedly daunting, as the corpus of texts was huge and ever-expanding. The oral form of documentation in India was alien to the British. In this, the texts are heard, remembered and passed on, usually with impeccable precision, over centuries and millennia. They started being put down in the written form, as estimated currently, only from the early centuries of the first millennium CE. There were many versions and interpolations along the way, which made the task of dating when the original was composed, when it was partly or largely revised, and which was the most correct and complete version, an intricate and cumbersome challenge.

The explorers were almost exclusively British, with Indians as mere providers of basic information if and when the British needed it, and they just provided whatever they were asked for. And the compilations, readings and conclusions, including those on the chronology, were totally done by the British. The 'why' of the exploration, though often initiated and interspersed with genuine scholarly inquiry, was always overlaid and mostly overwhelmed by the desire to subjugate and rule India for their own purposes.

From religious Indian texts and the pre-existing Greek and other comparative writings on history, in case of Jones, the exploration widened to non-religious texts and astronomical and calendar calculations with Cunningham. The deciphering of the Kharosti and Brahmi scripts was a major breakthrough that opened the gates for numismatics and inscriptions, which generated more substantive and reliable data. Archaeological excavations commenced in the late nineteenth century. While the type of sources increased, the exploration for older sources grew more incisive, for instance Müller's exploration of ancient texts. British officials, who had now experienced India as they worked here for decades, joined in this exploration, leading all the way to Smith. The four contributors make for a fine exposition of the 'movie' or the process of understanding the contours of Indian history and chronology. They are also representative of the contribution of numerous others, often as significant and important, and encapsulate the process well together.

A scholarly critique is frank and dispassionate, to the point and precise. It does not flinch from being bold and severe, as science progresses from falsification, and it is entirely for the sake of the advancement of understanding. The corrections, small and major, and the process of hypothesizing, theorizing and reconstructing theories and knowledge anew are all essential steps. In a critique, one's respect for the efforts, the contributions, howsoever minuscule, as well as for the person, is implied and inherent. While the context and timing of a work is always kept in mind, all critiques have the benefit of hindsight and of assessing something done before with the advantages of additional data, analysis and conclusions that have come in the interregnum.

The Indian chronology that was arrived at in the early twentieth century prevailed as such till Independence. As noted in the previous chapter, there have been some broad interpolations subsequently, and this brings us to the 'snapshot' as it exactly stands now.

THE SNAPSHOT

Besides the book *Early India* by Romila Thapar, we shall consider for this snapshot Upinder Singh's *A History of Ancient and Early Medieval India*.[26] It came out in 2009 and is widely used as a textbook for undergraduate and graduate students. The two books, each having a 2021 edition or reprint, give a true picture of the Indian chronology that prevails currently, both individually and together.

We found a line each on the two long periods—1500–500 BCE for the 'composition and compilation of Vedic corpus' and 2600–1700 BCE for 'Harappan urbanization: Mature and Late Harappan'—patched in Thapar's chronology. The earliest dates for any historical event are the accession of Ajatshatru around 493 BCE and Buddha's death in 486 BCE.[27] Her system of dating, in effect, confines itself to the 600 BCE limit or the beginning as laid down by Smith over a century ago. The period for the compilation of the Vedic corpus is exactly the one proposed by Max Müller in 1860, which we know was done very tentatively and abruptly. Thus, her chronology is still stuck—in terms of the design, construct or dates, and plausibly in terms of its orientation as well—to that of the colonial era.

Harappa could not be ignored but was made exogenous to Indian civilization, as if it had no prior or consequent linkages with the rest, soon after its discovery in the 1920s. It has largely remained so despite the huge and wide-ranging archaeological findings in the post-Independence period. Singh, while adhering to the term 'the Harappan Civilization' and broadly to the timeline, does allude to this being an indigenous 'Sindhu-Sarasvati civilization' and notes the significance of the early-Harappan phase and the recent discoveries and changing perspectives.

She identifies a period, 7000–2000 BCE, 'The Transition to Food Production: Neolithic, Neolithic-Chalcolithic, and Chalcolithic Villages.'[28] An earlier period, 'Hunter-Gatherers of the Paleolithic and Mesolithic Ages', is undated.

This takes back the continuity to 7000 BCE and beyond. Harappan time and space are incidentally bursting at the seams, with large urban settlements getting dated back to 5000 BCE, and these are preceded by smaller urban, semi-urban and rural settlements for another couple of millennia.[29] The spread, too, is up to northern Maharashtra and a good part of western Uttar Pradesh, covering well over a third of the Indian subcontinent. Singh's titles and periods fall short of the timeline and descriptions therein, and are often at variance; for instance the contention that the settlements are not just villages, but that they range from the rural to sophisticated urban conglomerations.

It is as if she is finding the Harappan Civilization conception restrictive, but is still unable to break out from it completely. The alternate and perhaps better conception is that this is all a continuous, integrated Indian civilization, spread over other regions of the subcontinent too, which evolved from 7000 BCE and earlier. The label 'Harappan Civilization', particularly the latter word and connotations therein, was wrong to start with and has been a distraction—and preferably should be got rid of now.

Another conception, that of Alexander's attack as the anchor point and its contemporaneity with Chandragupta Maurya being the basis of Indian chronology, is still not in the realm of a research question for Singh as well. The narrative, however, has been considerably toned down and corrected since Smith. For instance, Thapar devotes just two pages to the attack and writes, 'The Greek campaign in north-western India lasted for about two years. It made little lasting impression historically or politically on India, and not even a mention of Alexander is to be found in early Indian sources.'[30] Similarly, Singh takes a page to describe it and concludes, 'Alexander's invasion is generally seen as having briefly grazed the north-western rim of the subcontinent, not leading to any major or long-term impact.'[31]

This conception is a relic of the colonial era. It seems to have fallen below the radar, but has thoroughly bedevilled the Indian chronology. A peripheral thing or a non-event cannot be the right anchor for the writing of history. Since chronology is the backbone of history, a correct and complete one is essential for its proper exploration and writing. In its absence, history will be hard to explore and impossible to fathom. The narrative will frequently fall apart and short, making it the cause of further confusion and conflict—a situation that prevails currently in relation to the Indian antiquity.

◆

This 'movie' and 'snapshot' of the Indian chronology is a cogent illustration of how a body of knowledge takes shape in real life. It was a formidable quest to start with, especially in the circumstances of the late eighteenth century.

Ancient Indian texts that presented themselves in the beginning for exploration had to be carefully sourced, compiled, filtered and often translated into English, and have proven hard to track and date even after two and a half centuries. The analytical tools and methods of the discipline of philology that came in handy were put to use initially by colonial administrators such as William Jones. Their primary vocation was to build and run a new-found empire. The discipline itself, more inclined to find broad trends and patterns, was ill-suited and inadequate to cater to the required mathematical specificities of chronology.

They expectedly and perhaps inevitably jumped to conclusions, which were, at best, just intelligent and smart-sounding conjectures. These, unfortunately, turned out to be wrong turns. The accumulation of hard, precise scientific data, consequent to the deciphering of Brahmi and that accruing from coins, stone and metal inscriptions, added a certain grounding to the data and evidence, but that was not used to question or confront the earlier philological conjectures. From the mid-nineteenth century, this stream sought to calibrate their findings to the fast accumulating mathematical and chronological data—from astronomical observations and the related eras and calendars, in regard to which India was particularly rich and advanced.

These philological conjectures had, as it often happens, gained a strong constituency and momentum by the second half of the nineteenth century. Several others joined in and some from the academic and public domains, for example Max Müller, tried to build a career around it. This led to a spiralling of mutual attestations. It was useful for the colonial administrators and those allied to them, but the excessive momentum overpowered the findings on eras and from inscriptions, for instance those unearthed by Cunningham. This culminated in the blunt stances of Vincent Smith, who, while compiling and writing the history of India, chopped off everything prior to 600 BCE, and put it out of the contention. It was guided by colonial motives and fell well short of scholarly intent as well as its application.

This newly-defined Indian chronology and the historical narrative of the early twentieth century got endorsed by the ruling administrative and education system, and became the authoritative and the official version of Indian history. Generations of Indian students had to imbibe this in order to qualify through schools and colleges, and this informed their worldview. A small number, but mostly from very privileged backgrounds, made it to British universities to join government services subsequently or to pursue research and a career in academia.

A construct once established is hard to break. The Indian chronology outlined by 1920 still prevails, and has stunted the understanding and advancement of the study of India's deep past. A world-redefining discovery such as Harappa remains largely exogenous to Indian civilization and its chronology. It was made as early as the 1920s and has since been found to cover over a third of the Indian landmass and was extraordinary in terms of urban planning, crafts and trade. Its antecedents and consequences, too, are not fully accounted for.

India-based teachers and researchers, such as Romila Thapar and Upinder Singh, have been able to make inroads into correcting these narratives. The latter is able to state the data as it stands, up to 7000 BCE in the past and earlier for the earliest settlements, but she does it separately and does not integrate it into the continuum of Indian history. However, they have not yet questioned the chronology itself, which is its backbone. A correction has been overdue for over a century, which can only be wholesome for the chronology of Indian antiquity, and going all the way back and forth till 1192 CE. The following table puts together at one place the contributions, anomalies and gaps found during this unfolding movie and snapshot of the Indian chronology, and the implications thereof going further.

TABLE
Movie and Snapshot of the Indian Chronology

	Contribution	**Anomalies–Gaps**	**Implications**
William Jones	1780–90s • Compilation, translation of ancient Indian texts • Asiatic Society, discourses, journals	• Proto-Indo-European language, Aryan invasion? • Alexander–Chandragupta Maurya contemporaneity?	The two anomalies remain unverified and contested, but still pervade the construct of the Indian chronology and history.

	Contribution	Anomalies–Gaps	Implications
Cunningham	1860–80s • Validation of the Kali era starting in 3102 BCE and other Indian calendars, going up to 6777 BCE • Brahmi script, coins and inscriptions, the founding of Indian archaeology	• Reconciliation of the Yuga system and estimates for the precession of equinoxes? • Dating the Gupta dynasty and the validation of the 154 kings list handed over to Alexander?	While the precession is validated, the debates persist on the Yuga system, genealogies; a stout defence of Indian eras could have prevented the wrong turns taken by subsequent research on the chronology that still bedevil it.
Max Müller	1860–80s • Philological and comparative study of Sanskrit, Greek, Latin and other languages • Methodical analysis of the Indian literary corpus; highlighting the importance and respect it deserves	• Locked into Jones's contentions to the exclusion of all else, later data, and to build the axiomatic 'Aryan' precept into AIT • Abrupt, arbitrary dating of the corpus, based on an otherwise sound classification	His poorly based AIT, the corpus periodization, and also the dates for Buddha still permeate historical thinking and the chronology, a task for which the discipline of philology and Müller were clearly unsuited.

	Contribution	Anomalies–Gaps	Implications
Vincent Smith	1900–10s • Grounded Indian history on the emerging hard data, especially epigraphy and archaeology • Articulated and wrote well, to advance the popularization of Indian history	• Impatient, even haughty, and much like an administrator, to put all that was prior to 600 BCE out of the contention • Jumps to conclusions on the dating of the Maurya, Gupta dynasties; puts forth a one-sided, external, colonizing narrative of the Indian history, in particular Alexander's attack, for example	Continued reluctance to date any specific event prior to 600 BCE and the dynasty dates that have stuck; these have stunted the progress and prevented later generations of historians from updating the Indian chronology and hindered the further exploration of Indian antiquity at large.
Romila Thapar	1990–2010s • Correction of some narratives, for instance that of Alexander's attack	• The chronology is untouched, and the bulk of old and new data on Indian antiquity is not accounted for	Without realignment and updation of the chronology, this narrative tends to be limiting and distorted too.

	Contribution	Anomalies–Gaps	Implications
Upinder Singh	2000–2020s • Recognition of Indian settlements as far back as 7000 BCE and even earlier • Perceiving the integrity and continuity of Indian civilization along time-spaces	• The chronology construct and datings remain untouched; the recognition is sort of an implant and the continuity is still conjectural and in narrative alone	There is a sense of convergence and clamour, because of the burgeoning data and the narrative side, for the reconstruction of the backbone of the Indian chronology.

3

FINDINGS–ADVANCES

Archaeology, Astronomy and More

Mid-December 2022, on a foggy winter morning, I set out on a drive from Delhi to Rakhigarhi in the Indian state of Haryana. It took just over three hours, going past the airport and the exurbs of one of the largest human settlements in the world. On to the high-speed national highway that stretches all the way to the Pakistan border, I swerve off much earlier into the countryside and drive for around 30 kilometres. The terrain is very flat, allowing one to peer all around and see up to the horizon. Vigorous agricultural and allied activities make it one of the most prosperous regions in India currently.

A set of dwellings in the midst of fields marked the destination. It served as a 'hotel' for visiting archaeologists. Vasant Shinde, who has been leading the excavations in Rakhigarhi for over a decade, had asked the caretaker to show us around. The archaeological site was a kilometre away and on driving through a large, densely populated village, the landscape suddenly opened up, breathtaking in its expanse. A mound gently arose from the flatlands—ancient habitations, when abandoned generally, take the shape of a mound as dust, water, vegetation accumulate around it over centuries and millennia—and 11 of them were identified around the village by

2016. The total area is 550 hectares, making it by far the largest archaeological site in South Asia when compared to Mohenjo-Daro, Harappa, Dholavira and Ganeriwala, which are 300, 150, 100 and 80 hectares,[1] respectively.

Since the first excavation at Rakhigarhi in 1969, the earliest findings are dated to 4500 BCE or 4470 +/- 110 BCE as per the radiocarbon test samples done in 2014. Its mature phase was between 2600 and 1900 BCE. Thus, the site was occupied for nearly three millennia, which is much longer, often by a multiple of 10, than most of the prominent cities or habitats in the world at present. The mounds have many layers, as generations of people would have built new dwellings and moved around in the same locality. And one can visibly discern the stages in the evolution of the construction material and design, and the patterns of living, consumption and culture. There are many important findings to come as barely a small fraction of the site has been excavated.

Around Rakhigarhi, there are many similar sites, such as Kalibangan, Banwali, Siswal and Bhirrana, which tend to form a cluster. They lie along the River Ghaggar and its tributary Chautang. Kalibangan was among the first sites to be excavated in post-Independence India and has been extensively documented. Bhirrana is reckoned to be the oldest site, dated to 7570–7180 BCE from the charcoal samples found in 2013, and to 6689–6201 BCE from samples found in 2008.

These sites, during their mature phase, were well-developed urban centres, with well-planned and designed roads, drainage facilities, residential areas and housing. The elaborate granaries point to close linkages with the surrounding rural areas. And a factory-like site at Rakhigarhi, with several stone and metal-processing units, which used the raw materials sourced from far-off mountains and coastal areas, indicates wider trade flows and connections. Moreover, an urban centre cannot emerge and sustain itself without the two-way transportation of food and other supplies. The necessary flow of information, communication and monetary exchanges, as well as the requisite language, well-defined barter mechanisms or currency units for economic transactions, and record-keeping would have existed.

These archaeological findings are virtually from the core of India, within 200 kilometres of Delhi, and from a civilization that is urban and sophisticated, with wide and long links to the rest of the world. Thus, the Indian civilization indeed extends way beyond the Vincent Smith timeline that started in 600 BCE. He is off not by centuries but many millennia, for which hard, multifarious scientific evidence is now available. It would easily pass muster with the ideal of Goethe's that he espoused, of being true, certain and beyond any doubt.

One must note that such evidence was not available at the turn of the twentieth century when Smith started to write his dispassionate, authoritative history of India. Harappa, along the river Ravi in Punjab, was taken up for formal archaeological excavation in the 1910s. There have been reports of the presence of a huge pile of bricks, large mounds and stray artefacts for many decades, and the bricks were being pillaged and used for laying the railway line to Lahore. It was finally confirmed as an ancient, pre-Buddhist site in 1921. This was aided by the discovery of a much larger, undisturbed site at Mohenjo-Daro along the Indus, which was reckoned as similar in origin and antiquity to the earlier site in 1922. This was dated to the third millennium BCE.

These findings opened a new vista for Indian history and its chronology. Later, archaeological excavations have extended the timeline to the eighth millennium BCE, and the geographical spread of the evidence covers nearly a third of the subcontinent. It could conceivably stretch further back and get richer in terms of details and conclusions in the years to come. This timeline, however, is articulated as stray pieces of data or in patches, in relation to particular sites. The chronological sequence has been limited to a few periods, of around a millennia each, and not broken down into years and for individual or clusters of sites.

Moreover, the chronology formulated from the Harappa sites has not been integrated with other evidence for similar periods, and particularly for Indian civilization after 600 BCE. The major reason, as well as a handicap, has been the conception that the Harappan findings are somehow exogenous to the Indian civilization. This is totally untenable, given the extent of the timeline and the spread of evidence.

The conception was speculated upon in the 1920s, as the most extensive range of information came from Mohenjo-Daro and a few other sites discovered soon afterwards around the Indus. It, however, took root—perhaps because of the colonial administration and its proclivity to deny Indian civilization such a great measure of antiquity, and perhaps because anything otherwise would have meant a lot of work to redefine and reorder what had already been concluded—and became the norm. A term was coined: the 'Indus Valley Civilization' (IVC), and the mounting documentation and writings on its basis gave the conception a life and wings of its own.

Both the conception of exogeneity and the term IVC should have been discarded a long time ago. They became untenable, particularly after the extensive excavations at Kalibangan in the 1960s, and as more sites were discovered along the Gaggar-Hakra and their tributaries as well as in other regions. The conception and the term were yet another major wrong turn in the writing of Indian history. In their absence, or with an early correction, let's say by the 1950s, the research would have been suitably redirected on to a productive path. And it would carry on with much greater vigour and focus, since the deployment of a faulty conceptual lens and terminology is both a hindrance and a distraction.

The Harappa findings or the sites—using the archaeological convention of reference based on the first identified location—are best seen as one and integral to the continuum of Indian civilization. Dabbling with a few other terms, such as 'Sindhu-Saraswati Civilization', can distract one or make things worse by potentially adding another layer of confusion. The conception of an integrated and continuous line of Indian civilization would imply not only doing all the work that may have become apparent in the 1920s but also bringing to bear the data that has accumulated during the century gone by to the existing body of research and using it to reorder things suitably and find new conclusions about history. This endeavour, however, is about getting started, and it centres on what will eventually become its backbone—the rediscovery of the Indian chronology.

TIMELINES FROM ARCHAEOLOGY

The earliest evidence of agriculture and settled living comes not from Northwest India, but from Lahurdeva. Located in eastern Uttar Pradesh, bordering Nepal's Terai region, a five-year-long excavation from 2001 around a lake site yielded charred micro-samples of rice as well as the remains of wild and domesticated animals. They were radio-carbon dated to 8813–9171 BCE. Pot shards of coarse handmade red-ware were dated to 7000 BCE. Mehrgarh in Baluchistan, west of the river Indus, has yielded evidence of wheat and barley cultivation prior to 7000 BCE.

If we add Bhirrana, where settled but small and rural habitats could arguably extend to beyond 8000 BCE, the trajectory of the beginning of Indian civilization—with agriculture, animal husbandry, pottery and year-round occupation at a site—can go all the way back to the Holocene period or just after the end of the last Ice Age. The three sites are nearly 2,000 kilometres apart in aerial distance from Lahurdeva in the east to Mehrgarh in the west, and they are in fairly different climatic zones too. Plausibly, several such settled habitats would have existed in between and towards southern and eastern India as well. They are as yet undiscovered and unknown to us. Thus, the time and space of double unknowns, the fact that we don't know what we don't know, is arguably huge for the early settling period. We have to make careful and maximum use of whatever bits of data are currently available to gain as much understanding, for instance through spatial or geographical analysis, techno-socio-economic projections and scenario-building.

The end of the Ice Age, leading to the melting of the snow on the land and the seas, would have set in motion one of the most important climatic phenomena of the world. It was the monsoon winds, which rise in the vast waters of the Indian Ocean during summers and move into the subcontinent from the southwest direction. They soon cover most of its landmass and bring the bulk of the rains. These winds are blocked by the Himalayas, which prevents them from dissipating, leading to heavy precipitation and snow there, and form the mightiest rivers of Asia that are also perennial. Monsoon had probably started stabilizing within a millennium, or around 8000 BCE, and the rivers had probably evolved and forged their path from the high to the low ranges of the Himalayas, through the plains and finally into the seas.

River banks and valleys were the most inviting places for hunter-gatherers to stay put for a long time and make the major transition to round-the-year, permanent and settled habitations. 7000–8000 BCE could be such a period, and Bhirrana and Mehrgarh are the two corresponding sites known to us—Lahurdeva is located beside a lake and in a region that receives high precipitation; thus, it could have conceivably been settled even earlier. But inventions in agriculture, animal domestication, pottery, dwelling construction and other areas may have travelled back and forth among the settlements. The erstwhile hunter-gatherers were highly mobile and ingenious, often crossing hundreds of miles a year and entire continents over decades, for instance through the Bering Strait into the Americas.

These settlements mark the beginning of Indian civilization. A question the early settlers would have had to confront soon afterwards, perhaps within a few years and in the early decades of settling down, concerned the occurrence of the bulk of the rains in the span of a few months, followed by a long lull. Some knowledge and prediction was important for engaging in agriculture and related activities, although it was not essential for their survival, due to their proximity to perennial rivers. Farming also leads to a sedentary life and many possible long periods of little work. It would inevitably prompt innovations to make agricultural yields and living conditions better, greater family and social interactions, and would encourage people to start brooding on the ways and whys of life. The luminous and crowded-looking night sky and particularly the waxing and waning of the moon would also have invited their attention and speculation.

While there is little evidence as yet from the Gangetic Plains, these settlements expanded and proliferated along the Indus and Gaggar-Hakra rivers—and in between and around their tributaries. Their evidence has survived due to the availability and use of some varieties of stone, but primarily because of the quick upgrade to sun-baked bricks in the region. A standardized size, precision-made furnace-fired bricks and ceramics emerged around 5000 BCE, which also led to larger dwellings, simple community amenities, and thereby urbanization at sites such as Rakhigarhi. It would have also meant the use of cattle for cultivation and for transportation and the invention of the wheel. The latter is essential for carrying grains and construction materials, for instance from rural to urban areas.

The Gangetic Plains abounded with forests and the structures did not need to go beyond that made of wood, which was easy to handle. This lack of need would have persisted despite the contact and exchange of innovations with their northwestern counterparts along the Harappan sites, which were likely and certainly cannot be ruled out. Some findings may emerge in the future and new clues may be found from the coastal and other regions of India, but till such time, we have to make do with what we know from the northwest. The fourth millennium BCE is particularly important for findings on the use of metal.

Gold is the first metal known to mankind. It occurs in a free form, requiring just sieving and cleaning, and small finds have been made even in hunter-gatherer caves in Europe.[2] But this is not the case in India, and the earliest that gold seems to appear is much later and is likely to have arrived through trade. This is so for silver too. Copper, which needs simple heating or smelting to process, was the next metal that was put to use in India. India is well-endowed in copper ores, with large and easily accessible deposits in northern Rajasthan, for example. Furnaces and smelting material found at Kunal, near Bhirrana in Haryana, points to the production and usage of copper in the fourth millennium, or around 3500 BCE. The site precedes the culturally analogous Rehman Dheri in Khyber-Pakhtunkhwa and Kot Diji in Sindh, which is in present-day Pakistan.

Copper was alloyed soon afterwards with tin, another metal simple enough to extract, and with ores available in Khyber-Pakhtunkhwa to produce bronze. It was better suited for being used in ploughs, tools and various forms of implements, such as weapons and armour. Bronze reigned as the primary metal of civilizations for over two millennia. Its timeline could extend further into the fifth millennium, as an archaeological find only fixes the nearer bound in time, and just a point in space confirming the extent of its prevalence. What we do not know in the case of Indian civilization is indeed vast. A lot of Harappan sites are still totally or largely unexcavated. The Gangetic Plains and other regions of the country have not yet been put to archaeological studies at all for these timelines, but they were certainly populated and would not just have abandoned their trajectory of evolution, let's say, from Lahurdeva.

The third millennium BCE saw the Harappan sites attain maturity and reach their full extent.[3] Most of them displayed the most evolved public amenities, such as roads, water supply and sewerage facilities; the demarcation into two or more settlement areas, having distinctive dwelling sizes, layouts and functionalities;

as well as the use of sophisticated material like terracotta, a wide range of stones and some metal artefacts. Several sites have unique features to suit local conditions. For instance, the port site Lothal has dry docks and warehouses, and Dholavira, located in the rain-sparse region of the Rann of Kutch in Gujarat, has an elaborate system of water channels and huge reservoirs built entirely in stone. Among the frequent finds are the inscribed small flat tablets or seals made of a soft stone—steatite, and occasionally of terracotta and other stones, and gold. These were most likely utilized for the identification of goods and as bills of exchange in trade. There was extensive domestic trade among the smaller and larger sites using bullock carts, and certainly international trade with West Asia from its many port sites, as well as the use of coastal shipping.

All the sites have extraordinary similarities and these can be clearly marked out. They underscore a high degree of interaction, mobility and interdependence but also civilizational integration. This is extraordinary, as the sites are spread over nearly a third of the Indian subcontinent and occupy an area larger than the Mesopotamian, Egyptian and Chinese civilizations, its contemporaries, put together. They are numerous too, with around 1,400 sites having been discovered, 925 in present-day India and 475 in Pakistan. The larger sites are actually cities, with the population estimates of Mohenjo-Daro and Harappa being 30,000 and 60,000, respectively, and Rakhigarhi could have exceeded 100,000 people. Such population sizes would place the latter among the world's hundred largest cities up to five millennia later in 1800 CE.

An intriguing feature is the absence of written records. They rarely go beyond the symbols or pictures inscribed on the tablets and seals. The longest is a ten-symbol signboard found at Dholavira,[4] where the symbols are 37 cm high and the board three metres long, and one of the symbols is repeated four times.

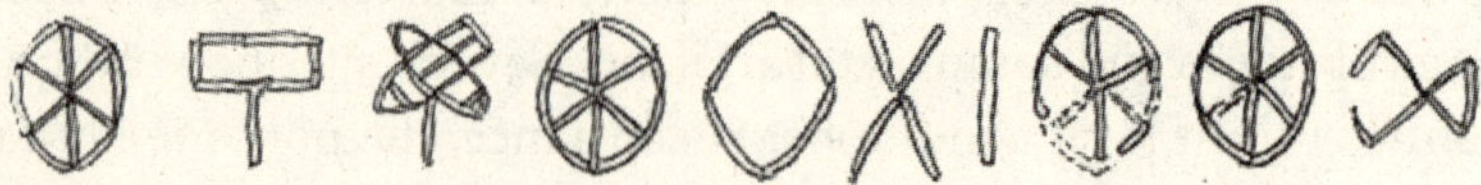

This is no evidence for a written script. And after a century of widespread excavations, one can conclude that the people at Harappan sites did not write. It is a surprise, as writing and the use of a script had been invented over a millennium ago in the evolving forms of the cuneiform in Mesopotamia around 3200 BCE, and the hieroglyphics in Egypt almost simultaneously. Harappan sites were in a state of active trade engagement with the first and would also have come across the writing system of the latter.

Harappans had bigger, spread-out and numerous settlements. They were socially, economically and culturally integrated into a civilization. This is not possible without the massive amount of communication carried over long distances, including the involvement of third parties and intermediaries. Moreover, trade with the Mesopotamians would have to be suitably handled and reconciled. It had to account for the exchange of goods and considerations, and most importantly, correct and timely information needed to be conveyed. There would have been several points of contact and transactions from, let's say, the rural producer to the urban aggregator, land transporter, shipper and finally, the buyer at the destination, and then it would just keep going back and forth.

The most plausible answer is that they did have a communication system that was adequate to meet the needs of widespread civilization. It would have allowed for the required variety and complexity of information exchange, backed by the standardization of learning, usage and understanding. It should have also been scalable enough to meet the requirements of international trade with a counterparty that uses writing. For such a communication system, language is necessary, but which, rather inconceivably for Harappan sites, did not need writing and thus a script.

They would have found, or at least believed, that their communication system was superior, too, in some ways. That would have obviated their need and inclination to learn the art of writing from other civilizations. In the absence of written documentation, the oral part of language has to be stronger and far more meticulous. The vocabulary, meaning, pronunciation and grammar need to be much more detailed and unambiguous, and the learning process exacting, disciplined and highly standardized. Since a non-written communication does not leave a record for reference or clarification, the clarity and the consonance of what is said, heard, understood and remembered has to be perfect. Interestingly, as oral communication need not be one-to-one, the civilization could always have witnesses or 'authorized listeners' for the contracts and administrative orders. Their testimony could have been considered equivalent to the truth in case of disputes, for instance in the court of law—and akin to a 'notary plus.'

You may be getting a sense that all this amounts to the Shruti communication system and the Gurukul learning tradition of ancient India. It is famed to have carried through a great number of texts orally, some of which were huge, for centuries and millennia without the loss of a single syllable or a speck of meaning. Max Müller noted, 'Shrotriyas in India [...] learn the Veda by heart, and they learn from their Guru, never from a manuscript and still less from a printed edition [...] I have had such students in my room at Oxford, who not only could repeat those hymns, but who repeated them with the proper accents (for the Vedic Sanskrit has accents like Greek), nay, who, when looking through my printed edition of the Rig-Veda, could point out a misprint without the slightest hesitation.'[5]

Before we let go of the Harappan sites, another intrigue confronts us. Most of the sites were abandoned almost suddenly around 1900 BCE. As with a lot else, this is also a subject of conjecturing, based less on the data than on wild and convenient speculation. The wildest one being the idea of invaders coming from up north and killing or driving away all the inhabitants, which is inconceivable given the size of the civilization, the number of sites and its spread from the mountains to the Arabian Sea and the edges of the Gangetic Plain. In any case, no invasion or victory ever leads to the abandonment of something that was sought after and resourceful, for a long time or permanently. A reasonable explanation lies in the forces of nature, when the river Ghaggar ceased to be perennial and started drying up, perhaps due to a tectonic event and some prolonged deterioration in the monsoon system.

Validation from the River Isotopes Study

A 2019 paper[6] in *Scientific Reports,* which is the fifth most cited journal in the world,[7] reported on the argon and strontium-neodymium isotopes along the 300-kilometre stretch of the Ghaggar basin. It established that during the 78,000–18,000 BCE and the 7000–2500 BCE phases, the river was perennial and received sediments from the higher and lower Himalayas.

The latter phase was attributed to the reactivation of the river by the distributaries of the Sutlej, since the other neighbouring river, Yamuna, had abandoned the Ghaggar channel much earlier. During the phase, it also flowed into the sea with its delta in the Rann of Kutch. There is tentative evidence of tectonic activity in the lower Himalayas around 2500 BCE and the Sutlej does takes a sharp westward turn on entering the plains, which is unusual for Himalayan rivers. This turn may have led to the flooding of some of the western sites, possibly Harappa itself, as it lies along the former course of the Ravi that the Sutlej merged with upstream.

Nevertheless, the river Ghaggar ceased to be perennial around 2500 BCE. Thereafter, nearly a thousand sites that have been found along its path became dependent entirely on the local monsoon rains. Groundwater levels would have dropped and the wells would either be rendered unusable or would need to be re-dug deeper. Moreover, the monsoon has often tended to be fickle and the rainfall varied, so a prolonged dry spell would have meant hardships—and a disruption and uncertainty in economic, trade and social activities.

The paper correlates the Ghaggar with the river Saraswati.[8] The latter finds frequent mention in the oldest Indian text, the Rig Veda, and several others, while the Ghaggar is altogether missing from it. River Saraswati is stated to be mightier than and just as revered as the Ganges in the early books of the Rig Veda, and this is correlated with its perennial phase; then, subsequently it is counted as one of the dozen rivers flowing between the Yamuna and the Sutlej after 2500 BCE. This fits well, and going by the importance of the river from the trail of archaeological findings in the region across time and space, as well as our discussion, it is the river Saraswati.

The Ghaggar is presently a monsoonal, intermittent river that flows through a channel that is many times larger than what it could have ever created or needed. It is arguably a latter-day name that somehow came into common parlance well past the perennial phase of the Saraswati, when it had mostly dried up and disappeared into the sand, and the sites had been abandoned. Thus, Saraswati was the name of the river when it engendered the settling and evolution of several Harappan sites—recalling the archaeological convention of identifying and naming a set of sites by the one that was first discovered. This river from that time is the subject of our discussion, and Saraswati is the right name for it. And thus, we shall switch to going further and term the whole cluster of settlements as being in the 'Indus-Saraswati' or the northwestern region of India.

The abandonment of the western sites in present-day Pakistan, almost at the same time, points to the socio-economic core of Harappa being in the Saraswati region. This core would have been shaken up and weakened when the river lost its perennial character around 2500 BCE and a gradual decline commenced. A few years of failed or deficient monsoons would bring the civilization to its knees and a collapsing core would take the rest of the sites along as well due to economic and trade links. There would have been the out-migration of people, which tends to start as a trickle and then turns widespread, overwhelming the entire population.

Fortunately, the Harappan sites and particularly those in the Saraswati region were proximate to the vast Gangetic Plains, fed by many perennial rivers that they were certainly aware of. It would have facilitated an eastward migration. But this does not imply, by any means, that the Gangetic Plains were less populated or socio-economically developed, as the natural resource conditions have been comparable, if not better, all along since the Holocene. However, it was large enough to absorb the bulk of the people from the Harappan sites easily. We do not yet know about that time in the Gangetic Plains, archaeologically, but that cannot imply the non-existence of similar sites there, or that we shall never know.

The continuity of the settlements in the Indus-Saraswati region that spanned over five millennia is indeed breathtaking and unparalleled. No other habitat comes anywhere close in terms of proven archaeological longevity, outside India, in the world at large. The continuity of the Indian civilization, which could have covered most of the subcontinent even during the time of the sites in northwestern India, persisted. The eastward migration from there, since 2500 BCE, would have certainly strengthened the socio-economic scene of the Gangetic Plains. This migration may not be much different from what has been going on all along and currently, when people move to more happening places within India and beyond.

Archaeological findings do thin out for a few centuries after 1900 BCE. Much of this could be due to the hindrance and confusion caused by infirmities in the construct of Indian history and the inefficacy of the dating anchor, as discussed in the previous chapters. These need to be redressed, starting with the rediscovery of the chronology, for the requisite progress. We now enter the realm of data from other sources that are often more precise for the purposes of dating, in comparison to the archaeological finds that are usually calibrated to a period or a range of years.

TIMELINES FROM ASTRONOMY

As ancient Indians settled into the practice of year-round occupation of habitats and agriculture, they soon needed to get a fix on the onset of monsoons. It needed to be accurate enough, as a variation of just a few weeks could jeopardize the availability of food for the entire year and their survival itself. No other ancient civilization, perhaps with the exception of the Egyptians who depended on the Nile floods, faced such a contingency.

We can surmise, putting ourselves in the shoes of these early Indian settlers, that they would have known about the weather turning from cold to hot and the days getting longer, and the heavy and frequent rains that came in their wake from their hunter-gatherer days. They would certainly know of the waxing and waning of the moon, and perhaps that the point in the horizon where the sun rises changes gradually, as also its trajectory during the day. These would have opened the gates to the study of astronomy.

The easy next step would be noticing the cluster of stars above the horizon just before sunrise and that they do not remain the same. A major breakthrough, after many rounds of seasons, would be the observation that clusters of stars reappear and repeat their positions and that they can be distinguished and identified. It is not hard to expect that they would have identified the clusters of stars and the existence of a rudimentary yearly cycle in a few hundred years after settling down or by the early eighth millennium BCE.

The numbering and naming of the clusters of stars that repeat in a year as the 27 constellations or Nakshatras marked the formalization of astronomy as a discipline. As the monsoon broadly coincided or occurred just after the longest day of the year, the year began from the summer solstice. The annual projection was usually termed 'Varshaphala' for the year and the rain, or both, analogously. The cycle of the moon, from it being full and bright, then waning to a new moon and waxing back again, provided another equally important yardstick. Together, these cycles of the moon and the sun made for the lunisolar construct of Indian astronomy.

A lunisolar construct poses additional challenges. The duration of the moon cycle or a sidereal month is about 27.32 days, but what appears to us is about 29.53 days, or a synodic month. This is due to relative motion—on completing one rotation around the earth in a sidereal month, the moon has to go further by the angle-time that the earth has travelled for us to note the completion of a rotation: that is a synodic month. Astronomy was entirely observational and descriptive before the Common Era, and till underlying scientific principles started being explored in the latter half of the second millennium CE—so, the synodic duration of 29.53 days made for a month. The 12 months equalled a little over 354 days, which was less than the duration of just over 365.251 days that the earth takes to complete a revolution around the sun. The need to match the 12 lunar months with a solar year, as they appear and in the real, calls for frequent adjustments by the insertion of a corrective intercalary month. In comparison, European astronomy uses the solar year and the Islamic the lunar year exclusively.

Indian astronomers found a workable solution pretty early on and perhaps by the mid-eighth millennium BCE. They introduced an extra intercalary month or *adhik-masa* every three calendar years or so. Another phenomenon that adds a dimension of complexity but could be important for the dating of ancient events is the precession of equinoxes. It is caused by the gravitational attraction of the moon and the sun on the earth's bulge around the equator since it is not a perfect sphere. This leads to the slight precession in the earth's rotation on its axis and it taking an ecliptic orbit and the equinoxes lagging at 50.4 arc-seconds per year. The 360-degree cycle takes precisely 25,771.5 years.[9] As a result, the apparent north from the earth will keep changing. The pole star, which ought to be forever stationary and point at the true north, will lose its meaning every few hundred years or so due to the precession of equinoxes. In 2100 CE, such a star will be Polaris and in 3942 BCE, it was Thuban, but there was no clearly distinguishable pole star for a long time in between.

Therefore, if we know the identity of the pole star corresponding to the occurrence of an ancient event, then we can date it. But given the gaps in our knowledge of the identifiable, referential pole star in the chronological past, precession-based dating can be applied only to very few events, for example around 4000 BCE. Information about any other star will not do, as they all move and rotate around the stationary pole star. Their positional parameters vis-à-vis the pole star that are needed for dating cannot be generated and recorded by the simple observations done with the naked eye in the ancient past. Thus, the precession of equinoxes may lead to tangible outcomes in dating for just a few ancient events and in very special circumstances.

One can conceivably work with the data available on the moon, the sun and the planets, as their locations and movements can be accurately noted through simple observations from ancient times. The dating conclusions, however, should be made cautiously and with many caveats. A number of planetary bodies should preferably be in some rare conjunction when one tries to date an event thousands of years in the past—as the planetary cycles repeat after a duration that ranges from under a year in case of Mercury and Venus to 12 to 30 years for Jupiter and Saturn. It is also useful to work with the data sets of more than one event, which are linked and separated by a known, verified period. The planetary data-based dating of an ancient event should be corroborated and supported by findings from other non-astronomical sources before being definitively concluded upon.

In the earlier chapters, we noted the two dates from Indian astronomy that have been ascertained—6777 BCE as the beginning of the Saptrishi era and 18 February 3102 BCE as that of the Kali era. The Saptrishi era corresponds to the rare conjunction of the sun, the moon and all the planets in the Aries constellation, observed on 22 February 6778 BCE. They were within 13 degrees of ecliptic longitudes and visible to the naked eye.

The Saptrishi conjunction can be validated by astronomy software, such as *Planetarium* and *Stellarium*, which simulate sky views well into the ancient past and have been available for the last couple of decades. It currently appears for 22 February 6778 BCE as per the prevailing Gregorian calendar and calibrated to 3 December 6777 BCE as per the *Vedanga Jyotisha*—in which the year began on Magha Shukla and the month with the full moon or late January. The *Vedanga Jyotisha* is the oldest surviving astronomical text from India, and it covers one of the six subject areas that are to be studied as part of the Vedic corpus.

The oldest Vedic text, the Rig Veda, has frequent references to the pole star as Dhruva. Since there was no identifiable pole star due to the precession of equinoxes till a few hundred years around 4000 BCE, the text is referring to either Thuban or some older pole star. Thus, around 3500 BCE is the nearer bound for the date of the Rig Veda, and it could go back a few thousand years too. This is interesting but not very useful or conclusive as a date of the text.

Similarly, other references to the helical rising of the Ashvinis, Orion's head near the vernal equinox, the helical rising of Magha on the summer solstice, the dogs of Yama and the direction of Pitraloka in the Rig Veda yield dates that are thousands of years apart. This is expected in case of star-related naked-eye observations, especially when relying on the precession of equinoxes for dating events in the ancient past. Fortunately, the other dates rely only on planetary data, as was the case for the beginning of the Saptrishi era.

A pre-eminent astronomer of ancient India, Aryabhatta, ascertained the conjunction of the sun, the moon and all the planets on 18 February 3102 BCE, marking the commencement of the Kali era. This date is closely related to the Mahabharata War that had happened 36 years earlier. There are several definitive references to planetary positions along the events described in the text, which is the longest epic poem in the world and 10 times the length of the Greek *Iliad* and *Odyssey* put together. Recently, in a comprehensive study, Saroj Bala analyzed 11 specific astronomical references for dating events through the views of the sky projected by the *Planetarium* as well as the *Stellarium* software.

The dating of events across software and the 11 events—which deploys the cross-referencing and triangulation research method over an extended data set—were found to be consistent and were validated. The references were spread over 53 years in 3100–3200 BCE and carried a high discriminatory variety among themselves because of being spaced over a range of days and months. The chain of events include, for example, the solar eclipse when the Pandavas leave for the 13 years' exile about 14 years before the war; the lunar eclipse on the full moon of the Kartika month, followed by a solar eclipse within 14 days before the war; Krishna imparting the guidance of the *Gita* to Arjuna on the commencement of the 18 days' war, which was on the new moon and when it was in the Jyestha nakhshatra or the Scorpio constellation; the winter solstice 67 days after the beginning of the war and a day before Bhishma's demise; and the solar eclipse 13 days after the full moon and in the thirty-sixth year after the war, when Krishna's Dwarka was destroyed.

Saroj Bala's dates, however, are about a year later as compared to those given by Aryabhatta, and there is a difference of around a month between the two software programmes. This small error of estimation of an event over five millennia ago could be due to the systemic limitations of software, and for the want of suitable calibration among calendars. The chain of events was not validated for 3067 BCE, 1792 BCE or 1472 BCE, the other dates proposed for the Mahabharata War in the past. But these papers and studies were much less elaborate in their data and their analysis. They have been critiqued and improved upon by Bala, in collaboration with a few of their authors—for instance, the accurate translation of shlokas in the Bhishma Parva.

Thus, we shall stick to Aryabhatta's timeline, which marked 18 February 3102 BCE as the beginning of the Kali era and 3138 BCE as the year of the Mahabharata War. Moreover, these two dates were often used as a point of reference for marking events and declarations in ancient India and for a long time thereafter. Several hundred inscriptions that use the Kali era have been found, and the two that have been formally archived and correspond with each other closely are: the Aihole inscription of the Chalukya king Pulekesin II dated to 634 CE, which notes it as the year 3735 of the Kali era, and the Paliyam copper plates referring to Karunathdakkan in 865 CE stating that 14,490,871 days of the Kali era have elapsed.

This discussion illustrates the challenges of scientifically dating ancient events through astronomical data. The Mahabharata is a sound but exceptional case. Its accurate dating was possible only because of the rare conjunction that is closely related and the large number of precise astronomical references we find in it. This was not the case for the Rig Veda—we could not make much headway and ended with just the lower bound. The other Indian epic, the Ramayana, also contains astronomical references, but they cannot be referenced like the Mahabharata to an irrefutable, close-by and well-known conjunction and need a starting base and corroborative findings from other non-astronomical sources for the dating to be done. However, the takeaways from archaeo-astronomy are indeed important and critical for the formation of a chronology of ancient India.

The two major dates are defined up to the year, month and day, which is the chronological ideal. But this level of precision cannot be vouched for, though it is pretty evocative and illustrative, and the accuracy of dating is certainly within a margin of more or less one year. The scientific validation of the beginning of the Saptrishi era from 6777 BCE, the Kali era from 3102 BCE and the Mahabharata War in 3138 BCE are breakthroughs that were a long time coming. These will act as important anchors for using the evidence from various disciplines to rediscover the string of Indian chronology. In addition, some of these astronomical findings could be supportive of those arising from other disciplines as well. This will be the multidisciplinary research method at work to scientifically unravel and align more of the ancient past chronologically.

MORE INPUTS, ADVANCES

Just like the dating of the Kali-Mahabharata events, the beginning of the Saptrishi era in 6777 BCE is very important in the Indian chronology. It is a pivotal event and date in the Yuga system, which is the primary method of long-duration time-keeping in India all through its history and vast geography. The system is the first and overwhelming recall in any discussion on ancient chronology among the experts as well as the masses and will be taken up in the next chapter. In the meantime, we return to the findings allied to archaeology.

Genes and their mutation or changes are at the core of the evolution of any living organism. They hold important markers and insights for human beings too, in terms of when and what happened during their evolution to the present and how they vary from place to place. Every individual has a different DNA and genes, which are inherited from one's parents and carried by the chromosomes present inside cells. It occurs as a unique, repetitive sequence of a few components. It is possible to go all the way to the origin, a generation at a time, by mapping and matching individual genes.

A 'complete' set of all possible genes for scientific reference and analysis, the human genome, was announced in 2004. It was not entirely done though, and remained 5 to 10 per cent incomplete, but was good enough for the bulk of applications and has since progressed further to fill most of the gaps. The concurrent advancement in computing and communication capabilities and infrastructure during the last couple of decades gave an immediate fillip to genetic studies. There were several collaborations, for instance between the Harvard Medical School (HMS) and the Centre for Cellular and Molecular Biology (CCMB) Hyderabad. It published a genome-wide survey of the Indian people in 2009.[10]

The clustering of the Indian gene pool into a few categories and their respective geographical prevalence is notable and interesting. As also are their similarities with that of other countries and regions to the west and the east. A survey of people living in India currently, however, is by definition cross-sectional, which, as the method of scientific research, cannot lead to definitive longitudinal or historical findings. Some tentative hypotheses can be put forth. But the paper runs ahead of data, jumps to sweeping conclusions and plugs into some convenient, though unfounded, precepts about migration. It was publicized widely by the vested socio-political constituencies in India and has added to the confusion. Such migrations could easily have been the other way round and differently sequenced historically. No genetic data from ancient India was available at that time, and the title of the paper itself is misleading.

These are very early days of using genetics for archaeological and historical studies, or archaeo-genetics, but it has potential.

The samples collected from the skeletons of ancient people from various geographies are adding up and our knowledge base is rapidly expanding. From India, the genome analysis of one ancient sample was published in 2019.[11] It was collected from the skeleton of a woman who lived in Rakhigarhi between 2800 and 2300 BCE. For want of any other comparably dated sample from India, the paper compared its results with a few samples from nearby regions with which Rakhigarhi and other Harappan sites were in contact. But it toed the line of the 2009 paper and indulged in a similar amount of over-theorizing. Both the papers are the outcome of the HMS-CCMB collaboration. The results of an ancient Indian sample notwithstanding, these are very early days for archaeo-genetics and it is far from yielding any definitive conclusions on historical dating and allied patterns.

We shall have more ancient Indian genome sample data in the future. The progress, though, will be slow and hard, as the proportion of burial sites that are being found is lower here and the hot and dry climate leads to fewer usable samples. Archaeo-genetics is a young discipline, and it should try to develop its original hypotheses and theories. It uses a new form of data and analysis, and this certainly bodes well for useful insights and advances of our knowledge of ancient India in the years and decades to come.

Archaeo-genetics should not tie itself into old, outdated precepts. These will put it off track, affect its credibility and delay its progress for a long time. We saw in the case of the similarly placed archaeo-astronomy discipline how newly available computing techniques, even when applied to age-old data but without the blinkers of past theories, led to the important and definitive dating of the Kali era and the Mahabharata war.

The findings from archaeology and allied disciplines point to the continuity of Indian civilization from the Holocene or the end of the last Ice Age. There is a chain of evidence from multiple and spread-out locations to start with, that deepens along the basins of the Indus and the Saraswati, and then widens to cover a third of the Indian landmass. These can be placed in a chronological sequence, although approximate, around the two dates of 6777 BCE and 3102 BCE that can serve as anchors. The prevailing Shruti communication system in ancient times is another interesting turn that we need not only to properly ascribe historically and chronologically but also to actually thrive upon. This is a fascinating and unique feature of Indian civilization, which holds the treasures of the past.

Fortuitously, a portion of the Shruti material was documented subsequently and is thus available to us. It poses the challenge of distinguishing the original and its timing and of separating the whats and whens of important interpolations, over centuries and millennia. The other challenge is of deviation and errors, and these, however, are considerably less, given the premise of the Shruti system, and the wherewithal of accurate transmission in terms of content and tone that continues even till today. This implies that the bulk of the material considered important enough for religious-philosophical or socio-economic purposes has been well preserved. It is a nice and welcome observation to make for the understanding of Indian civilization and our traditions of scholarship.

This also implies how unfortunate it was to disregard and label Indian texts and all that lies therein as mythical in the last couple of centuries. The early exploration and documentation of the texts for nearly a century and till the late 1880s were indeed vital and important. But the wrong turns thereafter, including the haughty colonial exclusion of anything prior to 600 BCE, was unconscionable and damaging. This became the official version of Indian history and chronology for learning and research, and it continues largely the same way even in the post-Independence period. It is a huge distraction for generations of learners. It may take a long time to dismantle fully and for research to get back on track and make up for the lost couple of centuries.

'We know what we don't know' is vast, as the pivotal Rakhigarhi site is reckoned to be still barely one per cent excavated, after more than five decades of the initial explorations. This is the aggregate level of exploration for all the Indus–Saraswati sites combined. 'We don't know what we don't know' from the Gangetic Plains, the Deccan Plateau and coastal areas and similar timelines can only be in the realm of imagination.

The discussion attempted in this chapter, however, proves the continuity of Indian civilization from the eighth millennium BCE to the present, and that makes it by far the oldest in the world. This antiquity pushes human civilization itself further by at least a couple of thousand years. The Mesopotamian and Egyptian civilizations do not extend beyond the fifth millennium by any stretch and the Greek and Persian ones barely past the first millennium BCE, with the Chinese somewhere in between.

This is a bold conclusion to make, which, in effect, leads to the reconstruction of the evolution and timelines of human civilization as a whole. But it can be made definitively at this stage itself and is a major advance in our understanding of the Indian as well as the world civilization at large. In the coming chapters, we shall try to put flesh around the skeleton and wreathe the string of events and chronology around the two anchor dates.

4

FINDINGS–ADVANCES

Genealogies and Yugas

I am setting a tall order for the reader in this book. The bulk of it is 'research in action' at the frontier of not one but many disciplines. Research is inherently complex and could be intimidating. The awareness and understanding of all that has been known and the urge to question and cross frontiers to find something new, which is inherent to research work, are often demanding to the reader as well.

The research also aims at developing new hypotheses and theories by abstracting and generalizing from a piece of data for the larger reality or context. These call for high precision in expression and writing and that may sometimes come at the cost of the easy flow of the text. That this book is for the general reader is always kept in mind, and I rely on clarity and brevity and intersperse the text with background information for better readability. You may also slow down or return to particular sections at times to comprehend the content properly. The quest to answer big questions about the chronology of India's ancient past is certainly meaningful. The discovery of the unknown and resolving the confusion is always an interesting experience. The research process is indeed exhilarating on occasion and at its conclusion.

We take the findings of a discipline as the input data in our endeavour. Data has to be first assessed for being correct, and trustworthy or valid, based on the credibility of the source and the coherence with comparable findings from within the same discipline and those from others. The sequence of significant findings in a discipline along time acts as the rough tool to order data. The relevance to the rediscovery of a chronology along the spaces or types of findings is the tool to select those for detailed consideration.

Infirmities, wrong turns and gaps in the understanding of Indian history were identified in the first and second chapters. These and the chronology being the essential first step to address them scientifically, directs the line of questioning, the analysis and the interpretation. A fresh, original look and the data-driven approach, without being biased by any pre-existing theory, saw us make insightful and definitive conclusions on the basis of data from archaeological and astronomical disciplines in the last chapter. We continue here with two other major sources of data for ancient India. The Yuga system gives the big, long-run picture of the chronology. And the genealogies, describing the accession of kings in a dynasty or region, provide local and short-run information, often for just a few decades. The data is voluminous and there is much confusion in both the sources. We shall first try to get a fix on the long sweep of the chronology.

THE YUGA SYSTEM

The Saptrishi era, beginning in 6777 BCE, is replicated and recognized precisely in the traditional Yuga concept of Indian time-keeping. The concept revolves around the cycle of four Yugas—Krita, Treta, Dvapar and Kali—termed the Chatur Yugas, which follow sequentially and get repeated. The year 6777 BCE marks the beginning of Treta within the present twenty-eighth

Chatur Yugas that is in progress. The duration of the twenty-eighth Treta Yuga was slated to be 1,200 years, or up to 5577 BCE, and thereafter, the twenty-eighth Dvapar Yuga would last for 2400 years.

These dates are the result of the understanding and alignment of a plethora of material that exists on the Yuga system, in terms of how it has evolved and where it stands now. It is, in effect, the 'Movie-Snapshot' analytical method we employed in the second chapter, but here, we begin with the big and all-encompassing snapshot. A lot of this will be based on the work of Vedveer Arya,[1] who combines the study of ancient texts with that of Indian and foreign calendars and astronomy, and has tried to put them together in three volumes on chronology and numerous presentations. His analysis of ancient India is forthright, integrative with regard to the material at hand and internally consistent, and thus can be taken as a reference to be suitably critiqued and built upon for our purposes.

Yuga–Chatur Yuga–Manvantara–Kalpa

The concept of time in the Indian tradition is cyclical, in which various units have fixed durations and they repeat themselves, much like a wheel. These units of time range from Yuga to Kalpa. The duration of the Kali Yuga was increased to 432,000 years, sometime after the Mahabharata war, which is 1,200 multiplied by 360 or the number of days attributed to a year, and it prevails currently. The units of time often referred to in India, mostly from the later texts, the *Puranas*, are:

- A Chatur Yuga, of Kali and three other Yugas, has a number of years in the ratio of 1:2:3:4 respectively; thus Dvapar–864,000, Treta–1,296,000, Krita–1,728,000 years, and Chatur Yuga–4,320,000 years.
- A Manvantara has 71 Chatur Yugas and a transition period Sandhyamsha of varying duration; we are currently in the twenty-eighth Chatur Yuga of the Vaivasvata

Manvantara that has, in total, 306,720,000 years (4,320,000 multiplied by 71).

- Kalpa, or one day for Brahma, has 14 Manvantaras and their respective transition periods, or 1,000 Chatur Yugas; thus Kalpa–4,320,000,000 years (432 crore or 4.32 billion years).
- A Pralay, or one day and night for Brahma, 864 crore years, one year for Brahma, that is 864 crores multiplied by 360, is 311,040 crore years. Brahma's lifespan of 100 years is 31,104,000 crore years.

Brahma has completed 50 years of his life, or 15,552,000 crore years (155,520 billion years) since the 'beginning', and his life cycle also repeats.

These numbers cannot be taken as scientific, as they far exceed the life of the earth and the solar system, estimated to five billion years, and of the universe, which is 10–15 billion years. A figure over 10,000 times the age of the universe, which dictates the period of time that Brahma has already lived, is beyond the pale of validity. Scientific evidence starts from just after the Big Bang or the formation of the universe, which is still expanding. It will reach a maximum limit and will then take the same amount of time to shrink back cyclically, but Brahma's current age, as stated, exceeds this several thousand times or cycles, and thus cannot be considered for scientific analysis and drawing conclusions.

Such projections of time cannot be based on observation, the sine qua non of the scientific method, either through naked-eye astronomy or some other form thereof in ancient India. Even today, no tool or technology exists that is able to peer beyond the Big Bang. It is also a scientific or mathematical impossibility, as time-space collapses on approaching the Big Bang, going by Einstein's special theory of relativity. These units of time and their duration thus cannot serve the purpose of evolving a scientifically validated Indian chronology. The multiplication by 360 to increase the duration of the Kali Yuga was another wrong turn in Indian history. It perhaps opened the gates for conjecturing even bigger units of time. These may satisfy or awe the believer or serve the purpose of divinity and faith-based constructs, but they come in the way of being grounded in scientific reality and its understanding.

On the other hand, we must note that science is a philosophy too, which, like any other, could be at variance with other branches of knowledge. These include religious philosophies, whether Islam or Christianity or the *darshana*s of the Indian civilization. A philosophy is distinguished by its ontology, or its understanding of the reality of the external world, human life and existence, and epistemology, its understanding of the way or method to know reality in terms of the data or evidence and the interpretations or analyses that are valid. While science considers only perceptual data, which is observed directly by sensory organs or with the aid of some tools, as valid, religious philosophies and darshanas consider some other forms of evidence as equally valid. It could be the writings in a holy book or texts and the sayings of a great saint, person or god.

Indian darshanas, which broadly correspond to philosophy, have a rich tradition consisting of distinctive schools and are a repository of their ontological and epistemological discussions. They range from the *astika* schools, such as Mimansa, Nyaya and Vedanta, which accept, for instance, 'Shabd Pramana' or the sayings of the Vedas and sometimes the Puranas as proven or valid. *Nastika*s, which include Buddhism and Jainism, accept some other texts. But the atheist schools, for example Charvaka and Ajivika, are generally 'Pratyakasha Pramaanwadi' and accept only perceptual data, akin to science.

Scientific philosophy evolved about half a millennium ago in Europe, whereas the West Asian and Western religions and Indian darshanas are much older. Christianity, in particular, has an interesting history of challenging, accommodating and cohabitating with science. Some aspects are still contested or lie in the grey zones of indifference. In India, which has a history of divergent and often conflicting philosophies co-existing together, science has not faced an Europe-like challenge or conflict. It never will, as all schools of philosophy are taken to be on a quest for the truth. Science has come into this belief and space of co-relevance in India, and it will do well to respect the age-old darshanas and symbiotically thrive—albeit without compromising on its ontology and epistemology and thus advancement.

Returning to our chronology, the '360' multiplier for extending the duration of the Kali Yuga, although somewhat convenient, is also a deviation from and an approximation of reality. It does not correspond to the duration of the lunar year of around 354 days, or the solar year of 365.25872-plus days, and thus does not aid in the better calibration of calendars or in avoiding fractions. This wrong turn is similar to that committed by Max Müller, assigning exactly two hundred years each to the three stages of the Vedic corpus and proposing AIT, which we set aside from the purposes of the chronology.

The units of time and their duration going up to a Kalpa would certainly have befuddled the British when they tried to make sense of the Indian civilization from the mid-eighteenth century. They were not steeped in the tradition of the peaceful co-existence of alternate philosophies and constructs, and being colonial in inclination and purpose, they overreacted by consigning the bulk of the ancient Indian corpus to the realm of the mythical. We, however, shall try to separate the wheat from the chaff judiciously, for the purposes of the Indian chronology, and draw out whatever is scientifically valid and useful.

The System as It Evolved

The Rig Veda, the oldest Indian text, makes a mention of Yuga in books one and ten. The youngest of the Vedas, the Atharva-Veda, refers to the Kali Yuga. The other Veda Samhita texts, the Brahmana's *Aitareya* and *Taittriya*, mention Krita, Treta, Dvapar and Kali as the four Yugas, although the Shadvimsha calls Krita 'Pushya'. The *Mundaka* Upanishad refers to Treta Yuga. The astronomy text *Vedanga Jyotisha*, which is a part of the Vedic corpus, states a Yuga to be of the duration of five lunisolar years.

Thus, the Yuga concept exists from the very first Indian texts, and during the compilation of the Vedic corpus, it was:

- A Yuga, consisting of 5*366 days per lunisolar year, or 1,830 days. It would have 60 solar months (30.5 days each) or 62 lunar months (29.5 days), including two intercalary lunar months.
- A Chatur Yuga, consisting of 20 lunisolar years.

The next major development, which redefined the Yuga concept, took place in 6777 BCE. It was linked to a major conjunction of the sun, the moon and all planets in the Aries constellation or Nakshatra, which marked not only the start of the Saptrishi era, as discussed in earlier chapters, but more importantly, it also marked the beginning of Siddhantic astronomy and calendars based on the *Surya Siddhanta*. The redefinitions were:

- An increase in the duration of a Yuga to 1,200 years, and a Chatur Yuga to 4,800 years.
- The recognition of the current Chatur Yuga as the twenty-eighth one, and the year 6777 BCE as marking the end of the Krita Yuga of the current cycle.
- The twenty-eighth Treta Yuga was to be from 6777 BCE to 5577 BCE.
- The years elapsed in 6777 BCE were 545 years (27*20 plus five years of the twenty-eighth Krita Yuga). In effect, the Indian Yuga system started from 7322 BCE.

The increase in the duration of the Yugas was to calibrate them with the hundred Jovian cycles of 12 years each, with the latter being the period of Jupiter's revolution, which would have been found accurately by then. A Jovian year of 4,331.572 days yields 360.96 earth-days per year and with 24 hours 11 seconds per day, which is closer to the reality and needs much less calibration or intercalation of months. It may have also started the tradition of the 12-yearly Kumbh Melas. Importantly, the beginning of the calendars from 7322 BCE tallies well with the archaeological findings, for instance the oldest of the Indus–Saraswati sites in Bhirrana and Mehrgarh.

Then, some time later, the duration of the Chatur Yuga was increased to 12,000 years and the ratio of 1:2:3:4 between the durations of the Kali, Dvapar, Treta and Krita Yugas was adopted. This meant:

- The Kali Yuga would have 1,200 years, the Dvapar 2,400 years, the Treta 3,600 years and the Krita 4,800 years.
- The duration of the twenty-eighth Treta Yuga was not explicitly restated, which, having begun in 6777 BCE, but because of being conceptually and acceptably longer than Dvapar, would have meant a degree of vagueness about its end date.
- The twenty-eighth Dvapar Yuga was to be from 5577 BCE to 3177 BCE and the twenty-eighth Kali Yuga from 3177 BCE to 1977 BCE, but these would also have suffered from vagueness and a lack of precision, perhaps at both ends, around their beginning and end dates.

The change to the 1,000 Jovian cycles for a Chatur Yuga would have further improved the accuracy and the alignment of the calendars. This realization would have come well after the beginning of the twenty-eighth Treta Yuga, but it is hard to say when it actually came. The Ramayana was in the Treta Yuga and the Mahabharata in the Dvapar, and the events of the latter are validated to extend up to 3102 BCE, making it the nearer bound. The change, though, was considered important enough to be adopted.

This tendency to change the time cycle of the Yugas before the current one ended was repeated some time after the beginning of Kali Yuga. The changes, however, were far larger and many:

- The duration of the twenty-eighth Kali Yuga was increased to 432,000 years, which is 1,200 multiplied by 360.
- But on this occasion, the ongoing Yuga itself was disturbed, and the twenty-eighth Kali Yuga was now to end well over 400 millennia into the Common Era.
- The concept of the Manvantara was introduced, each consisting of 71 Chatur Yugas and a suitable transition period.
- The current one is the Vaivasvata Manvantara, which is the seventh of 14 Manvantaras in a Kalpa or one day of Brahma; the Pralay is one day and one night of Brahma, and then there is Brahma's year, with 50 years out of his 100-year lifespan having been completed.

These implied that the Kali Yuga will continue forever for all practical purposes. The extraordinary length of the timelines also imparted a sense of timelessness to the god Brahma and created space for all others.

Tidying up the System Together

The above snapshot and the movie actually explain the system well in terms of the whats of the units of time, their duration and how they came about. The underlying reasons, or the whys, were essentially the quest for accuracy and the alignment with respect to the reality. It was also to keep pace with unfolding astronomical phenomena, with new learning and the expansion of the knowledge base by making suitable adaptations and changes. The quest was excruciating, as the revolution periods of both the moon and the earth are not whole numbers, and one can go up to an infinite number of decimal places in case of the latter.

A lunisolar calendar further complicated the matter in India, as it meant grappling with two separate cycles of different approximations. The switch to Jupiter or the Jovian cycles was daring and showed enterprise and innovation, but that was not a whole number either and was just slightly better and neater in approximation. The realignment was qualitatively simpler in case of the Islamic calendar that already used lunar astronomy, as it was for the European system that only used the solar one.

The latter went through the well-known switch from the Julian to the Georgian calendar in 1582 CE. It was ordained by the head of the Church, and it meant skipping the dates from 4 October to 15 October and adjusting four days in the vernal equinox during the same year. This corrected for about one more day per century that the earth takes for the 1,400 years of the Julian calendar and provided a formula for the correction of one day every 400, 4,000 and 20,000 years going further. Indians, however, have managed to achieve such accuracy since Aryabhatta's time.

One can surmise that another major conjunction of the sun, the moon and the planets observed on 18 February 3102 BCE precipitated the last set of changes. Aryabhatta and his student, Latadeva, calibrated the Indian calendar from that date, and it has retained the accuracy thereafter. This date, and not 3177 BCE, was to mark the beginning of the Kali Yuga or the Kali era. Thus, the twenty-eighth Dvapar Yuga would have been extended to 3102 BCE, lasting 2,475 years from 5577 BCE to 3102 BCE—or some other, as the date of transition from the twenty-eighth Treta to the Dvapar Yuga has never been clearly stated, which if, for the sake of illustration, it was 5100 BCE, would mean a 2,677-year-long twenty-eighth Treta Yuga (6777–5100 BCE) and a 1,998-year-long twenty-eighth Dvapar Yuga (5100–3102 BCE). And thereupon, the 432,000-year-long twenty-eighth Kali Yuga, stretching from 3102 BCE to 428898 CE!

The major conjunctions, such as those in 6777 BCE and 3102 BCE, evidently had a defining impact on Indian astronomy. This could be due to a lack of central authority, such as the Pope in Europe, and the corrections and switches had to be based on an astronomical event that was clearly visible to the naked eye and hard to ignore or err on. Since 3102 BCE, with the accuracy and the alignment of the calendar no longer a constraint, others could have a field day. The stupendous increase in the duration of Kali

Yuga to 432,000 years, in effect, made the Yuga system irrelevant to the calendar, especially its use for marking the seasons, months and days, and festivals and other religious and social activities. Perhaps that is why Aryabhatta's contribution is considered so pivotal in Indian astronomy.

The others went on to invent the new Chatur Yuga, though still around the 1:2:3:4 ratio between the numbers of years belonging to the four Yugas and the remaining system of the Manvantara, the Kalpa and Brahma's lifespan. It must have been done with a design and a purpose in mind—that, having expanded wide and continued for so long, it will be useful enough. The last set of changes, leading to the invention of the concept of the Manvantara and further, have little relevance to astronomy and calendars and to our rediscovery of the Indian chronology.

A truly novel insight and conclusion, based on the twenty-eighth Treta Yuga from 6777 BCE, was on the beginning of the Yuga chronology from 7322 BCE onwards. This, being in alignment with archaeological and other scientific data, brings the Yuga concept, which is often projected and perceived as esoteric, within the purview and under the precepts of formal research. It also ascertains the scientific foundations, astronomical and mathematical consistency, and robustness of the Yuga chronology.

This was so from the beginning and continued well after the Mahabharata and the commencement of the twenty-eighth Kali Yuga or the Kali era. It went on until the introduction of the Manvantara, the Kalpa and other terms, which, anyway, were not relevant or applicable while preparing the astronomy-rooted calendars and the chronology. The periods of the twenty-eighth Treta and Dvapar Yugas—especially the clarity around the start of the Treta Yuga in 6777 BCE and the end of the Dvapar in 3102 BCE, and the ambiguity on the Treta-Dvapar transition year in between—the conclusion on the commencement of the Indian calendar from 7322 BCE and the reaffirmation of the Kali era from 3102 BCE are important takeaways from this exercise.

THE RAMAYANA AND THE GENEALOGIES

The ambiguity about the year of transition from the twenty-eighth Treta to the Dvapar Yuga opens up the right space for suitably assessing the findings related to the Ramayana. It is a defining event and a text about Indian history and civilization, along with the Mahabharata. The data for the Ramayana, however, are of a different type in terms of the sources and incontrovertibility for the purposes of dating; and we have to travel across the disciplines of astronomy, geography and genealogies for this.

Similar to the Mahabharata, the positions of the sun, moon and the five planets in various constellations, which can be observed by the naked eye, are described with clarity in the Valmiki Ramayana. They are sufficiently detailed for astronomical analysis and describe many sequential events, allowing for cross-verification. The validity of the text and the astronomical references are well established. These positions have been mapped by *Planetarium* and other astronomy software for dates in several studies[2] in the last couple of decades:

- At the birth of Rama, the sun was in the Aries constellation, the moon and Jupiter in Cancer, Venus in Pisces, Saturn in Libra and Mars in Capricorn, and on the ninth day of the waxing moon in the Chaitra month, which corresponds to noon on 10 January 5114 BCE.
- The reference to the Putra-Kamesthi Yajna, a Vedic ritual praying for the birth of a son, is dated to 15 January 5115 BCE; the planned date for Rama's coronation, which ultimately meant him leaving for the forests, to 5 January 5039 BCE; the start of Rama's Sena or his army's march to Lanka to 10 September 5076 BCE; Ravana's killing to 4 December 5076 BCE; and the completion of Rama's forest exile and his coronation when he was 39 years old to 2 January 5075.

These dates, unlike the Mahabharata, cannot be referenced, for instance, to a major conjunction such as that of 18 February 3102 BCE, which has been recorded by Aryabhatta and several other ancient astronomers. That became the point of reference for the calibration of the subsequent eras and for dating major events in many texts and inscriptions. But the end of the twenty-eighth Treta Yuga with Rama's demise, let's say, 50 years later around 5025 BCE, is consistent with our dating and the periods of the twenty-eighth Chatur Yuga—based on the two ascertained anchor conjunctions, the farther one being that of 6777 BCE.

The mid-point of the two conjunctions is 4950 BCE, which is close to the estimated end date of Treta in 5025 BCE. The margin of error is +/- 15 years, depending on Rama's life and his regnal period realistically ranging from 64 to 104 years and 25 to 65 years, respectively. The astronomical possibility of all the positions at Rama's birth and other referenced events being repeated—within a thousand years on either side of 5025 BCE and that being the maximum space available from our Yuga analysis—is mathematically zero. Thus, Rama's birth in 5114 BCE, his coronation after the victory in Lanka in 5075 BCE, and the end of the twenty-eighth Treta Yuga in 5025 BCE, with a margin of error of +/- 15 years, are validated.

Corroborative data from geography relates to the sequence of scores of places visited during Rama's exile. These are recorded in the Valmiki Ramayana and form a verifiable and cogent route up to the sea coast from Ayodhya. The bridge-like structures noticeable along the 30-kilometre stretch of the sea between Rameswaram on the Indian coast and Talai-Mannar on the Sri Lankan side are recorded in the maps and government notifications from the fifteenth century onwards, and it is unmistakably perceptible even now.

Most of the places visited carry the same name till today, which is generally considered to be a strong indicator of the historicity and authenticity of the information under consideration. The visit has been woven into vivid tales and customs at most of these places, which also carry distinctive identifier points and locations. The places are greatly revered all along, at the local, regional and national levels, and Rama's visit there is mentioned in religious and other texts. Some interesting data in the text, which is further researched and refined upon, is the genealogy of 94 Suryavansha rulers, also referred to as the Iksvaku dynasty[3] of the Koshala kingdom in Ayodhya. Rama was the sixty-fourth ruler.

The absence of archaeological finds with respect to the Ramayana, which are correspondingly dated to the sixth millennium BCE, is currently a missing link. While this cannot rule out those events and timelines by any means, either scientifically or archaeologically, our validation poses new research questions and directions. It certainly moves the questions into the domain of 'we know that we don't know' for the discipline of archaeology. Given the centrality of the Ramayana to Indian history and civilization, there is a strong case for greater vigour and wide-ranging excavations and for the adoption of suitable tools and techniques.

The Lahurdeva site, not far from Ayodhya and dated to around 8000 BCE, provides a few important pointers. Such settlements would have continued and progressed as the region was highly hospitable and a trajectory similar to that in the Indus-Saraswati region is most likely to have existed here. Areas such as the Gangetic Plains, which primarily used wooden structures, could be explored in a few innovative ways and at locations particularly around the places specifically mentioned in the Ramayana and which are still revered. On the other hand, not all events leave archaeological evidence. In a research initiative, one deploys all that exists and is available at a point in time, and here, it is the data from archaeo-astronomy and geography and the conclusions from Yuga analysis in the case of dating the Ramayana.

A View of Timelines from the Ramayana

The genealogy of the Iksvaku dynasty is a veritable treasure, given its antiquity in particular. A key unit in the genealogical-chronology analysis is the average duration of a king's reign. In the Ramayana, the earlier ruler, Dasaratha, had been ruling for a long time and was in his old age when Rama was born in 5114 BCE. The latter was crowned king in 5075 BCE at the age of 39, and the next ruler, Kusa, was born thereafter. Rama would have reigned for 30 to 40 years to establish the famed Ram Rajya, and handed over the reins when Kusa came of age and was ready.

This indicates the prevalence of long reigns and the orderly and mature transition between rulers in the dynasty. A few rulers, let's say around 25 per cent, may have reigned for shorter periods due to early deaths or other reasons. Thus, an average 30-year regnal period is justifiable. It implies:

- The first ruler, Manu, was crowned in 6965 BCE, that is 5,075 plus 1,890 (63 rulers for 30 years each); which is well beyond the twenty-eighth Chatur Yuga that started in 6782 BCE (five years of its elapsed twenty-eighth Krita Yuga plus 6777 BCE).
- The reign of the last ruler, Brihatksaya, would have ended in 4125 BCE, that is 5,025 (the end of Rama's reign) minus 900 (30 rulers), and the second-last ruler, Brihadbala, would have reigned from 4185 to 4155 BCE.

Brihadbala's regnal period does not tally, as he participated in the Mahabharata war on the Kaurava side and was killed by Arjuna's son Abhimanyu in 3138 BCE. The gap of over 1,000 years is bridgeable if the average regnal period is around 60 years, which is unrealistic. Else, the genealogy we have is not complete, or there should have been twice the number of rulers or 60 of them post-Rama.

The recent work of Vedveer Arya, although differing slightly in dates, concurs that the Iksvaku dynasty weakened after Agnivarna and led to a split in the kingdom.[4] There is no information for over 1,000 years, till Brihadbala and his few ancestors are mentioned in the Puranas and the Mahabharata, who would have ruled just the rump of a great dynasty. Agnivarna, the eighty-fifth ruler in our list, is dated to around 4400 BCE, and the genealogy thereafter can be considered to be uncertain and suffused with missing names of rulers. The gap too, in terms of the dating of Brihadbala's death and the Mahabharata, can be taken as accounted for.

On the farther side, Manu is the first Suryavansha ruler who is reckoned as the earliest king of Indian civilization. He is also identified with the *Manusmriti*, a treatise on Dharma, constitution and law, and ways of conduct of society. The Smriti texts attributed to individual authors, for example Yjnavalkaya, Vatsyayana or Manu, are derived from the older Shruti texts of the Vedic corpus. The Ramayana itself is a bridge between the Vedic and post-Vedic culture and a commentary on the Vedas portrayed in a narrative or story form.[5] While the Rig, Yajur and Sama Vedas are mentioned in the Ramayana, the youngest, Atharva Veda, is not so specifically. Its themes and elements are present though, and in abundance, and this could be due to Atharva having yet to attain the status of a Veda, and the Ramayana events being concurrent. The Valmiki text may be written sometime along the way or later.

This will put the Atharva Veda just before or within the 5000–5500 BCE period. The other three will be earlier, and the Rig Veda could plausibly date back to 6500–7000 BCE. Such a date will fit with the observation of the 6777 BCE conjunction, requiring the knowledge of five planets, cycles of the moon and the sun, and Nakshatras or constellations; and the dating of archaeological sites at Bhirrana and in northwest India, which is ascertained as broadly the location for the compilation of the Vedas from their content.

A remarkable feature is the longevity of the Iksvaku dynasty. It runs unbroken and holds pre-eminence from Manu to Agnivarna, which is a period from 6985 BCE till the end of the eighty-fifth ruler's reign in 4445 BCE, or for over 25 centuries. The continuity of the dynasty, though in a much-emaciated state, is recorded up to the Mahabharata in 3138 BCE. This is extraordinary in the history of Indian and world civilization, where dynasties last a couple of hundred years but rarely more than half a millennium. That is perhaps why Rama's exile soon after the announcement of his coronation was such an earth-shaking event. He was to become the sixty-fourth ruler and his conduct in accepting the exile and thereafter was exemplary, making him so revered as a person across the length and breadth of India, till today and perhaps forever.

The Iksvaku dynasty was located in Koshala and its capital was Ayodhya, in the eastern part of the present-day Uttar Pradesh. It is around 750 kilometres and a twenty-five days' walking distance from the Bhirrana area, as per Google Maps! Conceivably, the region in between the Gangetic Plains and the vast expanse of the subcontinent all the way to Sri Lanka during Rama's exile and reign around 5050 BCE was not only populated but was also a thriving civilization.

This shows how little we know of Indian civilization and history. That little was also not handled well, unfortunately, in terms of the care and sensitivity ancient data deserves and the unbiased analysis and conceptualization, and it thus failed to direct further research suitably. The wrong turns were taken and they piled up, as illustrated in the summary table at the end of Chapter Two. It led to the wrong and brutal amputation of ancient India's longevity and the denial of its geographical spread, which has demonstrated its continuity since 7000 BCE for sure. The rightful exploration of Indian civilization was hindered and wrongful teachings got propagated in the colonial period and also the post-Independence decades. The Iksvaku dynasty, the Ramayana and the Vedas are among the greatest heritage of humankind. And their appropriate understanding and appreciation is important for India and the world at large.

The Emergence of the First 'Imperial' Dynasty

The pre-eminence of the Iksvaku dynasty would have been established over generations. Its origin from Manu would have meant that they had a head start in the organization of society and in the running of a monarchy-based state, which the habitats in various regions would have emulated. An interesting observation, based on the emergence of Shruti texts and the Vedas in the Indus-Saraswati region and the subsequent Smriti texts in the eastern Gangetic Plains, is that the latter was more densely populated—thus needing the shift from a clan-based to a monarchy-based order at the earliest and leading it.

The late eighth to early seventh millennium could be the period of transition from clans to an organized society in the Gangetic Plains. This is not that incredible as the antecedents of the Mesopotamian civilization have been archaeologically traced to its northwest in the hilly regions and before 7000 BCE. An expanding society needs someone to frame, interpret and enforce rules, and Manu was the pioneer. He linked and derived his authority from the Vedas, which had been written earlier and was thus well known by his time and established as a point of reference. Passing on authority in a hereditary fashion is the usual evolutionary next step observed in emerging societies, leading to the creation of a ruler or a king and the dynasty.

The influence of the Iksvaku rulers would have spread, as the people and their clan or local heads started adhering to the *Manusmriti* in particular. It is a rule book or a code book of 'Dharma', and the right and righteous conduct of the Iksvaku rulers would have become a point of reference or model for it. Their authority would have been largely moral and would have been strengthened over generations. Social groups in nearby and far-off regions, while getting organized under kings, came to consider the pioneering and most evolved Iksvakus as the kings of kings or the Maharaja-Dhiraja, the 'emperors'.

In this King-Emperor framework, the latter is not collecting tributes or entering into formal treaties or enforcing authority by force. The influence though was no less powerful, built on the frame and the specifics of Dharma. The Iksvaku dynasty commanded recognition and respect, as is evident from the description of Rama's journey and interactions during exile, across the length and breadth of India. He was asked to put an end to many individuals who had forsaken Dharma, often termed *rakshasa*s and demons—for example, Khara-Dushana and Baali. In fact, the march to Lanka and the battle with Ravana and his clan is called a Dharma-Yuddha, or a war to uphold the right code and conduct.

The Continuity of Genealogies

With the Iksvaku dynasty, the emperor or imperial framework emerged and took root in Indian society and civilization. There was acceptance, actually expectation, of such a central authority that rulers across the nation looked up to. The imperial dynasty was also identified with a capital city and region. Ayodhya and Koshala were the first such central locations within Indian civilization, which stretched from the early seventh millennium to the middle of the fifth millennium, for nearly 25 centuries.

The Indus-Saraswati region, particularly the area around Bhirrana and Rakhigarhi, must have been comparably evolved and perhaps competitive to the Ayodhya–Koshala part of India. The latter took the lead with the Smriti texts and instrumentalities but lost its prominence after Iksvaku emperor Agnivarna, whose reign is dated to around 4400 BCE. This could be due to better social-technological-economic developments in the Indus-Saraswati region, and prominence swung back to the place of origin of earlier Shruti or Vedic texts.

In the later fifth millennium BCE, the Kuru dynasty rose to pre-eminence or attained the emperor status in Indian civilization. Although there are some references to the founder of the dynasty, Kuru, in the earlier Shruti or Vedic corpus, we have the genealogy of 35 rulers from Puru to Yudhisthira.[6] As per our yardstick of the thirty years regnal period per ruler, this will add up to 1,050 years for the available genealogy. It will broadly align with the end of Yudhisthira's rule, coinciding with the beginning of the Kali era in 3102 BCE.

The wives of the Kuru rulers came from various kingdoms and clans—for example, Kekaya, north-west Punjab in present-day Pakistan; Vaideh, Nepal to the north of Ayodhya; Vidharbha, in eastern Maharashtra; Anga, in northern Bengal; Takshshila, Khyber-Pakhtunwa; Kashi, eastern Uttar Pradesh; Koshala-Ayodhya; Trigarta, Haryana; Magadha and central Bihar. This gives a measure of the civilizational extent in the fourth millennium BCE, in the spread of kingdoms and their deep socio-cultural engagement. The Kurus had married into the imperial Iksvaku dynasty around 3600 BCE, indicating their rise and the levelling of their relative status.

The Mahabharata War of 3138 BCE was a watershed in Indian history, a time when most of the kingdoms were forced to participate and take sides. While a bulk of the kingdoms were from the Indus-Saraswati region and the Gangetic Plains, which seems to be the most thickly populated, the spread was across the Vindhyas, the Deccan Plateau, coastal Andhra, Tamil Nadu and Kerala, and up to Sinhala or Sri Lanka, which sided with the Kauravas. The genealogies of some of these kingdoms are available. We shall, however, track the Indian chronology along the rulers of the dynasty considered pre-eminent or as emperors. It transitioned from the Iksvakus to the Kurus in the late fourth millennium BCE.

The information about genealogy and chronology becomes richer post-Mahabharata with the third set of ancient texts after Shruti and Smriti, the Puranas. They are much less abstract and written in the form of stories for the masses.

Four Puranas, namely Vayu, Matsya, Vishnu and Bhavishya, provide detailed family trees of various dynasties. They, however, need a good feel of the whole Sanskrit literature and the language, and may confound, such as the attempts of Frederick Pargiter in the early twentieth century. He made several errors[7], which have been addressed subsequently.

From Parikshita, who became ruler after Yudhisthira, the Kuru dynasty flourished for five generations or till around 2950 BCE. A defeat to the non-Veda adherent Salva tribe and the flooding of Hastinapur during the reign of the sixth post-Mahabharata ruler Nichaksu compromised its pole position and standing. Capital and people were shifted to the easternmost edge of the empire at Kausambi, near present-day Prayagraj. The Panchala kingdom, in the central and northern parts of Uttar Pradesh that were ruled by Drupad, Draupadi's father at the time of the Mahabharata War, rose in influence.

The Drupad kingdom's rise to prominence was nowhere near the level of the Iksvaku and Kuru dynasties. There were over a dozen large kingdoms from north-west India to the Gangetic delta. One of them was Magadha, with the capital at Patliputra or present-day Patna in Bihar. It slowly stole a march over others, in a millennium or so, to the imperial level. Magadha became a unitary political-economic entity and covered the bulk of India, or an empire by the medieval or modern yardsticks too, on a couple of occasions. To its genealogy and chronology, we thus shift our attention.

Based on the Puranas and other relevant texts, Kota Venkatachala[8] has compiled the consistent and continuous genealogy of Magadha rulers. The 1957 work addresses the anomalies and gaps that had confounded earlier attempts, and is arguably free of confusion and errors. Most of his work has been digitized and can be freely downloaded on web search.

The founding of the Magadha kingdom by Brihadritha, *c.* 3500 BCE [A descendant of Kuru; Brihadritha's tenth descendant, Jarasandha, fought Bhima and was killed; his eleventh descendant fought in the Mahabharata war on the side of the Pandavas]

23 rulers of the Brihadritha dynasty, post-Mahabharata:	3138–2132 bce
5 rulers of the Pradyota dynasty:	2132–1994 bce
10 rulers of the Sisunaga dynasty:	1994–1634 bce
2 rulers of the Nanda dynasty:	1634–1534 bce
12 rulers of the Maurya dynasty:	1534–1218 bce
10 rulers of the Sunga dynasty:	1218–918 bce
4 rulers of the Kanwa dynasty:	918–833 BCE
32 rulers of the Andhra dynasty:	833–327 BCE
7 rulers of the Gupta dynasty:	327–82 BCE
24 rulers of the Parmara dynasty:	82 BCE–CE 1193

[Four Rajput or Agni-Vansha dynasties—Parmara, Pratihara, Chalukya, Chahmana—ruled the bulk of India]

Venkatachala's work carries a detailed description, about a page each, of every ruler from Brihadritha to the Gupta dynasties, and also up to Prithviraj Chauhan. The latter, in a confederacy of the kings of three other Agni-Vansha or Rajput dynasties, fought with Mohammad Ghori in the second Battle of Tarain near Kurukshetra. It is now more accurately dated to 1192 CE, by the better alignment of the Islamic Hijri calendar and Indian calendars, where the start of a year could vary up to six months on either side.

The 4,331 years duration with 128 rulers that is covered makes for an average regnal period of 37 years. This genealogy and dating broadly align with the findings of other Indian scholars, who have used traditional sources and texts. They have also countered the readings of various colonial explorers and pointed out the errors they made. Vedveer Arya goes further and adds the extensive study of inscriptions by reading them afresh and outlining the specifics of the mistakes made line by line and word by word, whether in the understanding of the Sanskrit language or the transcription of the Brahmi or any of the other scripts used.

Arya dates the 29 inscriptions of the Guptas and orders them chronologically, from the fifth year of the dynasty in 330 BCE to its 224th year in 110 BCE.[9] His periodization of the Gupta dynasty from 334 to 89 BCE is almost identical to that of Venkatachala's. The two works, referenced here, are independent and have been produced over seven decades apart from one another. Arya's findings from the texts are corroborated by the methodical and comprehensive study of inscriptions and archaeo-astronomy.

They fit with our discussion and conclusions drawn in this chapter and the previous one. There is a longitudinal or chronological consistency of the events and their dating, from 6777 BCE to 1192 CE, for nearly nine millennia. The assessment and analysis of the findings and advances from multiple disciplines, ranging from archaeology to genealogy, stand the tests of cross or external validity, and continual and time-interval or internal validity, and meet the repeatability or reliability yardsticks of the multidisciplinary scientific research protocol. There is rigour, for instance, in the way the end period of 1192 CE is evaluated for accuracy up to the year; the Mahabharata and related events are at +/- one year validity; and the older Ramayana dates to +/- 15 years.

These chronology conclusions, however, are at a huge variance to the datings prevailing since the early twentieth century or over 100 years. They would call for a massive overhaul in the design and detail of the Indian chronology construct, and the periodization and dates of specific historical events. This is the subject of our exploration in the next few chapters. We shall assess our conclusions for the horizontal consistency with respect to other parallel chronologies in the world and other Indian regions wherever relevant and available; and for the dating of specific and pivotal events that have had major consequences, as case studies. We shall also make major changes and minor refinements wherever necessary, and will distil new research questions and hypotheses going further.

5

THE REDISCOVERED CONSTRUCT

This chapter is the fulcrum of our endeavour to rediscover the Indian chronology. We bring to bear the findings—advances outlined in the previous two chapters—for suitably updating and aligning it. A lot of ground has been covered so far. Our conclusions on the dates, which cut across and synthesize multiple disciplines, open a new window into India's antiquity. They point towards a fresh, original construct or the design of its chronology.

An altogether new construct is better, when the variance and thereby the correction required are major and conceptual. This is true for the ancient Indian chronology, which has not been updated for nearly a century or in effect since the work of Vincent Smith around 1910. And that too was an outcome of several wrong turns, as we saw in the second chapter, as much due to the initial, tentative stages of exploration and understanding as to the limitations of the colonial mindset, intent and haughtiness. In addition, and fortuitously, a huge amount of relevant data and findings have come up, from the discovery of Harappan sites and from multiple disciplines, in the past century. These have to be suitably accounted for and incorporated.

Moreover, a new construct helps us avoid any blinkers and biases from pre-existing, partial or outdated theories. We take the empiricist or data-upwards approach of the multidisciplinary research method. The new construct is outlined first in this method of theory-building. It ought to flow logically and cogently from the conclusions drawn in the previous chapters. Thereupon, the construct is assessed for internal and external consistency and validity, including squaring up with the chronology that is prevailing currently. Here, one moves from the conceptual to the specific—the assessment of the design or overall construct, then the key building blocks or periods, and on to the dating of a single event or a cluster thereof.

The plethora of anomalies that have sunk deep and wide and the phenomenal advances of the past century put this chapter on a very interesting footing. An open and curious mind will find the journey to be one of joy. One rarely gets an opportunity to research and rediscover something as fundamental as the chronology of a major world civilization's antiquity. It will, however, be a beginning. The task of setting the record straight will continue in the later chapters as well and will raise a new set of questions to be researched in the years to come.

THE 'FOUR PERIODS' CONSTRUCT OF INDIAN ANTIQUITY

A few conclusions stand out from our exploration so far. They are akin to a set of keys for unlocking the chronology of India's deep past. The vista that opens out is formidable and forms four clearly observable periods. Each period is a distinctive contour and the four of them together encompass and map the lay of the land. Their internal and external consistency, in the sequence and the placing of the events, extends from millennia and centuries to decades and years. The 'Four Periods' construct of Indian antiquity's chronology brings us to the classification stage of the theory-building process—an important juncture and a point of advancement in the scientific understanding of a phenomenon.

One of the conclusions is the **ten-millennia continuity of Indian civilization.** It is along the time dimension post-Holocene, without a break, and across the space of its subcontinental landmass. This time-space is validated by the data from multiple disciplines which add up together. For instance, archaeological findings related to 'year-round occupation and settling—agriculture—animal domestication—community habitats' from the eighth millennium and some extending beyond 8000 BCE, thus the civilization at Lahurdeva, Bhirrana and Mehrgarh in present-day Uttar Pradesh, Haryana and Baluchistan, respectively. Such finds continue thereafter for every millennium, though varying in their richness and expanse. That makes for the ten millennia of India's civilizational continuity, ascertainable from the turn of the eighth millennium BCE to the present.

Archaeological data is corroborated by the Yuga system of Indian timekeeping that is calculated to begin from 7322 BCE and the genealogies of the King-Emperor framework extending from around 7000 BCE till 1192 CE. These timelines are supported by astronomical observations noted in several ancient texts and inscriptions. Take, for instance, the occurrence of a major conjunction in the Aries constellation of the five planets visible to the naked eye and the sun and the moon on 3 December 6777 BCE and 18 February 3102 BCE. The dates are proven by the astrophysics analysis using software tools and technologies now at hand, and can be ascertained by anyone anywhere.

The findings cover the long and short of continuity in time—from the millennia and more offered by archaeology and the Yuga system to the decades and years offered by genealogy and astronomy calendars. Geographical continuity, too, extends from the Himalayas to the seas and the present-day northeast to Afghanistan and the Iran border. There would be a steady expansion in the time-space of Indian civilization post-Holocene and from the early settling nodes, such as Lahurdeva, Bhirrana and Mehrgarh that we know of. Similar nodes will have appeared in other parts, as hunter-gatherers abounded all over the Indian subcontinent. And the expanse of organized society throughout would have conceivably started emerging in the early eighth millennium BCE.

The links and coherence among regions would have progressed and intensified, unless broken by the extraordinary circumstances observed in the case of Harappan sites around 1900 BCE. This instance and also the availability of large and highly habitable but empty places would have invited migrations among the various regions. They would have continued all along, as it happens today from the rural to the urban, and the eastern to the western and southern regions, for better socio-economic circumstances.

6777 BCE and 3102 BCE are anchors in the chronology of Indian antiquity. These are defined precisely up to the day, which astronomy-based dating ought to do, and are recognized for their usefulness and veracity in preparing calendars. They were pivotal in organizing, improving and re-aligning the Yugas, the system of reckoning and recording time over long durations. 6777 BCE marks the beginning of the twenty-eighth Treta Yuga and the shift from five to 1,200 years Yugas and then to 12,000 years of Chatur Yuga. 3102 BCE is the year of the commencement of the twenty-eighth Kali Yuga, which is going on right now, and the re-statement of its duration to 432,000 years.

India invented the annual calendar way back in the early settling period, several millennia before the other ancient world civilizations. This was due to its primordial and specific need to accurately predict the onset of the southwest monsoon. The calendar was lunisolar, which posed the persistent challenge of synchronizing 12 30-day months in a 360-day year, to the 29.53 day cycle of the moon, and just over 365.251 days of the earth's revolution. Frequent adjustments were needed, through the introduction of half or full intercalary months in some years. Realigning the Yuga system to the Jovian cycle or Jupiter's revolution was a bold move—its cycle spanning 4,331.572 days translates to 12 years of the much closer 360.96 earth-days per year, and it led to the initial shift to the 1,200 years Yuga; then the 12,000 years Chatur Yuga, including the duration of the other three Yugas in a 4:3:2:1 ratio, to 1,200 years in the Kali Yuga. Finally, it led to the duration of Kali Yuga being multiplied by 360 to yield 432,000 years.

In the absence of a central authority in India—such as Pope Gregory, who mandated the corrected calendar for Europe in 1582 CE—the major conjunctions that were hard to miss out and err upon, and which were possible to cross-verify among widely dispersed astronomers, served the purpose. The Indian calendar was perfected for all times in the past and all times to come, with its anchor laid at 3102 BCE, within a century or so when the conjunction was still a living and shared memory. It implied a clarity in astronomical observations and mathematical calculations as well as their importance in outlining the relevant concepts and procedures for calibrations going further, including the introduction of intercalary months.

This is remarkable, being achieved over four millennia before Europe, and is a measure of the advances achieved by Indian astronomy and mathematics. The dating of hundreds of inscriptions in the Kali era, found across the subcontinent's geography till a few centuries ago, and its consistency with all subsequent calendars, sakas or eras, and their adherence to it, underscore the acceptance and validity of 3102 BCE—and correspondingly that of 6777 BCE, which also notably marks the beginning of the earliest Saptrishi era—as the meaningful anchors of the ancient Indian chronology.

325 BCE as the intermediary marker, between 3102 BCE and 1192 CE, is useful. Alexander's two-year-long campaign ending in 325 BCE, although reckoned to be of little historical importance or consequence to Indian civilization, anchored the chronology evolved in the early twentieth century. The consequent dating of events embodied the data and understanding of Indian antiquity that was available till then, to the colonial chroniclers in particular. It also marked the earliest application of the scientific method to Indian history and chronology, albeit clouded by the colonial mindset, intent and context and limited by their amateurish education, grounding and training in research.

Since the 325 BCE-based chronology still prevails, the dating is useful to serve as a point of reference and departure. It may be clumsy and deviant, but our endeavour for rediscovery needs to relate to and build upon something that exists, in terms of the design as well as the detail. The date is an important marker though, as some degree of alignment was achieved between the European and Indian calendars going further and the external accounts of India from Greek and other travellers started becoming available. Moreover, 325 BCE lies at the sort of a mid-point between 3102 BCE and 1192 CE, which aids in a balanced exploration of the 'before' and 'after' periods.

The Mahabharata war of 3138 BCE, closely linked to 3102 BCE, and the Ramayana a couple of millennia earlier, are by far the most defining events of Indian history and civilization. They retain their salience even today and will do so perhaps forever. Besides the philosophy, culture and way of life, the Mahabharata in particular was pivotal for the political economy of India then and subsequently. Most of the states and kings, from the southern Pandya and Sinhala and the eastern Anga and Banga provinces to almost everyone in the central, western and northern regions, participated, and sided with one or the other contestant in the war. It affirmed the shift in the centre of gravity or India's King-Emperor framework, underway since the late fifth millennium BCE, to the Kurus from the Iksvakus of Ayodhya.

The Kuru capital Hastinapur, though, was flooded not long after, during the reign of the fifth post-Mahabharata ruler around 2950 BCE. The consequent relocation of the capital to Kausambi near present-day Prayagraj set in motion another eastward shift of India's centre of gravity. Magadha rose to prominence in a few centuries, with its capital at Patliputra or Patna. It retained its empire-like eminence for over two millennia, with the Guptas being the last such Magadha-based dynasty. Thereafter, the situation becomes fuzzy, though the Surya and Chandra Vansha Rajputs and the Agni-Vansha dynasties—Parmara, Pratihara, Chalukya and Chahmana—and their sub-lineages could together lay some claim to pre-eminence. The Rajput kingdoms were indeed spread across much of India's length and breadth, and their lineages contain a good degree of continuity from the first century BCE. They came together as a confederacy in support of Prithviraj Chauhan for the Battle of Tarain in 1192 CE. Vincent Smith also reckons the five and a half centuries between Harsha's death in 640 CE and the Battle of Tarain, in particular, as the Rajput period.[1]

The conclusions—'the ten-millennia continuity of Indian civilization', '6777 BCE and 3102 BCE are anchors', and '325 BCE is an intermediary marker'—come together and create a classification of the chronology into the four periods. This is taken further and built upon, with the suitable titling of the periods around the string of major events and influential conditions validated in the earlier chapters, as the **Four Periods** construct of Indian antiquity:

i. **Early settling period** [*c.* 9000–6777 BCE]
End of the last Ice Age or Holocene in India, best estimated to around 9000 BCE; earliest evidence of year-round occupation, sedentary life, and agriculture and animal domestication, from Lahurdeva pre-8000 BCE and soon afterwards at Mehrgarh, Bhirrana, etc.; evolution of communication methods from the hunter-gatherer days into a rudimentary language and basic knowledge of monsoons, around 7500 BCE; observations of the cycles of planetary bodies and seasons, and the emergence of the Shruti tradition and its early precepts on life and living, around 7000 BCE.

ii. **Ramayana**–Mahabharata **period** [6777–3102 BCE]
Building blocks for the rapid civilizational advance in rural habitats, particularly in the Indus-Saraswati

region of northwestern India, seventh millennium BCE; identification of Nakshatras, planetary cycles and emergence of mathematics and astronomy-based calendars, early seventh millennium BCE; flowering of the Shruti tradition, into the earliest versions of the Vedas and allied vocational texts, and accompanied by the Gurukul learning system, late seventh millennium BCE; shift in the civilizational centre of gravity to Koshala in central-north India, which takes the lead in the Smriti tradition, and emergence of the King-Emperor framework, sixth millennium BCE; birth of Rama in 5114 BCE and the events of the Ramayana in the century that followed; formation of a large number of urban and coastal habitats or cities and towns, linked to a network of rural hubs or villages, all over the Indian subcontinent, and the shift of the centre back to northwest India with the rise of the Kurus, fifth millennium BCE; Mahabharata war in 3138 BCE.

iii. **Post**-Mahabharata **period** [3102–325 BCE]
Death of Yudhisthira and Krishna and ascension of Parikshita as Kuru emperor, 3102 BCE; delineation of Siddhantic astronomy and a perfected lunisolar calendar, based on planetary and 12-constellation observations and mathematical procedures, and recalibration of the Yuga system, with a redefined twenty-eighth Kali era of 432,000 years beginning in 3102 BCE, early third millennium BCE; flooding of Hastinapur and relocation of the Kuru capital to Kausambi near Prayagraj, around 2950 BCE; decline of the Kurus and rise of around a dozen comparable kingdoms, third millennium BCE; emergence of Magadha to pre-eminence with the imperial capital around Patliputra, along with the Brihadritha dynasty, late third millennium BCE; seven subsequent dynasties at Magadha, with empire-like recognition, although with continually

changing boundaries of the directly and indirectly ruled geographical areas, from 2132 to 327 BCE.

iv. **Gupta-Rajput period** [325 BCE–CE 1192 CE]
Ascension of Chandragupta from the Gupta dynasty, the last of the imperial dynasties from Patliputra-Magadha, that ruled for nearly two and a half centuries till 82 BCE; end of Alexander's two-year-long campaign in north-western India, 325 BCE; Samudragupta, the second ruler of the Gupta dynasty, expanded the boundaries of his empire to cover most of India and integrated it as a political-administrative unit; fragmentation into several competing kingdoms, of which the four dynasties that drew lineage as Agni-Vansha Rajputs were significant, marks the turn into the Common Era; consolidation of the Rajput dynasties, who tended to lay claim to imperial status jointly while administering separate kingdoms, early first millennium CE; Parmara, Pratihara, Chalukya and Chahmanas kingdoms covered the bulk of India, first millennium CE; confederacy of the four Rajput dynasties in support of Prithviraj Chauhan in the battle, 1192 CE.

There is clarity around the dating of periods, not only to the year verifiably, but also to the month and day plausibly. The titling of the periods after defining events, dynasties or cultural influence, for instance the term 'post-Mahabharata' in case of the third period, is to capture their respective and distinctive salience. Marking them up in terms of the titles of the periods adds a suitable amount of emphasis and adds to the recall of their impact in shaping the character of Indian civilization as a whole. This is also true for the trajectories of its evolution, at that time and in that period, up to the present.

The construct stands to the protocols of data and analysis of the multidisciplinary method and the mathematical ordinality applicable to a chronology. The validity of every data point is ascertained at its source, when it is first stated in a work, and then it is triangulated within and across other works within its discipline. It is then tested for reliability or repeatability in other disciplines, for example the dating emerging from astronomy and astrophysics is correlated to that in the Yuga systems, their genealogy and archaeology. The validity of the construct itself is ascertained for internal and external consistency within a discipline and across disciplines.

A Four Periods construct of ancient India's chronology considerably advances the understanding thereof prevailing since the early twentieth century, outlined and used, for instance, in the 1921 edition of Vincent Smith's book.[2] Archaeological excavations had just begun in India then and the Yuga system and genealogies were proving to be thoroughly befuddling. We have incorporated the burgeoning archaeological findings of the century gone by and have utilized the cleaning and digitization of ancient texts to gain clarity and cohesiveness in our understanding of the units of Indian timekeeping. These, backed by the much better ordering of the genealogies and insights from archaeo-astronomy in particular, have become possible only in the last couple of decades, and we have covered considerable ground in that regard.

This has been a long time coming, for over a hundred years. The incorporation is certainly belated and has been long overdue, from the perspectives of the scientific method and scholarship, for their timely deployment and in the suitable corrections and integration thereupon. The ground covered has taken us far beyond the mere updation of the chronology outlined in the early twentieth century and to its altogether new reconstruction. A dramatically altered 'snapshot' of ancient India's chronology has emerged, which takes its 'movie' many a leap and turn ahead. It certainly realigns the prevailing design or plot, and metaphorically speaking, will transform the scenes going further. The Four Periods construct is nothing short of a rediscovery of the chronology of Indian antiquity.

Science progresses through falsification of data from the mathematical and natural sciences and its analytical conclusions.

For the social sciences and multidisciplinary research, where data can be perceptual and often lead to many analytical interpretations, the progress could be somewhat meandering and slower. The 'replication and extension logic' comes into play, with a conclusion being corroborated, strengthened and logically extended, as the data and interpretations accumulate, or it gets weakened and is finally eliminated.

The chronology is clearly something related to natural science, with a date taken to be true until falsified and thereafter corrected. The consequent historical narratives, however, could range into the social sciences. A few of them could be rendered incomplete or proved to be poor in terms of understanding, and biased when the falsified parts of the chronology are corrected. Such narratives need to be suitably overhauled. They could have got deeply and widely ingrained otherwise—for instance, those based on Smith's twentieth-century chronology or Max Müller's assertions. But when the chronological backbone is reconstructed, many of the historical narratives will have to be corrected on reappraisal.

Our primary focus though is on the chronology, and we shall get into the narratives of India's antiquity only to the extent necessary. We need to move further from the overall design or construct to the details or the specific dating of events. Here, a comparative analysis of Smith's early-twentieth century chronology is necessary, as it is still influential, and is, in effect, our point of departure. It underlies all that is subsequently written and understood about Indian antiquity, and underpins all the historical narratives taught in schools and colleges and even researched upon at university.

We shall start with the 'across period' comparison to highlight the major advancements that have been made, and to identify the various aspects and dating of Smith's chronology that have been falsified and need to be corrected. Special attention will be given to dynasties and events that span more than one period. This will set us up for the 'within period' comparative study of significant events and dating systems. The 'across' and 'within' comparative studies shall take our Four Periods construct to the level of details and include that as well.

A JOURNEY ACROSS THE PERIODS

At the end of the second chapter, we summarized the 'movie' and 'snapshot' of the prevailing chronology in Table 1. It illustrated the path of understanding India's antiquity, since the late eighteenth century, and how its chronology got constructed and outlined over a century and a half later, around 1920. Taking cues from the 2021 editions of the books by Romila Thapar and Upinder Singh, we found how that chronology has stood still and has not been updated, though some narratives of the antiquity have been corrected.

We shall call the prevailing chronology the 1920 construct, and square it up with the Four Periods one that has been rediscovered and constructed anew. A quick glance at the two constructs is stunning in terms of the time horizons that open up and the magnitude of corrections. It is a relief, too, as the Indian chronology that has been bottled up for a long time is finally released with the full light and force of the scientific method. The data and the analytical tools and techniques now at hand and the best of the standards and ethics of multidisciplinary research make this happen. Its implications, going further, for the understanding of Indian antiquity and civilization and of the world at large, will be equally stunning and meaningful.

The Four Periods construct adds nearly three periods and over seven millennia to the existing Indian chronology and antiquity. There is some correlation with the 1920 construct towards the tail end of the updated chronology, with regard to Alexander's attack in 327–325 BCE and the Battle of Tarain, though the latter has been dated to 1192 CE after the dating system has gone through some fine-tuning through the better calibration of calendars. The advance in the classification and periodization is stark. Separating out the fourth period, 325 BCE–1192 CE, enables us to see beyond the 1920 construct and its self-inflicted constraint of 600 BCE and avoids the trap of either trying to fit every verifiable data within, or terming it conjectural and mythical.

A lot of such data was available in 1920, but Smith wrongly decided to ignore or undermine most of it which was available from sources other than the inscriptions. It will have plausibly taken the 1920 construct beyond 1500 BCE to the beginning of the Saptrishi era in 6777 BCE, as ascertained by Müller and Cunningham, respectively. In this, his frailty in terms of training and orientation as a researcher showed that any data or conjecture, however feeble, is important, particularly when it comes to antiquity which is hard to explore, and its understanding ought to be carefully built upon.

The third period could have been similarly handled, as the Kali era beginning in 3102 BCE was ascertained by Cunningham, Duff and several others, from the mid-nineteenth century onwards. In science, we can never claim to know everything, and for antiquity, moving from 'don't know that we don't know' to 'knowing that we don't know' itself is often a major advance. In hindsight, a '3102–325 BCE' period of Indian antiquity would have kept a space open to welcome the discovery of the Harappan sites in the 1920s and later. It would have stopped the fantastic 'Aryan homeland' and 'Aryan invasion' propositions in their tracks and avoided the mistake of trying to label the sites, in one fell swoop, as being somehow exogenous to the Indian civilization.

Ancient Sanskrit texts are categorized into the earliest Shruti period to Smriti, the Upanishads and then the Puranas. Müller classified them into the Chandas or Rigvedic Mantras, Brahmanas and Sutras, which, though inferior, is fairly robust. The first three are Shruti texts, but the fact that he assigned the equal period of two hundred years for the compilation of each set of texts and dated them from 600 to 1200 BCE is hard to comprehend and abrupt. He was a far better scholar and rarely made a mention of these dates after putting it forth in 1860, till his demise in 1900. He was perhaps trying to find his feet in England and conform to prevalent modes of thought in those colonial times. His writings on the Aryans spreading out from central Asia, which was still very thinly populated, into Europe and India, read like a poetic flight of fancy. It was an illusory attempt to make Sanskrit a contemporary of Latin and Greek in the antiquity and to add weight to Jones's grand conjecture of a 'proto-Indo-European' language as the common parent.

No textual or archaeological evidence for the existence of a proto-Indo-European language has been found anywhere for over two and a half centuries, and it ought to have been set aside by the 1920 construct. With that, the theory of the Aryans originating outside India would have gone out of fashion as well. This would have also ruled out any possibility of their invasion or conquest and the idea of any substantive migration. It was a wrong turn and an unforced error, but it bedevilled the inquiry into Indian antiquity and chronology and ended up sending it in the wrong direction. Errors of omission and commission piled up—for example, the undermining of the evidence from ancient texts and the exogeneity of Harappan sites.

A close miss, unfortunately, was the overpowering of the body of evidence that was available on Indian astronomy and calendars. Cunningham's work on the eras in particular would have brought the year 6777 BCE into play. This was ascertained as the beginning of the Saptrishi era. It concurred remarkably with the list of 154 great kings who had ruled India for 6,451 years and three months, which was handed over to Alexander some time in 327–325 BCE. Thus, the second period of the Four Periods construct, 6777–3102 BCE, was not out of the question even in the 1920 construct, but Smith and some of his contemporaries just got it wrong—though one should not jump to the conclusion that the error was intentional and mala fide.

We should note that the accurate dating of events many millennia ago in the antiquity can only be facilitated by astronomy and calendars. Archaeological data, subsequent to the calibration of carbon dating samples, usually has an error range of a few decades. Written or epigraphic documentation, such as texts or inscriptions on stone, rocks and metals, was then estimated as not extending beyond the latter half of the first millennium BCE in India, in comparison to the early second millennium, which is when it appeared in Babylon and Assyria, and the clay tablets and papyrus records from Egypt in the mid-third millennium BCE.

Astronomical data, by definition, is accurate to the day and the hour, and to the location when we use solar and lunar eclipses. Though the calibration of dates of the solar, lunar or Indian lunisolar calendars could be a challenge, it leads to a mathematical fact and one can be either precisely right or wrong. Astronomical observations can take us back tens of millennia in the past verifiably, given the knowledge of the precession of equinoxes, the exact 25,771-1/2 years cycle. This was known by Hipparchus in Greece and Parashara in India at the time of Alexander's Indian campaign, and subsequently by Aryabhatta, albeit with around one per cent error.

Thus, astronomical references strewn across several Indian texts are a treasure trove for dating the antiquity. They can be easily cross-referenced and proven by anyone with the Planetarium and Stellarium software programmes that are available now. Moreover, the genealogies act as an independent and additional source to ascertain the dates accurately down to the decade, extending well into multiple millennia before Christ. Besides, the list of the 154 kings handed over to Alexander, the 94 rulers of the Iksvaku dynasty, the 35 Kuru rulers till Yudhisthira, and several more genealogies are available and can be cross-verified across the Valmiki Ramayana, various Puranas and other texts.

With the veracity of the anchor point, 6777 BCE, in place, and that being ascertained in the 1920 construct itself, the 'Early

Settling' period is a mere logical extension thereof. Something would have existed prior to 6777 BCE, although its upper limit would have to be the end of the last Ice Age or the Holocene, which would have meant that they progressed to organized society and civilization from being hunter-gatherers over a couple of millennia. This progression is unlikely to be very different in India with respect to the 'Neolithic revolution' noted in the Hilly Flanks along the foothills of the Zagros and Taurus mountains in West Asia. It is also contemporaneous with them and similar in duration.

Therefore, and interestingly, the Four Periods construct of ancient India's chronology could have been incorporated in the 1920 construct as well. The new construct is 'stunning' in terms of the time horizon, only because we have been conditioned to accept an inexplicably short chronology. This led to a blinkered sense of history. The entire before the Common Era chronology and, therefore, the history of India got truncated and the point of its beginning reduced to the latter half of the first millennium, which was much less than even a tenth of its actual age.

The 1920 construct was a product of these wrong turns in conjecturing, and the inability to test and put them together. It wrongfully overlooked and rode over a sizeable body of data and knowledge already available, particularly on the eras and calendars. The scientific method does not permit a researcher to pick and choose data, or give preference to some, whether from one's own discipline or from some other. It is also against the structure of scholarship and its ethics, where each piece of data is important and valuable, even if partially validated, as it opens up new questions and avenues of inquiry. Naturally, the 1920 construct proved restrictive and stunted the progress of research and exploration, misleading generations of learners by encouraging them to fit data forcefully and draw erroneous conclusions. It thwarted the right understanding of India's antiquity and set it on a dubious footing and trajectory. This is just a case of poor scholarship, which has turned out to be pernicious for India and its civilization.

Among the 'Anomalies–Gaps' tabulated at the end of the second chapter, the Yuga system turned out to be the most challenging subject to understand and also the most important one for the rediscovery of the Indian chronology. It is, after all, the primary method for long-run timekeeping in India. Findings on the five-year Yuga and 20-year Chatur Yuga and the progressive increase in their duration to, for instance, the twenty-eighth Kali Yuga of 432,000 years, made by several studies in the last few decades, were pivotal for this project of rediscovery.

A careful analysis of the progression led to vital breakthroughs in our understanding of the beginning of Yuga timekeeping from 7322 BCE and our understanding of the reasons for and the ways of increasing the durations. And finally, it helped us get a fix on the dates of the events of the Ramayana and the Mahabharata. It also underscored advances in Indian astronomy and mathematics, which preceded Europe by three to five millennia. This was particularly evidenced in the recalibration and the correction of the calendars, the earliest attempts for which are dated to the fifth millennium BCE, and prior, and to the Ramayana.

The Four Periods construct rides on a couple more breakthroughs and analytical conclusions. First, the fact that India evolved a language around the eighth millennium BCE, but it continued without a script till at least the second millennium BCE, and much longer afterwards in the mainstream. This was because of the sophisticated Shruti and Gurukul learning systems, which could carry even the most extensive documentation and texts far and wide, and down the years and generations without a single distortion, even at the level of the word or the syllable. This made human habitation and civilization possible in the subcontinent, making it, plausibly, the earliest of its kind along northwest India, the region identified with the compilation of the Shruti texts.

The core of the civilization shifted to the central Gangetic Plains, where the bulk of the subsequent Smriti texts was located, and then back to the northwest, for the third set of the later Upanishad texts. It ties in well with the founding of the first dynasty, the Iksvakus, in the early sixth millennium BCE, and the commencement of the King-Emperor framework of Indian civilization. The framework continued with the rise of the Kurus in the early fourth millennium, then Magadha in the third millennium, and broadly lasted till the end of the fourth period in 1192 CE. The genealogical data extending all through this, which has been cleaned up and cross-validated, provides a body to the frame of the Yuga system of timekeeping.

The other analytical breakthrough is the information we have about the Saraswati river, in terms of its geography and its ebb and flow. It was a vigorous snow-fed river till 2500 BCE, although with certain twists deeper in its past, and supported the formation of settlements all along its path from the Himalayan foothills to the Rann of Kutch on the coast. These settlements grew into a wide network of rural habitats from the eighth millennium and further into towns, cities and ports. Along with the other large river, Indus, this evolved into the largest-known network of human habitation of that time, which, arguably, was closely connected to similar settlements in other parts of India—we do not yet have archaeological evidence, but the findings from astronomy and astrophysics, texts and genealogies definitely point to it, and there is a strong case for suitable excavations.

The sheer spatio-temporal extent of Indian civilization, from the Indus-Saraswati region to other parts of the landmass and beginning in the early-seventh millennium BCE, is a reality-redefining notion for the world. This was also the final nail in the coffin of another pernicious proposition, that of the Harappan sites somehow being exogenous to Indian civilization. The analytical breakthroughs open the gate for extraordinary inquiries; for instance, how a Shruti-based Indian civilization designed and managed the extraordinary public infrastructure and private habitats found in the Indus-Saraswati region, and how the economic transactions and social order were handled in the rural and urban habitats found up to the present-day western Uttar Pradesh and north Maharashtra, and for the trade overseas with Mesopotamia, for instance, which had a script.

The progress in our scientific understanding and explanations, from 'we don't know that we don't know' to 'we know that we don't know,' is significant in itself. The Four Periods construct of the Indian chronology does so for a swathe of time-space related to Indian civilization, inaugurating great possibilities and research questions. It also calls into question several dates that have been assigned to the events and personalities in the past century. This is what we now turn our attention to.

GETTING A FIX ON PIVOTAL EVENTS AND DATES

A chronology is a string of mathematical and sequential facts of events and their dates. Some of the events could be pivotal, as they act as a pole for deriving other dates, over decades or centuries and even longer periods. The best stand-out example of a pivotal event is Alexander's Indian campaign in 327–325 BCE, on which the 1920 construct was anchored and the bulk of the chronology of ancient India was derived from. We shall try to get a fix on such pivotal events and dates from the perspective of the Four Periods construct.

Pivotal events should preferably be important and consequential, for the construction of a relationship of coherence between the chronology and its corresponding historical salience and linkages, and thus its verifiability. The Mahabharata war of 3138 BCE was certainly such a pivotal and defining event of Indian civilization. Unfortunately, the 1920 construct chose Alexander's campaign as the anchor. We noted in the second chapter that the campaign barely grazed the northwestern rim of the subcontinent and made no lasting impression on India, historically or politically. No mention of Alexander can be found in ancient texts and inscriptions, either contemporary or thereabouts.

While it is hard to hold up Alexander's campaign as the pivotal event to serve as the anchor for ancient India's chronology, it wrought a major wrong turn and caused much trouble. Jones made the mistake of ascribing it as contemporaneous with Chandragupta of the Maurya dynasty. A much better philological correspondence can be inferred between the Greek references to 'Xandrames—Sandrokottus—Sandrocryptus' as the rulers of Magadha, and Chandrasri, also noted as Chandrabija and the last ruler of the Andhra or Satvahana dynasty, and later, Chandragupta and Samudragupta from the Gupta dynasty. Comparatively speaking, its correspondence with 'Dhana Nanda—Chandragupta—Bindusara' from the Maurya dynasty is hard to justify and even outlandish. This is by no means conclusive, but provides us with an important clue.

In the fourth chapter, we found that genealogical data from Purana texts and the coins and inscriptions broadly concur with the idea of the inception of the Gupta dynasty in 334 BCE. This included a methodical re-reading of the inscriptions, used for example by Cunningham, which indicated that the ascension of the first ruler of the Gupta dynasty took place between 25 CE and 75 BCE, as noted in the second chapter. In another wrong turn, this ascension was subsequently dated to 319 CE by the British civil servant J.F. Fleet, who became known as an epigraphist,[3] and this was used in the 1920 construct.

But it was based on an erroneous and wobbly conclusion. The Valabhi era, as stated by Al Beruni, came 241 years after the Saka era, beginning in 78 CE, and thus 319 CE was taken as identical to the Gupta era. Al Beruni himself noted that by 319 CE, the Gupta dynasty had ceased to exist, and would have plausibly started many centuries earlier. Fleet had also concluded that the Malava-Gana era is the same as the Vikrama era, beginning in 57 BCE, so that the Mandsaur inscription during the reign of Kumragupta-I of the 493 Malava-Gana era translates to 436 CE. This has not found any supportive evidence and there are contradictory assertions correlating the Malava-Gana era, for instance to the Krita era beginning in 719 BCE.

Besides the clear data on genealogies, much better data and analysis on the eras and calendars are now available. Arya took four inscriptions that noted solar eclipses in the Gupta era, tested them for consonance with sky positions given by astronomy, found 334 BCE as the valid date for the beginning of the Gupta era and that 319 CE was invalid.[4] He found similar results for the six inscriptions that mention the Jovian years in the Gupta era and for the detailed epigraphic analysis of the three inscriptions. This research is consistent with the genealogy-based post-Mahabharata dynastic lists and periods. It is much more recent and wider, and the analysis is rigorous and mathematically precise. We shall refine our estimation of the period of the Gupta dynasty and say that it began in 334 BCE and ended in 89 CE, in contrast to the earlier estimation, 327 BCE and 82 CE. This is par for the course, as the dates derived from genealogical lists often have approximations up to a few decades. Accordingly, the dating of the last three rows of dynasties put forth towards the end of the previous chapter will become:

32 rulers of Andhra or Satvahana dynasty:	833–334 BCE
7 rulers of Gupta dynasty:	334–89 BCE
24 rulers of the Parmara, other Agni-Vansha dynasties:	89 BCE–1192 CE

This is a significant rediscovery, leading to a massive realignment and an extension of around 653 years, on top of the 1920 construct. Re-dating the pivotal Gupta dynasty as beginning from 334 BCE instead of 319 CE opens up a vital space for the correction of several other errors of commission and omission. While the start and end dates of our Four Periods construct form a sound classification for an updation, a lot in the third and fourth periods will change. The first and second periods, however, will remain largely unaffected as they were way beyond the design and details of the 1920 construct.

In the third period, the ascension of Ashoka as the ruler of Magadha and the nirvana or death of Buddha are among the most pivotal events and dates. The latter, in particular, has seen much debate and uncertainty. Ashoka's ascension, as the grandson of Chandragupta, the founder of the Maurya dynasty and son of Bindusar, is erroneously dated to 268 BCE in the 1920 construct and its chronology, for instance in the latest edition of Thapar's book. It was based on the presumed contemporaneity of Alexander and Chandragupta Maurya, whose accession was dated to 321 BCE. When this presumption of contemporaneity was found to be invalid, and the Gupta dynasty that came 653 years later was found to be the right contender for the position, the consequent corrections would need to be at least by that much and possibly more. Buddha's nirvana, dated to 486 BCE on the same basis, would also call for such massive corrections and pushed towards greater antiquity.

Re-dating Ashoka's Ascension and Buddha's Nirvana

The Four Periods construct dates the Maurya dynasty from 1534–1218 BCE. Its founder Chandragupta ruled for 34 years and Bindusara and Ashoka ruled for 28 and 36 years, as per the genealogical data. This is cross-validated across the *Vayu, Matshya, Vishnu* and *Bhavishya Puranas*, the Buddhist texts *Mahavamsha, Ashokavadana* and the Lankan *Dipavamsha*, and the Jain text *Parishishta-parva* by Hemchandra.[5] Thus, Ashoka reigned from 1472 to 1436 BCE.

Similarly, Buddha is reckoned to have gained nirvana in the eighth regnal year of Ajatshatru, the sixth ruler of the Sisunaga dynasty.[6] This corresponds to his nirvana being in 1807 BCE, and his birth 80 years earlier in 1887 BCE.

The Sisunaga dynasty, 1994–1634 BCE, precedes the Nanda, 1634–1534 BCE, and Maurya dynasties. Incidentally, the 1920 construct also concluded upon Buddha's nirvana, after much jostling, and assigned it to the eighth year of Ajatshatru's reign. It proves the existence of a coherence between the 1920 and the Four Periods constructs as regards the dynasties and the number of rulers, certainly from Ashoka's ascension to Buddha's nirvana. The years that elapsed are, however, different, and they are 215 and 335 years, respectively.

The 1920 construct also linked and arrived at the dates of Buddha's nirvana and Ashoka's ascension on the basis of Puranic genealogies. But there was a tendency to pick and choose and to squeeze the periods at play. For instance, Pargiter[7] reckoned that 1,050 years elapsed between the Mahabharata war and the coronation of Mahapadmananda. It would have led to the nirvana getting erroneously dated prior to 2088 BCE, going by the Mahabharata date of 3138 BCE that was well ascertained by then, but this was not picked up for resolution and, instead, the Mahabharata itself was deemed mythical. The duration of the Nanda dynasty was squeezed to a mere 41 years, 362—321 BCE, in comparison to the well-documented hundred years' rule of Mahapadmananda and his eight sons.

This was primarily to assign a relationship of contemporaneity between Chandragupta Maurya and Alexander's campaign, which, as noted, was a grievously wrong turn in the chronicling of Indian history. It tended to overwhelm the data as well as the method of the 1920 construct. Buddha's nirvana was harder to track and many dates spread over a span of 60 years were debated for decades. This was also due to the plethora of data available from Persian, Tibetan, Chinese, Burmese and Siamese sources, which variously dated the nirvana to numerous points of time in a period stretching back to 3080 BCE.

The act of re-dating Buddha's nirvana to 1807 BCE and Ashoka's ascension to 1476 BCE, however, has been confronted by some obvious contentions. The most apparent of them is the 30 (or more) Ashokan edicts found on the pillars, rocks and caves all over the subcontinent. But all the dates indicated there are circular, pointing at some year of his reign, or the Gaya pillar's 'forty-second year after the death of his father,' and they do not cause any conceptual or construct-level inconsistency.

The recalibration of Brahmi and other scripts by around a thousand years in the past, to the mid to early second millennium, is actually welcome and coherent with the existence of scripts to the West and for longer. It will also stand clear with the archaeological data on the abandonment of Indus-Saraswati sites by 1900 BCE, where no substantive evidence of writing has been found. Ashoka may have been breaking the mould, being a pioneer in the use of writing in India, though the Shruti tradition continued to be the mainstay for a long time.

A good part of the backward shift in the dates is taken care of by the 653 years by which the Gupta dynasty is pushed back, and the rest conceivably by the pernicious and persistent tendency among chroniclers of the 1920 construct of squeezing the first and second millennium BCE periods to a period almost half its length. Re-dating these two pivotal events is a step forward and an important outcome of the Four Periods construct.

With some clarity on pivotal dates of Ashoka's ascension and Buddha's nirvana, all the dates given by the 1920 construct need to be replaced by those of the Four Periods construct, for its third or Post-Mahabharata period from 3102 to 325 BCE.

They were based primarily on Puranic genealogies anyway. Our construct unburdens them from their reliance on Alexander's Indian campaign as an anchor point, the mistake of considering it contemporaneous with Chandragupta Maurya, and from the tendency of picking and choosing dates and squeezing durations to somehow fit their scheme, which led to erroneous conclusions. This was poor science, in terms of the method, application and perhaps ethics, and these corrections were long overdue.

Indian civilization, contrary to general belief, is actually far richer than any other with respect to the material available for dating events in antiquity. Extraordinary advances in astronomy, mathematics and calendars provide dates not only for the years, but the month, the day and often hours, up to the early seventh millennium. These are often available from more than one source, allowing for adequate cross-validation, besides being tractable and verifiable through the astronomy software programmes now at hand and by anyone. They are also not stray dates, but conceptually and mathematically tied together by the Yuga system for long periods up to millennia.

Shorter periods of centuries, decades and further are backed by the genealogies of rulers. These, too, are available from many and wide-ranging sources, in several Puranas, references in the great epics and most other ancient texts, and from Persia, Tibet, Southeast Asia and other places that came under Indian influence, particularly Buddhism. No other civilization comes anywhere close in terms of the data available for chronicling its antiquity that is as reliable in the extent, accuracy, detail and multiplicity of its sources. Archaeological data is vast as well and extends to the late ninth millennium, though it is patchy and lacks uniformity particularly along India's vast geography. But that has a lot to do with the limitations of the 1920 construct, as the bulk of the excavations was done afterwards in the last century and were often stunted and misdirected in their exploration and findings.

For the fourth or Gupta-Rajput period, from 325 BCE to 1192 CE, most of the dating in the first half or till 500 CE given in the 1920 construct will need to be replaced. The word 'Rajput' in the title of the period is novel, but it is representative of the fact that the four Agni-Vansha lineages ruled the bulk of the landmass till 1192 CE and styled themselves the inheritors of the King-Emperor framework of Indian civilization. A majority of the leading rulers, such as Pulakeshin, Harsha, Kumarapala and Prithviraj, listed for instance in Thapar's chronology, belong to these dynasties.

Re-dating events in the fourth period is best done on a case-to-case basis. It also needs to take care of additional evidence, for instance, from the travelogues of Fa Hsien, Hiuen Tsang and Alberuni used in the 1920 construct, for suitable recalibration. We shall have a chapter each on the four periods to follow. The rounds of discovery will continue, as also on the errors of omission. Several great rulers such as Vikramaditya and Salivahana, who could not find space in the constrictive 1920 construct, will get reinstated into the chronology. This will lead to the correction and a definitive dating of many significant individuals like Varamihira and Kalidasa. A few of them, for example Chanakya, will get re-assigned to a different period and given their correct dates.

The root and branch overhauling of ancient India's chronology has indeed been a long time coming. While Ajatshatru's accession around 493 BCE is the earliest recorded date currently, this rediscovery of the ten-millennia continuity of Indian civilization posits the Four Periods construct—early settling around 9000 BCE, Saptrishi era from 6777 BCE, Kali era from 3102 BCE, Alexander's attack in 325 BCE—anchored by the Mahabharata War in 3138 BCE. More new dating and the fleshing of some narratives will make the periods come alive and impart a better sense of Indian and world history. The research, particularly the rediscovery of something as profound as the chronology of a major human civilization, is thrilling. There is plenty more in the offing.

6

'EARLY SETTLING' PERIOD: *c.* 9000–6777 BCE

The Four Periods construct of ancient Indian chronology comes as a relief and a release. To anyone with an interest or a stake in the understanding of human civilization, and India in particular, the construct clears doubts and confusion. They have plagued scholars and the masses alike since the mid-eighteenth century. It also finally releases the Indian chronology and history from the restrictive and flawed 1920 construct. Our Four Periods construct opens the gates for the rightful and vigorous exploration of India's antiquity, going further.

It is an enabling framework and was much needed, as the understanding of Indian civilization has lagged behind that of others, for instance the Mesopotamian or the Greek-Roman civilizations. A lot is still shrouded in the known-unknowns and even the double unknowns. The chronological backbone of Indian antiquity is now world-class in its clarity and superior in its precision in terms of periodization. It is the most advanced too, with respect to the diversity and validity of data and the analytical tools and techniques, which are tied together by the multidisciplinary method. Being late has, in some ways, turned into an advantage for it.

The construct is a breakthrough in the scientific method too, for its utility and application in the exploration of pre-history—which necessitates scouring whatever data from all possible sources—and the facility in cutting across disciplines. Going up from data to the construct or theory-building part is particularly appropriate, for areas where the partial, biased and outdated precepts prevail. This was the case for ancient India's chronology, and it may be so for some other civilizations too. Our multidisciplinary method could engender similar updations there as well.

Europeans took the lead in science and the scientific method in the latter half of the previous or second millennium CE. They came to define chronologies and write histories for the rest of the world, while tending to talk up and exalt their own. The histories of other civilizations carry the imprints of their limitations in the understanding of events and their context, the data available at the time, and their worldviews and interests. These have often remained frozen and perhaps need to be similarly overhauled. We shall touch upon some of the flaws in the current understanding of other non-European civilizations while exploring the external consistency of the rediscovered Indian construct. It may raise interesting possibilities for contiguous and contemporary civilizations. There was a global connect among the civilizations all along. Thus, there has to be an appropriate and adequate degree of coherence among the chronologies and narratives of various civilizations.

For now, we turn to the first period of our construct. The 'Early Settling' period is dated to around 9000 to 6777 BCE. This was preceded by an immensely long period of cosmological, geological and biological evolution that resulted in the formation of the Indian landmass and the presence of human beings therein. We shall very briefly explore this evolution and the beginning, primarily to get a sense of how recent and so accidental the civilization is. It will set us up for the first of two subsequent sub-periods. The time up to 8000 BCE saw the sprouting of localized human activity and the founding and invention of the basic building blocks for evolving into a civilization in due course.

The eighth millennium and the three centuries thereupon, or till 6777 BCE, is when Indian civilization took shape. We observe major advances that go on to define some of its core attributes for the long run. There is credible archaeological evidence, and moreover, a few key patterns are clearly visible. They align well with the happenings in what came to be known as the Hilly Flanks or the Fertile Crescent in West Asia. In the last three centuries of the Early Settling period, findings from astrophysics, the Yuga system and genealogies start filling up the knowledge base on Indian chronology and antiquity.

THE BEGINNING

We noted in the fourth chapter that our universe is 10–15 billion years in age. It is 13.8 billion years old based on the Big Bang theory; as the universe is still expanding and galaxies are moving further away, this conceivably began with the explosion of a unitary core. When the expansion ends, a contraction will take the universe back to a core or singularity, and then there will be another big bang and the cycle will repeat itself.

This is remarkably similar to the Indian concept of cosmological time, where the cycles of Chatur Yuga—Manvantara—Kalpa—Pralay—Brahma's lifespan are to continue forever. It is hard to assess Brahma's lifespan as it is postulated to be 311,040 billion years, which is conceptually similar to the time period between the two big bangs. The coherence in theorizing and postulating and the facility of Indian mathematicians with such huge numbers over four millennia in the past is a salient marker of the civilizational knowledge base and development.

The universe, while expanding, splintered into galaxies, and then into stars and planets. Our sun and its solar system is estimated to have been formed 4.571 billion years ago and the earth soon afterwards, 4.543 billion years ago. The moon followed quickly 4.53 billion years ago, as the result of the earth's huge collision with a pre-planetary body or a planetoid that carved away a part of it. The earth was molten initially and its rapid cooling and several accidents resulted in the formation of water shortly thereafter, by 4.4 billion years. A whole lot of geological events and stages later, the earth acquired a solid crust and the atmosphere around 750 million years ago.

The crust soon split up and then recombined into a super-continent called Pangaea, by 540 million years, which marks the beginning of the current geological stage. There was a break-up again and the southern part coalesced into Gondwana around 485 million years ago, moving towards the pole. A major geological event was the breaking up of what became the bulk of the Indian subcontinent, 125 million years ago. It drifted northeast, left the Madagascar part along the way, and eventually collided with the Eurasian landmass 50 million years before the present.

In the Indian cosmology, there is a vivid description of Mount Meru surrounded by four continent-like islands. Of these, the southern one is Jambudwipa. Within this island and to the south of the Himalayas till the seas is Bharatvarsha, named after its ruler Bharata. It is, conceptually, a somewhat apt description of the Indian landmass, from the perspectives of geological evolution and eventually geography, although quite sketchy and adrift in terms of the details.

Geological timelines are paralleled by the evolution of life on earth, the only such celestial body in the universe that is known. Life began very early, in the form of single-cell microorganisms around 3.5 billion years ago. A long, eventful evolution, interspersed by many near extinctions, the living on earth started to resemble its present state 350 million years ago—with insects and vegetation covering the land and a variety of species, including sharks, in the seas. The dinosaurs emerged 250 million years ago and came to dominate the land 40 million years later, and the mammals appeared 160 million years before the present.

While the Indian subcontinent was making its way towards Eurasia, dinosaurs became extinct 66 million years ago and the domination of mammals started. A range of large trees and flowering plants dotted the landscape. Most of the mammals, including horses, appeared 10 million years before the present. The first humanoid, Australopithecus, emerged four million years ago. The earliest man, Homo habilis, came about in East and South Africa, as did the ancestor of cattle, aurochs in India, two million years ago. Homo habilis evolved into Homo erectus, and the latter was the first human to leave Africa and spread across Eurasia. Heidelberg and Neanderthal men emerged 600,000 and 350,000 years ago, respectively. Modern human beings, the Homo sapiens, evolved in the northern parts and the Horn of Africa 250,000 years before the present.

Around 60,000 years ago, Homo sapiens started moving out of Africa and replaced the Neanderthal in Europe and other humans in Asia over the next 20,000 years. Earlier, the Toba volcanic eruption in Sumatra 70,000 years ago had caused a global cloud cover for nearly a decade and set in motion a millennium-long cooling, and almost decimated the number of living and genetic diversity. This greatly aided the rapid dispersal and dominance of Homo sapiens all over.

The first wave of migration of the Homo sapiens was along coastal Asia, to reach India by around 50,000 years ago.[1] They sped across most of South, East and Southeast Asia by 40,000 years from now, and then jumped across the sea to Australia soon after. Another wave moved northwards into West and Central Europe from 40,000 to 30,000 years ago. The two waves came together in North Asia, and spectacularly, Homo sapiens used the frozen Bering Strait to cross over into America 15,000 years ago. Here, they spread fast, perhaps unhindered by the presence of other humans, to reach the tip of South America in another 3,000 years.

Equipped with a large brain, the Homo sapiens not only eliminated all other pre-existing human variants everywhere but also came to dominate everything around. Adept at using and innovating tools and learning about the flora and fauna, they gained superiority over other mammals and species. They were social and formed highly mobile bands, which enabled them to hunt large animals such as mammoths or protect themselves from carnivores and to plan activities collectively—for example, moving large logs and using them to make rafts for exploring the seas, enabling them to cross over into Australia. The speed and spread of the Homo sapiens globally is a phenomenal saga of enterprise.

It wreaked havoc on the natural world too. The Homo sapiens hastened and contributed to the extinction of the mammoth, which weighed up to 10 tonnes and lived for over a million years, from most of Eurasia around 12,000 years ago. In Australia, they finished off about a dozen large mammals within a thousand years or so of their arrival.[2] The kangaroo is the only over-100-pounds mammal that survived and remains in the continent. The Homo sapiens marked a major step further in the evolution of living beings on earth. Early forebodings, whether the speed of their global spread or the scale of their impact, did put them in a different class altogether—among the handful of turning points in the evolution of the earth itself!

The Homo sapiens took shelter in cave nooks or camped near water and lived in groups, which was not very different from several other species. But they took to making fire, for cooking the food they hunted or gathered and for placing it at the cave entry to ward off animals. They also started to draw their experiences and themselves on the cave walls. The earliest cave drawings are dated to 35,000 BCE and later in Europe, barring a few exceptions, and to the arrival of the Homo sapiens in the area. In India, the drawings at the Ambadevi rock shelters in Betul district of Madhya Pradesh, bordering Maharashtra, are dated to 23,000 BCE.

LOCALIZED HUMAN ACTIVITY

We now get to the period of our direct interest and closer to the archaeological timelines, for instance, of the second chapter. The

Homo sapiens had evidently spread into the bulk of Eurasia and had not only come to dominate it but had also taken control of the life there by 25,000 BCE. They were truly thriving and would have greatly increased in numbers. Their hunter-gatherer ways had proven to be effective and superior, more than that of any other species at any time before that, including all the human variants that preceded them.

This was extraordinary, unprecedented and awesome. But the forces of nature continued to be at play, particularly the cosmological ones, including the sun's cycles and the earth's wobbles. There are variations in the solar radiation released along the sun's cycle spanning 11 years. The earth is not a perfect sphere, which introduces the precession of the equinoxes, as we know, but also a wobble in its rotation on its axis and variations in its tilt. It is called the Milankovich cycle, after the Serbian mathematician who discovered it, and it repeats every 41,000 years. These cycles, in a range of complex combinations, lead to changes in solar radiation received on the earth.

A drop in the radiation leads to cooling and the lowering of temperatures. Consequently, the polar ice caps expand and cover a larger, more substantial portion of the earth. It also means the dropping of sea levels and the icing up of several areas of the earth, and the receding of the seas and the opening of walkable channels and pathways. One of the most consequential of such pathways was across the Bering Strait, which made possible the spread of the Homo sapiens into the Americas. The impact of changes in solar radiations on the earth's temperature has been isolated and ascertained by tracking the thickness of the layers of ice that form annually in Antarctica, and other parameters.

In 2004, a European team drilled two miles deep under the ice in Antarctica and could go back 740,000 years in time.[3] An interesting pattern was visible. Soon after the Homo sapiens started moving out of Africa, the earth started cooling. It reached its trough around 20,000 BCE, called the 'Last Glacial Maximum', when the earth's average temperature was 10 degrees centigrade lower than the present. This was the peak of the last Ice Age, with the entire landmass and seas beyond 40 degrees from the equator frozen. Mile-thick ice and glaciers covered those regions, drawing in so much of the earth's water that the sea levels dropped by nearly 100 metres.

One could walk from Africa to Europe and then conceivably to America, but most of the farther regions were uninhabitable. Life around the equator was tough too, with brief summers, limited plant growth and low fauna activity. The Homo sapiens would have tended to stay put and huddle, mostly towards the equator. Their brains and skills would have strained just to survive, and this kept the population low. These conditions continued till 14,000 BCE, when the temperature started to rise and rapidly went eight degrees higher, or just a couple of degrees lower than the present, by 12,700 BCE. It led to massive melting of the snows, often floods, the formation of several large freshwater bodies, and the coastline came to resemble what it is at present. It also spurred the spread of the Homo sapiens.

This was a brief respite though, as the earth started cooling again. It reached the temperature prevailing three millennia earlier by 10,800 BCE. The period 12,700–10,800 BCE, termed the 'Late Glacial Interstadial', was followed by another rise in the temperature. The 'Younger Dryas', from 10,800 to 9000 BCE, brought it back to the earlier high. And by 8000 BCE, the temperature reached the current level and has largely remained so. The periods and timelines of the earth's cooling–warming cycles align closely with the evolution of the Homo sapiens, which was by far the dominating species on the earth.

The two and a half millennia and till 8000 BCE was a period of massive 'global warming', and temperatures rose by around 10 degrees celsius. It meant an explosion of flora and fauna. Hunter-gatherers (Homo sapiens) flourished, in numbers and well-being and all over the globe. The climatic change had stabilized around

9000 BCE, termed the 'Holocene', and particularly in what came to be known as the 'Lucky Latitudes' of the earth. The region between 20 and 35 degree latitudes in Eurasia, for a variety of factors, provided the best conditions for life and living. It covered the largest landmass in India, besides parts of southern China, West Asia and Turkey, and the Iberian Peninsula.

The Lucky Latitudes region abounded in vegetation and a variety of plants. Thus, it was the most hospitable place for the Homo sapiens to hunt animals and gather seeds, roots and other eatables. They could find a good bit nearby and regularly, and could afford to stay put at a place for long periods of time, where they had taken shelter. The Hilly Flanks, an arc extending across Israel, Syria, southern Turkey, northern Iraq and western Iran and curving around the Tigris, Euphrates and Jordan valleys, was one such area.

An archaeological site, Ain Malla in northern Israel, has evidence of round dwellings using stone for walls and tree trunks for supporting the roof. It is dated to 12,500 BCE, the time of peak warming before the Late Glacial Interstadial set in. Bones of deer, foxes and birds, burned scraps of nuts and plants, and a few human graves indicate prolonged occupation at the site, possibly over many years. The grave of a woman cuddling her dog, dated to 11,000 BCE, points to animal domestication. Such activities would conceivably be happening in other parts of the Lucky Latitudes too, particularly India, which claimed the largest portion of the Lucky Latitudes.

While marking the beginning of long-term dwellings and animal domestication, evolution would have slowed and activities remained subdued till the end of Younger Dryas in 9800 BCE. The next millennium, till 8000 BCE, was the period of spectacular revival and advance. Long stays at a location would have meant finding some leftover seeds sprouting into plants and closely observing those growing around, and sowing some of the seeds intensively was a small step forward but a major advance in terms of its implications and the invention of agriculture.

Similar developments, paralleling those in the Hilly Flanks, would have been happening in India too. The probabilities are assuredly higher, as a larger contiguous landmass is considered helpful. It is put forth as an argument for much lesser activity in the region similar to the Lucky Latitudes in the southern hemisphere, where comparatively the area is barely a tenth of the one up north. The dwellings and animal domestication in India too could have first happened around 12,500 BCE. And from 9800 to 8000 BCE, the scale and scope of evolution would be comparable, if not faster and higher. Besides a larger landmass, India was better endowed in terms of rainfall and perennial rivers, due to the southwest monsoon and the Himalayan snows, and thus more hospitable.

Localized settlements would have certainly emerged in India by the early ninth millennium or soon after 9000 BCE. Archaeological evidence of rice cultivation and animal domestication, from Lahurdeva in eastern Uttar Pradesh in particular, largely belongs to this millennium. If we add the evidence of round, sunken dwellings at Bhirrana along the Saraswati in Haryana and of wheat and barley cultivation and pit burial with personal effects at Mehrgarh west of the Indus in Baluchistan, we have some kind of an arc of settlements in India too. Bhirrana and Mehrgarh are currently dated to the millennium later, but they and other nearby sites could extend into the ninth millennium on further exploration.

This is more of an arc of the current evidence, which is indeed very scanty in the case of India. The settlements will conceivably have spanned all around the three nodes and beyond, given that the conditions here were more favourable than anywhere else in the Lucky Latitudes. For want of direct evidence from India, we need to depend on the extrapolation of findings from elsewhere. In the Hilly Flanks, which is far better explored, cultivation started in full earnest from 9300 BCE. The cultivated wheat and barley seeds were slightly bigger than their wild version and the granaries were 10 by 10 feet in dimension in the Jordan valley and are dated to 9000 BCE.

The bigger seeds are largely a result of careful selection over multiple rounds of cultivation and advances in agriculture. Granaries indicate a sizeable degree of production and the knowledge of storing grains properly for a year or more. It also indicates the year and multi-year-long occupation of a site and localized human activity, and a shift away from the hunter-gatherer ways. There are several similar sites in the Hilly Flanks. The settling-down can be dated to the ninth millennium and taken as well-established in the region by 8000 BCE. Such dating can also be ascribed to other areas of the Lucky Latitudes, particularly India.

The lack of data for the ninth millennium in India, barring the exception of Lahurdeva, is a major gap. The comparison with similar sites, within India and that, for instance, from the Hilly Flanks, will greatly enhance our understanding of the localized living stage of human civilization. Tracing links from the hunter-gatherer sites and towards nearby river valleys and lakes could help find such localized settlements. Areas around Bhimbetka, the Narmada valley in Madhya Pradesh, other locations in the Gangetic Plains and a wider exploration of the Indus-Saraswati region, with an eye for greater antiquity, holds promise.

THE MAKING OF A CIVILIZATION

Within the first period of our chronology construct, which spans from around 9000 to 6777 BCE, it is the latter half that sees Indian civilization taking shape. Round-the-year localized living for many years led to the invention of animal domestication, agriculture and the construction of dwellings by 8000 BCE. These are the basic building blocks of settled and social living for humans—at a place, often in large numbers, and plausibly for decades. This weaned them away from their earlier hunter-gatherer ways, mostly forever.

These basic building blocks are essential for the settled living of humans anywhere. These are then impacted by the local climatic and topographical conditions, for instance the weather and rains and the level, rocky terrain or otherwise. Local conditions could be different; within the Lucky Latitudes region, let's say between the Hilly Flanks and Indian plains. The latter received the bulk of its rains in the burst of the monsoonal four months and the terrain is largely not rocky, mostly even and the soil clayey and alluvial. These differing local conditions set the settlements on varying trajectories.

Civilization is a techno-economic and socio-cultural entity. Its features are similar and cohesive within, and distinct from those outside and others. In the eighth millennium, Indian settlements, particularly along the Indus and Saraswati rivers, started acquiring such features. And these were identifiably different from those in the Hilly Flanks, which were also evolving simultaneously. Bhirrana and Mehrgarh are the two nodes that give us a fair sense of the emerging civilization, which is distinctly Indian. Northwest India was climatically better placed. It was drier than the Gangetic Plains, which was heavily forested and needed more sophisticated tools for clearing and making them habitable.

At Bhirrana, the Hakra Wares culture is dated up to the eighth millennium or 7500 BCE. It is termed a 'culture,' as the people were reckoned to be living in organized societies. They had innovated on a variety of technologies for the construction of dwelling pits that had clay-plastered walls and floors, and the manufacture of a range of pottery, jewellery of lapis lazuli and other stones, and terracotta bangles and other items. This implies the availability of tools and techniques to handle a variety of materials and high precision.

It would have been a sophisticated economy, as the technologies required dedicated learning and application of years, implying the specialization, division of labour and thereby economic transactions among various occupations. A lot of material, such as lapis lazuli, was available only a few hundred kilometres away, thus there was trade involving travel and means of transportation, measurement, valuation and exchange. It also necessitated a mutually comprehensible language and communication system. A civilization had indeed taken shape by the mid-eighth millennium in India.

There are several sites nearby which indicate the spread of civilization too. A radius of at least a couple of hundred kilometres is required to foster and support the socio-economy around Bhirrana. Moreover, 800 kilometres to its southwest and west of the Indus river is Mehrgarh, which is definitively dated to 7000 BCE. It could plausibly extend a few centuries into the eighth millennium. The techno-economic and socio-cultural civilization at Mehrgarh is almost identical to Bhirrana. Additional findings of sea shells indicate overland or river-based travel and trade with the coasts, and of dentistry and the requisite fine molar drilling tools and techniques. A nearby site, Kili Gul Mohammad, similarly dated, indicates a cluster of socio-economic connections around Mehrgarh as well.

Visualizing concentric circles of civilization around the nodes of Bhirrana and Mehrgarh, the Indus-Saraswati region comes across as a large civilization by the late eighth millennium itself. An archaeological find and its dating need to be interpreted correctly. The dating often has a calibration range running into decades, and even centuries for finds in the deep past. Moreover, there could be similar objects that have not yet been found which are older, at the same site or nearby. Archaeologists, too, are generally conservative in extending antiquity. In addition, the finds, let's say, of unbaked mud-brick constructions or fine beads are a result of the long process of techno-economic and socio-cultural evolution over a few centuries and more. The duration of such a process needs to be compounded to that of finds dating to get a better sense of the antiquity of the civilization in which it was embedded.

Civilization in India had taken a different trajectory as compared to the Hilly Flanks, and had advanced further by 7000 BCE. Largely devoid of stone, but well supplied in alluvial clay, Indians innovated with its use. They certainly led and progressed further in knowledge and sophistication with the usage of clay for manufacturing sun-baked or unbaked bricks for house construction and the wider range of pottery, beads, bangles and terracotta. Greater finds in the Hilly Flanks indicative of socio-cultural emphasis were related to burial rituals and defensive fortification rather than material goods and related advancements. This is particularly evident in the archaeological sites at Cayonu in southeast Turkey and Jericho along the river Jordan. Much less long-distance travel, communication and trade are comparatively plausible for the Hilly Flanks.

In India, the situation takes a very interesting turn towards the end of the eighth millennium or around 7000 BCE. All the civilization's progress along the techno-economic and socio-cultural dimensions comes together in two remarkable developments. The first was in the field of mathematics and astronomy, both of which were engendered by a major need and something only specific to Indian civilization. It was the need to predict the monsoon season accurately, as it deeply impacted agricultural production, manufacturing and trade, and thereby the bulk of their socio-cultural activities and well-being.

The discovery of the linkage between the passing and recurrence of seasons and the movement of the sun and moon along constellations was a breakthrough. This scientific conclusion, however, was of no use as a technology to outline the onset and duration of the monsoon—unless backed by the techniques to take note of astronomical observations accurately and make credible projections. It led to the invention of numbers and mathematical procedures. And of the abstraction of a 'zero' and the place value system of numbers, in particular. These enabled the preparation of the annual calendar and the projection of longer cycles of years.

A need is premised to be the mother of discovery and invention. The breakthroughs in astronomy and mathematics are among the earliest examples of the premise. They converged together before 7000 BCE, preceding the rest of the world by an astonishing five millennia and more! Indian calendars and the longer time cycle, the Yuga system, was fairly developed by 6777 BCE. The beginning of the Yuga system is calculated to 7322 BCE.

The second remarkable development was the language, Sanskrit, albeit without a script, and the Shruti ecosystem to go with it. A language is essential for the emergence and continuation of a civilization, from techno-economic as well as socio-cultural requirements. We date the compilation of the oldest Sanskrit text, the Rig Veda, to 6500–7000 BCE. It is largely based on the observation that the youngest, the Atharva Veda, was yet to gain the status of Veda in the Ramayana period and can thus be assigned to 5000–5500 BCE.

The Sanskrit language was still evolving at the time of the Rig Veda, which is in *chhanda* or short phrases, and the first text in its fully evolved *laukika* form is the Valmiki Ramayana. Thus, the emergence of Sanskrit as a language can be placed in the 8000–7500 BCE period. This is in the eighth millennium, and concurs with the time of the shaping of Indian civilization. The forgoing of a script was a very interesting turn, though not entirely inconceivable or accidental at that time.

There were no scripts anywhere in the world in the eighth millennium BCE, and for a long time afterwards. Writing is a technology that requires preceding inventions of writing implements or tools and the medium. None of the latter, which became the usual writing media in Indian antiquity, such as palm leaves or birch bark, grew naturally in the Indus-Saraswati region. Clay tablets, which could be manufactured and made locally, were cumbersome for long texts, but came to be used a couple of millennia later for noting a few representative and abstract symbols at the time. Forsaking a script is not all that dissimilar from writing by hand with pen on paper as a medium, and this may soon go extinct!

We explored the viability and efficacy of Shruti, accompanied by the invention of the Gurukul system of learning, in the third chapter. It still continues in a very small niche, and its practitioners take pride and consider the Shruti to be as effective if not superior. Indian civilization in the eighth millennium was spread over a thousand kilometres and engaged in vigorous socio-economic transactions. The Shruti–Gurukul ecosystem would have grown further geographically, and in sophistication and perfection.

The two developments—in astronomy and mathematics and the Shruti ecosystem—set Indian civilization apart from the rest. These make it vastly distinct from the other world civilizations. The distinctiveness is hard to comprehend from the present, particularly given the lenses we have come to wear, which also make the period of antiquity to the eighth millennium so astonishing. It is borne by archaeological evidence, which when properly analyzed and contextualized, is adequate by itself. The evidence, as it turns out, is not less ascertaining either, in comparison to that for the Hilly Flanks. More and wider socio-economic linkages are evident from the material evidence found at archaeological sites in the Indus-Saraswati region, to bestow greater validity and reliability on the conclusions on Indian antiquity.

Data and conclusions from the astronomy, calendars and Yuga system of reckoning long periods of time are available for Indian civilization alone. They yield scientific and chronologically precise dates, and add another layer of validity and reliability to the archaeology-based conclusions. That is what any scholar would dream of, for instance, while researching the Hilly Flanks. There is a third layer too. It is genealogy, which goes back all the way to the crowning of the first ruler, Manu, in 6965 BCE. The genealogy is unbroken for the pre-eminent king or emperor of India till 1192 CE, stretching for over eight millennia. The estimation error for the dating of Manu is not more than a couple of hundred years, which is not only par for the course but also better than the archaeological evidence-based dating for a period of such antiquity.

The genealogical data, besides being unbroken in continuity, is detailed up to around a decade and verifiable across half a dozen different ancient texts. No other world civilization comes remotely close, whether in terms of the volume of information available or the fine granularity of periodization. These also square up with the socio-cultural and political shift in the centre of gravity of Indian civilization. For instance, Manu's ascension marks the transition of ancient literature from the oldest set of Shruti to the succeeding Smriti texts.

It also underscored the evolution of the concept of the political-administrative state. As it did the concurrent shift in the centre of gravity of Indian civilization to the Gangetic Plains and the emergence of its King-Emperor framework. These lead us to the next chapter.

7

'RAMAYANA–MAHABHARATA' PERIOD: 6777–3102 BCE

A significant takeaway from the previous chapter and the Four Periods construct is that Indian civilization took shape in the eighth millennium before the Common Era, which is between 8000 and 7000 BCE. This makes the civilization ten millennia long. It is by far the oldest in the world, and pushes the advent of civilization itself by a few millennia into antiquity.

Assigning the antiquity and continuity of Indian civilization to a period of ten millennia, or 10,000 years, could appear startling. This, however, is based on the rigorous application of the scientific and multidisciplinary method, on the validity of definition and construct, and the repeatability and external and internal validity of the data. We define civilization as a techno-economic and socio-cultural entity, which is similar and cohesive within and distinct from those outside and others. The distinctive features, once shaped, set a civilization apart and provide continuity along a trajectory of its own.

In his 1996 work *The Clash of Civilizations*,[1] Harvard political scientist Samuel Huntington defines civilization as the highest cultural grouping of people. The emergence of a distinctive culture is recognized as the primary identifier of a civilization, in the century gone by—and up to Arnold Toynbee,[2] who started publishing his 16 volumes on the study of history from 1934.

Culture, in turn, is an outcome of technological advance, means of communication and economic transactions, the division of labour and social stratification. We found evidence and a plausible case for all of these things around the nodes of Bhirrana and Mehrgarh in the Indus-Saraswati region, during the eighth millennium BCE.

Comparatively, evolution appears slower in the Hilly Flanks. It could be because the area was much smaller, narrow in width, and punctuated by several isolated mountain settlements. The progress into a civilization happens much later, around 5000 BCE, when the lowlands of southern Mesopotamia start to get populated and they learn to tame and channelize the Tigris and Euphrates river waters into canals. This is a larger contiguous region and allowed for continuous social interaction and exchange. Structures on brick platforms are found, for instance, at Eridu[3] in present-day Iraq from 5000 to 3000 BCE. Such archaeological finds were also encountered in the Indus-Saraswati region, in much greater intensity in terms of diversity and area, from the eighth millennium BCE.

This conclusion turns the prevailing understanding of the evolution of world civilizations on its head. That is where and when it began—India, instead of southern Iraq, and around three millennia earlier! From the later centuries of the eighth millennium, astronomy, the calendar and the Yuga system findings are available for India, which is corroborative of this conclusion. Such inputs from other disciplines, which are mathematically precise and presently verifiable, do not exist in any other civilization, particularly in the Mesopotamian civilization of southern Iraq in West Asia.

The conclusion, for instance, will contradict Ian Morris's contention about the 'West' taking the lead early on around 5000 BCE in terms of social development, and going on to rule the 'East' till and for now. It is the other way round. His definitions are flawed too, as he labels Mesopotamia as the 'West' and, by implication, subsequently linked to Europe and America. For him,

China is the 'East' and for his own convenience, India is wrongly ignored for want of evidence. Ian Morris is an archaeologist and an academic at Stanford University who taught at Cambridge earlier. He floated the contention in 2010, which surprisingly is still along the lines of what Vincent Smith and William Jones said a century and two ago, respectively, but has since backed out. A lot of such contentions or partial, half-baked and biased theories continue to prevail and need to be methodically corrected.

We shall take the evolution of Chinese civilization into consideration, which is currently traced to the late second millennium BCE, mostly in the subsequent chapters. In India, though, the date of the ascension of the first ruler, Manu, and the beginning of the Iksvaku dynasty is estimated to 6965 BCE. This marks the emergence of a political-administrative state. The *Manusmriti* extensively defines the precepts and procedures of an organized society and state, and it is truly the origin of political order in the world.[4] This is regarded as the most advanced and final piece in the emergence and existence of a civilization. The text itself is remarkably prescient and influential, as it is still referred to and debated in present-day India, often fiercely, nearly nine millennia later.

Such a text can only be the outcome of a long process of trial and error, thinking, debating and practising a political order and a state, and thereby its evolution, for at least a few centuries. That adds up to the continuity of Indian civilization over ten millennia. It is indeed a fascinating conclusion. Its footing could not have been firmer and surer, going by the data sources and the rigour of multidisciplinary research. This gives us the requisite bearings and powers our exploration of the 6777–3102 BCE period.

The period saw the flowering of Indian civilization. A lot of it, particularly in the social, cultural and philosophical domains, is as alive today as it was in those times. We shall take around a millennium at a time to gain a sense of the period and the events that shaped it. The exploration of external consistency with the other civilizations that emerged and progressed will add an important layer of richness to our understanding thereof. It will open a new window into the subsequent flow of ideas, tools and technologies, goods and trade, and of people among civilizations.

Resetting the timeline of Indian civilization from the eighth millennium BCE and ascertaining the continuity of its history over ten millennia make for a plethora of insights and a range of possibilities, and a lot of corrections to our understanding.

A WORLD-LEADING CIVILIZATION

The early part of the 'Ramayana—Mahabharata' period saw Indian civilization spreading. Conceivably, its geographical boundaries expanded too, though the greater expansion consisted in the sprouting of newer rural settlements and their growth into small and then larger urban habitats. With the basic techno-economic and socio-cultural building blocks in place by the late eighth millennium BCE, their progress would conceivably be rapid. The next millennium will be important for setting the long-term patterns of India's civilization.

Unfortunately, there is not much archaeological data specific to the seventh millennium, 7000–6000 BCE. There is continuity among the settlements at Bhirrana and Mehrgarh, and some more superior civilizational artefacts have been found and dated. A few sites around these two nodes have also been located, for example Kunal and Kot Diji, where the settlements would have begun in the seventh millennium. The excavations in the northwest region have been slow, still very patchy and quite incomplete, for instance even for Bhirrana. We know far less than a small percentage of what is possible archaeologically.

This is not just due to a lack of resources. Strangely, there is an appalling lack of enthusiasm and sense of purpose in finding things that are new, significant and path-breaking. And there is hesitation and a lack of confidence in stating and dating archaeological findings deeper into antiquity. Digging at the pivotal Rakhigarhi site for this 'season' had not even started till mid-December 2023. It was delayed the previous year too, and in 2020–22, the pandemic ruled out virtually any excavation. Moreover, the archaeological digging 'season' from around early November to late March, around five months a year, is a relic of the colonial era procedures, conveniences and constraints.

The infrastructure and living and working facilities that are now available can easily enable round-the-year digging in India, as is the case for projects in other sectors. New technologies can enable exploration that is a few times faster. In addition to this, the documentation of archaeological finds takes years and their publication, decades. A suitable overhaul, including the redesign and updating of procedures, can exponentially expedite the pace of exploration. This is much needed, else we shall take 50 years to know what is possible in a single year!

Our Four Periods construct should be a major facilitator for exploration in future. The chronology outlined in the 1920s was conceptually limiting and flawed, and thus a source of confusion and a hindrance for the exploration of Indian antiquity. However, the civilizational patterns discerned from the archaeological finds at Bhirrana and Mehrgarh would not only be valid but also extendable to the seventh millennium BCE. Technological innovations and progress would have plausibly continued and the socio-economic linkages would have deepened. The identification and dating of the dozens of sites to the next or the sixth millennium, which are much larger and spread throughout the Indus-Saraswati region, underscore the continuity and progress of civilization during 7000–6000 BCE.

For the early part of the Ramayana—Mahabharata period, no major findings or their dates come forth from archaeology. Thus, we rely primarily on the Yuga system and ancient texts for the pivotal events and chronology. The period begins with the Saptrishi era and the twenty-eighth Treta Yuga, calibrated to

3 December 6777 BCE as per the *Vedanga Jyotisha*. It also marked a shift to the 1,200-year Yugas, based on the Jovian or Jupiter's cycles. This underscores a significant advance in astronomical observations and mathematical calculations, and their application for enhancing the accuracy of calendars.

Jupiter is the second farthest planet visible to the naked eye, and not an easy one to identify and observe. It takes close to 4,331.572 days to complete a revolution around the sun. This works out to 12 years or 360.96 Earth days, which is significantly closer to the 360-days-per-year estimate of the Indian luni-solar calendar, than the earth's own revolution period of around 365.251 days. Therefore, basing the long-term reckoning of time under the Yuga system on the Jovian cycle would necessitate much fewer and less frequent corrections.

On the other hand, it would have needed to observe at least a dozen Jupiter cycles to find the duration and confirm it exactly enough to make this shift. This makes for nearly 300 years of observations before the shift in 6777 BCE. Ascribing a similar duration to older calendars based on the cycle of the sun and the moon, we get ascertainably close to the start of Indian calendars being dated to 7322 BCE. This is as per the Yuga system, with 27 Chatur Yugas, each spanning 20 years, and the 28 Krita Yuga of five years, or 545 years, preceding the 6777 BCE mark.

The mathematics needed to note and process such observations will include the zero and the place value of numbers, arithmetic operations from addition to division, and the knowledge of fractions and decimals. Thereby, these inventions can be estimated to have been made prior to 6777 BCE in India. The period is plausibly 7500–6777 BCE. The fact that the knowledge of mathematics in India goes back to such antiquity, and mathematics arguably being among the greatest inventions of the human mind and at the core of all the sciences and the bulk of our knowledge, would be enough to place India ahead of all the civilizations in the world by far, and for over five millennia. It was applied not only to astronomy and calendars, but also became intricately woven into social, cultural and religious practices, as were technological advances, economic measurements and transactions, and the evolution of areas such as architecture, medicine, literature and the arts.

In the schema of Indian knowledge, astronomy and astrology are inseparable or are the two sides of the same coin. The latter defines an individual's conduct through a day, a month, a year, up to a lifetime, and connects it to the social arena, from small groups and clans to entire villages, states and overall civilizations. The *Vedanga Jyotisha* is the oldest surviving text on astronomy and astrology in India. It is linked to the Vedas by way of practice or discipline. The five other Vedangas are—*Shiksha*, on phonetics and recitation; *Kalpa*, on ways to conduct Vedic rituals through one's life; *Vyakarna*, on grammar and the formation of sentences; *Nirukta*, on etymology and the explanation or linguistic analysis of words; and *Chandas*, on prosody or the metres and syllables used in verse.

The Vedangas are the applied texts of the Vedas. We dated the compilation of the earliest, the Rig Veda, to 7000–6500 BCE, in the previous chapter. The Sama Veda and the Yajur Veda are estimated to have been composed between 6500–6000 BCE and 6000–5500 BCE, respectively. The Atharva Veda is the Ramayana's contemporary, thus it can be dated to 5500–5000 BCE. Each Veda has four components—the Samhitas or hymns and mantras; the Aranyakas or the 'what' of rituals and ceremonies; the Brahmanas or the 'how' of rituals and ceremonies; and the Upanishads, or philosophies. There are up to a hundred texts on the various components of every Veda. The Vedangas transcribe them into practical procedures, for instance the Kalpa connects directly to the Brahmanas and the Aranyakas. Also among them, for example, the time and date of a ritual would be identified through Jyotisha and conducted as per the Kalpa and on the basis of the other Vedangas too.

The dating of the Veda will certainly include the compilation of the Samhita component and a good part of the corresponding Aranyakas and Brahmanas. The last two would plausibly have continued further, as did the Vedangas. The composition of the Upanishads continued even later and their compilation did not happen until the end of the Ramayana–Mahabharata period. The Vedic corpus is indeed huge. The main texts themselves run into over a hundred, and all of the lesser and subsidiary texts could add up to a thousand. Max Müller was right in asserting that the volume of ancient Sanskrit texts amounted to many times that of all the Greek-Latin texts combined. The Vedic corpus would also exceed the volume of texts belonging to all the other world religions put together, by quite a few times with ease.

There are a couple of other highlights. First, there is an extraordinary emphasis on grammar, etymology, phonetics and diction in the Sanskrit texts and language, from the very beginning. This level of detailing and the insistence on perfection are not found in any other language, including the modern ones. There is mathematical precision, which rules out any possibility of ambiguity in understanding, and that is why the Sanskrit language is currently rated as the most suitable for computer programming. This also aligns with the absence of a script, or any need for such a thing, and thereby the inherent self-sufficiency and confidence of the Shruti tradition.

Second, the language itself is evolving, and towards perfection. Here, the seventh millennium is pivotal, as this was when Sanskrit evolved from the chhanda stage of the Rig Veda towards the fully fledged laukika of the Valmiki Ramayana. Rig Vedic Sanskrit comes across as an abstraction and an abbreviation of a developed thought struggling to find expression in language and being put forth in a way similar to a mathematical formula. Laukika took over a millennium to evolve, with an expansive grammar and the intonations and disciplines necessary for Shruti. It was a language in which great literature, whether in verse or prose, could be created.

Geographically, northwest India or the Indus-Saraswati region is the area of the compilation of the earliest Shruti texts, such as the Vedic Samhitas and the initial Aranyakas and Brahmanas. The compilation needs to be understood clearly. A chhanda or hymn is attributed to and mostly identified with an individual sage, who realized it through deep thought and reflection and articulated it. Many sages would have plausibly discussed and debated thereupon, who may have numbered in the hundreds given the range of the hymns, and they might have done it over many decades, going by the complexity of their thought and articulation. These were then put together in one or more texts, and some hymns were repeated across the Vedic corpus, based on the need for continuity and consistency of thought and the zone of exploration. This was all verbal, but adhered to the strictest discipline of language. Thus, there was clarity and absolutely no ambiguity in the compilation process, which has lasted many millennia till the present day.

The subsequent Smriti texts start emerging from the early seventh millennium. They can be judged to correspond to the ascension of Manu, the founder of the Iksvaku dynasty that is estimated to have happened in 6965 BCE. 'Smriti' is that which needs to be remembered, and thereupon to be put into practice. The Vedangas are often classed with the Shruti as well as the Smriti, and they could be transitional texts, as they relate to practice. The Smriti texts fall into a wide range and they have a long chronology. They can be reckoned as the other part of the ancient Sanskrit texts, while the first part is the Vedic corpus. The Dharma-shastras, the epics Ramayana and Mahabharata, the *Bhagavad Gita* and the Puranas, taken together, cover a formidable expanse of subjects and texts. They were largely compiled in a chronological sequence, albeit with considerable overlap.

The Dharma-shastras are the earliest Smriti texts, and can be dated to the first half of our Ramayana—Mahabharata period. The Ramayana, the Mahabharata and the *Bhagavad Gita* all fall within the second half, and the Puranas in the next Post-Mahabharata period. Although Manu's ascension is estimated to have happened in 6965 BCE, the *Manusmriti* could have been given its final shape in the few hundred years that followed, or around the mid-seventh millennium. The other major Dharma-shastras are attributed to Yajnavalkaya, Parasara and Narada, and would have followed in the latter half of the seventh millennium BCE and further.

The Dharma-shastras are an important step in the evolution of civilization and the state in India. It long preceded a similar development in any other place in the world, and the next oldest one, the Mesopotamian civilization, by at least two millennia. One needs formal rules and laws for managing the socio-political order in a large, expansive society and an economy that has progressed to the division of labour and the development of specializations. This necessitates the conception of a state which has the authority to formulate laws, regulate conduct and employ coercive power if and when required. The question is how a state with such authority and power could come about.

Having a king or a chief was the first answer to this question for all civilizations. But the king was just another individual, unless bestowed with the requisite powers by something superior. It was often god or the deemed creator of everything. A king was assigned divine powers either directly in person, as an embodiment of the creator or as his assigned representative. We have now moved ahead, and reached a point where the king's powers are bound by a rule book or a constitution and other institutions such as the judiciary and an elected parliament, and further on to a republic, where no king is needed and the constitution alone counts. The *Manusmriti* is actually doing both, giving the king a demigod status and an extensive rule book.

There are 2,700 verses divided into 12 chapters in the *Manusmriti*, which conceives order and society around the concept of *dharma*, broadly translated as morality, rights and duties. It organizes society into four *varna*s—Brahmin, Kshatriya,

Vaishya and Shudra—and the life of an individual along stages or *ashramas*, Brahmacharya, Grihastha, Vanaprastha and Sanyasa. Dharma for each varna and ashrama is outlined and they all converge into the king, who is the embodiment and upholder of dharma as a whole. The Manu and the other Smritis detail civil and criminal law, punishment and atonement, the rules of inheritance, the adoption of law and procedures of governance, and righteous wars and society.

The Dharma-shastras could compare with the constitution of any modern state in its sophistication, detail and the checks and balances it has in place. Kingdoms in the Indian civilization aspired to adhere to this concept and code from the mid-seventh millennium. It continued to be practised in the Hindu kingdoms till the modern times in pre-Independence India, and in Nepal up to a couple of decades ago, and it is still practised, to a degree, in Thailand; it would have influenced other civilizations too. The image of the 'oriental despot' was totally misplaced in case of the rulers in India. Despotism was the norm, however, for the kings in other civilizations, especially in the West and Europe till well past the Renaissance in fifteenth century CE.

As noted in the fourth and fifth chapters, the Smriti texts, starting with that by Manu, were compiled in the Gangetic Plains. Iksvaku, the first ruling dynasty in India, was established in the Koshala region around present-day Ayodhya. It is estimated to have commenced in 6965 BCE with Manu, and named after his son and the succeeding ruler, Iksvaku. The dynasty gained primacy largely due to its conceptual breakthroughs in organizing a society and a state, and their pre-eminence over other rulers led to the creation of the King-Emperor framework in India. This prevailed till the end of our period of study, 1192 CE. With the rise of the Iksvaku dynasty, the centre of gravity of Indian civilization shifted to the Gangetic Plains.

The seventh millennium was a period of immense significance to Indian civilization. In the centuries prior to 6000 BCE, Indian astronomy and mathematics reached their full bloom, the Sanskrit language evolved to perfection and the bulk of the Shruti texts were compiled, and the conception of an orderly society and state was ironed out. The Smriti texts originating in the Gangetic Plains by the mid-seventh millennium BCE point to the existence of urban and rural settlements there, similar to those in the Indus-Saraswati region, and conceivably in many other parts of India.

But we do not have a shred of archaeological evidence from the Gangetic Plains and also very little that is new from northwest India that can be dated to the seventh millennium BCE. The discipline has been a weak link in the rediscovery of the Indian chronology. This underscores the need for a huge amount of reinvigoration and for far greater and faster archaeological excavations, and perhaps an overhauling of the entire set-up. It needs to mobilize the ways and means to be a world-leading power, which is what the exploration of India's antiquity and its richness calls for. It finally has to shed the colonial mindset and procedures that have imperilled the right extent of input and output with regard to its history and civilization for a long time.

THE RAMAYANA BECKONS

The sixth millennium, 6000–5000 BCE, is an eventful period in the Indian chronology. It culminated in the epic Ramayana towards the end of the millennium, which is among the most defining events of India's civilization, and reverberates in the socio-political arena today, just as much as it did in the past. We still have no archaeological evidence from the Gangetic Plains, the loci of the epic, but it makes a re-appearance in the Indus-Saraswati region. Data from astronomy and astrophysics, the calendars, the Yuga system and texts and genealogies, however, becomes richer and more fine-grained in terms of the chronology. There is often more than one source to draw upon and cross-validate.

At the beginning of the millennium, The *Manusmriti* emerged as the undisputed text for the organization of society and state in India. The Iksvaku dynasty had by then established its pre-eminence all over India. The Koshala region, around present-day Ayodhya, is almost at the centre of the Gangetic Plains, albeit slightly to the north. Ayodhya is not far from Lahurdeva, the pre-8000 BCE site that provided the earliest evidence of rice cultivation and animal domestication in India. The area between the two, across a distance coverable in about five walking days, and the flat and unchanging terrain could hold important clues for the evolution and continuity of civilization in the region.

The discipline of archaeology comes up short when it comes to excavations relating to this antiquity, from the sixth to the eighth millennium BCE. Its findings on 'Northern Black Polished Ware' (NBPW) culture from the region, based on pottery and other artefacts, are from a much later time, i.e., the first millennium BCE. This culture could have been discerned from a later and higher layer as the region was always populated, and the archaeological digging and excavations have yet to reach the lower layers. Here, the limitations of the 1920s construct, which chronicled Indian civilization starting from 600 BCE, could be at play. It may have thwarted deeper excavations and caused blind spots in the process of identification and reporting older finds. A bad theory or construct can be insidious. There is a case for the archaeologist to undertake a re-examination and actively seek useful clues.

In the Indus-Saraswati region, a few sites such as Rakhigarhi are dated prior to 5000 BCE. But this, the largest of Harappan sites, has been barely explored, and the exploration has covered barely a small percentage of its total area and depth in the last six decades since the excavations first started. And the lower layers, which correspond to the late sixth millennium BCE, have been looked into very sparingly and superficially. There is an enormous amount of hesitation to explore and document anything beyond the third millennium BCE among archaeologists in India.

In research, one often observes a tendency either to force fit or to ignore any outlier data. This is poor scholarship and a sign of a lack of self-confidence. It should be the other way round for anyone curious and committed enough to the advancement of the discipline.

The sixth millennium was a significant period for the recalibration of the Yugas, primarily to improve the accuracy of Indian calendars. A shift from the Yugas with durations of 1,200 years was considered appropriate. The Jovian cycle remained the basis, but the duration of the Chatur Yuga was recalibrated to 12,000 years with the durations of the respective Yugas in a 4:3:2:1 ratio—implying the respective duration of the Krita to be 4,800, the Treta 3,600, the Dvapar 2,400 and the Kali 1,200 years. The shift underlined the identification of the need and the willingness to improve on the accuracy of calendars, even if it is a slight improvement. Consequently, the duration of the twenty-eighth Treta Yuga was fixed at 6777 to 3177 BCE. While the sixth millennium, from 6000 to 5000 BCE, belonged fully to the Treta Yuga, there was soon a twist in the tale in the next millennium, and that is the matter of the following section.

Over 30 generations of the Iksvaku dynasty would have ruled by the beginning of the sixth millennium BCE, if we take the average regnal period to be 30 years. Besides establishing its pre-eminence in India, its continuity since 6965 BCE would make it the longest-reigning dynasty in any civilization anywhere in the world, at that point and right up to modern times. As the originator and torchbearer of dharma, their influence would have reached every settlement in the Indian landmass. Since it was extensively outlined and detailed, and there was no other alternative, the entirety of Indian society would have largely come to accept and adopt the precepts, procedures and ways of Manu's Dharma-shastra as prescribed.

Society would have got organized along the varnas and every individual would have known and tried to adhere to the four ashramas in his life by the early sixth millennium. Duties, as they were accorded by the constructs of Varna-ashrama and citizenship and operationalized through civil and criminal laws, would have formed the bedrock of the political economy. An important cog was someone who would enforce the laws, and do so judiciously. The *Manusmriti* clearly envisaged a ruler bestowed with divinity. Such a ruler, king or raja could be installed by the Brahmin varna from among the Kshatriyas.

A few individuals, who were socio-economically influential and belonged to a higher or an elite strata, would have staked their claim to be the king. After some struggle and jostling among pre-existing clans, such a person would have emerged. The territories would be small, broadly determined by the areas populated by the participating clans, though his authority would be based upon his adherence to the Dharma-shastras, and subject to the checks and balances therein. Their legitimacy would crucially depend on their affiliation to the Iksvakus, who were the originators and had survived as a model for such a long time.

Thus, the King-Emperor framework based on dharma or moral authority within Indian civilization evolved, and it continued for over seven millennia till 1192 CE. India is a vast landmass, and no single individual or state could have directly enforced law and order and dispensed justice centrally in those times. Rishi Agastya is credited with being the anchor of dharma in the southern region and Rishi Vasishtha in the north.[5] The Indus-Saraswati region that had led the civilizational evolution earlier, during the composition of the Vedic Shruti texts, would have been co-opted into this concept of socio-economic-political order.

Over the first half of the sixth millennium, the integration and homogeneity of Indian civilization would have been realized. The *Manusmriti* had envisaged a hereditary ruler who was brought up and conducted himself, on his ascension, as per the well-laid-out and strict disciplinary procedures and schedules of the dharma. This provided for the continuity and convergence of the stakes for the king and other members of society, through the bulk of India. The forested parts of the Deccan Plateau could have been circumvented or partially influenced, but the coastal regions were certainly integrated. The Iksvakus were the pre-eminent dynasty for the whole civilization, from the Himalayas to the seas and from the Brahmaputra to the outer fringes of the Indus Valley, and they were as good as being the ordained emperors for all of India.

The dharma texts set a tall order, which was consistent and clear, and they were continually embellished by subsidiary texts and commentaries. There was always a lot to understand, do and improve, for every individual in society and for the king and various parts of the state apparatus. This kept the whole civilization engaged and in multidimensional loops, in order to be fully absorbed and become self-preserving and propelling. The economy and vocations also got organized along varna lines and the various clans and individuals would have been classified under one or the other. Clans could have retained their earlier identities and lineages, while belonging to a varna now, in the form of an identifier surname; then they went on to become distinctive *jaati*s.

The jaati was a sub-grouping within a varna, and could comprise one or more surnames or family lineage names. Since the whole system of dharma was hierarchical and hereditary, the sub-group jaati and the varna would have soon become defined by one's birth. We prefer the term 'jaati' instead of 'caste', as the latter gained currency many millennia afterwards, in the early seventeenth century, with the advent of Europeans in India. They linked it to the Latin 'castus' and its Portuguese derivative 'casta', but that had different race-related connotations. The jaatis were derived entirely from the same race, and within the same varna, but they were distinguished and surnamed according to the small localized village or area they hailed from, or the occupation and family lineage they belonged to. The jaati acted as an identifier and a social binder, and a way of propagating specialized vocations and skills. The jaati also came in handy in preserving bloodlines and avoiding incestuous marriages, and for advancing suitable socio-economic interactions, liaisons and mobility.

By the mid-sixth millennium, around 5500 BCE, the varna-jaati system of Indian civilization would have been institutionalized. This is phenomenally advanced with regard to the time and spaces of evolution, as the second oldest world civilization in Mesopotamia would start its journey at least half a millennium later. At this time, the pre-eminent Iksvaku dynasty would be nearing its fiftieth ruler. Several other rajas or kings spread across various region all over India would have established their own lineages comprising more than a dozen rulers each. The King-Emperor framework, the concomitant and multifaceted characteristics of political economy, the stratification and homogenization of society that bound every individual into a cohesive whole, would have developed and stabilized in the entirety of the Indian landmass.

A string of pilgrimage centres, which were major instruments of the socio-cultural as well as economic integration of the civilization, would have sprouted all over the landmass. Incidentally, the largest such congregation, the Kumbh Mela, is based on the 12-year cycle of the Jupiter. It would have surely been linked with and started from the recalibration of the Yugas and the calendars to the Jovian cycle from 6777 BCE. The Kumbh Mela is organized at four pivotal locations within Indian civilization—Haridwar, where the snow-fed Himalayan river Ganges enters the plains, Prayagraj in eastern Uttar Pradesh, at the confluence of the Ganges and the Yamuna, Ujjain in central Madhya Pradesh, where the zero meridian of Indian astronomy intersects with the Tropic of Cancer, and Nashik, on the western edge of the Deccan Plateau in Maharashtra, just 30 kilometres from the point of origin of the river Godavari, which is the longest river in South India and flows east to Telangana, Andhra, and empties in the Bay of Bengal.

This was the socio-cultural and political make-up of India when Rama was born in the Iksvaku dynasty. He was the eldest son of Dashratha, the sixty-third hereditary ruler of the lineage that founded and embodied the dharma construct of civilization. Rama was born very late in Dashratha's regnal period, in 5114 BCE, which cleared away the clouds of anxiety that had gathered about the continuity of the illustrious dynasty. He was a precocious child, who stood apart in calibre and the respect and affection he could command from everyone. A strict regimen of education in the Gurukul of Rishi Vasishtha followed.

Rama demonstrated his prowess in slaying 'demons', essentially men and sometimes women, who had fallen foul of dharma. They used to trouble citizens spending time in the forests during the Vanaprastha and Sanyasa ashrama (stages) of life. His marriage to Sita—the daughter of king Janaka of Mithila up north in the Himalayan foothills that traverses present-day Nepal and India—in a wedding contest followed soon after this. Rama was to be crowned the ruler at the age of 25 but was instead forced to go into exile in the forest for 14 years, honouring the pledge his father had made to his stepmother Kaikeyi. Her son, Bharata, refused to be crowned ruler, indicating that the precept of primogeniture was well established, especially in the pre-eminent Iksvaku dynasty.

These developments would have sent shockwaves across the civilization—Valmiki, who was the contemporary of Rama and wrote the epic Ramayana, construes the Indian landmass as a cultural continuum and comes pretty close to the conception of a unified nation, particularly in the latter 'kandas' or chapters, such as the Lanka and Uttara kandas. The text is in the fully formed and free-flowing verse of laukika Sanskrit. Rama had an eventful life that tested his morality, prowess and fortitude. His journey through the Indian geography and across the Palk Strait to defeat Ravana makes for one of the greatest accounts of human endeavour in the history of civilization in the world.

Rama was duly crowned as the ruler in 5075 BCE, and went on to establish the ideal of a state—called 'Ram Rajya', extolled by several thinkers, including Mahatma Gandhi, all through history and right up to modern times. Here the ruler upheld dharma, served the 'praja' or the populace, and his own interests and comfort were subservient to those of the state. There are indications of Rama expanding the dynasty's direct rule when the need or the opportunity arose. He sent his youngest brother Shatrughana to subdue the king of Mathura, who had deviated from the path of dharma, and established his rule there.

Bharata was deputed to Gandhara in the northwestern region. His mother belonged to the nearby and contiguous Kaikeya kingdom. Remarkably, Takshshila and Peshawar in present-day Pakistan have been named after Bharata's sons, Taksh and Pushkala. His other brother, Lakshmana, who had accompanied him into his 14-year exile, is credited with establishing Lucknow in Uttar Pradesh, and he set up his rule in the Anga and Banga regions, corresponding to eastern Bihar and northern Bengal, and the southern part of West Bengal and southwestern Bangladesh, respectively. In another deviation, Rama, instead of choosing one inheritor, divided his realm between his twin sons. The northern part went to Lava, with its capital at Shravasti, where Buddha too lived after his enlightenment. The southern part went to Kusa, whose capital was Kushavati, and it extended up to the Vindhya Range in Central India.

This takes us close to the end of the sixth millennium, around 5000 BCE. Kusa is reckoned to be the direct descendant of Rama and the sixty-fifth ruler of the Iksvaku dynasty in terms of the genealogy. Koshala, however, acquired a different shape after Rama. At the turn of the millennium, Rama and his brothers' descendants or cousins would have directly ruled a vast swathe of the Indian subcontinent. This would have extended from the northwestern borders to deltaic Bengal and the foothills of Nepal to the Vindhyas along the river Narmada.

FAST-FORWARD TO THE MAHABHARATA

The contours of civilization were established across the bulk of the Indian landmass by the early fifth millennium BCE. They would have taken root in the far-flung and peripheral areas as well. Bharata's presence and rule in the northwest region, for instance, would have inculcated the best of the dharma practices there. This would also be the case for the coastal parts and the hinterland plains of Bengal and in Telangana and Andhra.

In the southern Indian states, the efforts of Rishi Agastya would have carried forward and expanded to cover the whole region. He was a contemporary of Rishi Vasishtha, to whose gurukul Rama was sent for education, and is extensively referred to in the first texts of Sangam literature in Tamil. Besides Agastya in the south, the link between Mehrgarh in Baluchistan and the coastal region in Sindh had been well established for a couple of millennia before this time. Indian civilization progressed apace till around 4500 BCE, when the new findings and contours started emerging.

More sites and evidence of advances in the Indus-Saraswati region get identified for which we have the archaeological data. Rakhigarhi in Haryana and near Delhi, and Mohenjo-daro and Harappa in the Sindh and Punjab provinces of present-day Pakistan appear as much larger nodes. These and the coastal sites of Lothal and Dholavira in Gujarat and the inland Kalibangan in Rajasthan were subjects of major excavations. The antecedents or the inception of all these sites can be traced back to the late sixth millennium to the early fifth millennium BCE. A significant find, particularly in Kalibangan, are the fire altars used for Vedic rituals in almost every large dwelling or built space. The sites were advancing towards becoming urban centres and the landscape of the Indus-Saraswati region was evidently becoming similar to any modern nation—large and small cities dotting the region and each with its respective rural hinterland consisting of villages.

This landscape would certainly prevail in Koshala and many other regions of India by the mid-fifth millennium BCE. It would be so for longer and on a much grander scale in the case of Koshala, the seat of the de facto emperor and the lead and core of civilization for over two millennia. Archaeological data will eventually be found from the region, and hopefully soon. An important piece for our rediscovery of the Indian chronology, noted in the third chapter, was the discovery of copper furnaces and smelting material at Kunal near Bhirrana.

The use of copper and its close cousin, bronze, is a major advance, and marks the next step or age in the evolution of human civilization. It is particularly critical for the political economy, as the metal gives a huge boost to the warfare equipment and capabilities and the tools for clearing forests, ploughing fields and allied activities. The Kunal finds, though currently dated to 3500 BCE, could imply the use of copper and bronze from a few centuries to even a millennium earlier in the Indus-Saraswati region. It could extend by another millennium or so, to the late sixth millennium BCE, when Rama perfected his bow-arrow skills and went on to wage a campaign in Lanka.

In the Ramayana period, the century from 5100 to 5000 BCE, Rama and other princes of Koshala seem to have had a significant advantage in the range of arrows and the techniques of using them. At Janaka's congregation, he outshone all the other kings though he was only in his late teens, and no one else barring Ravana and his brothers from Lanka appeared to possess comparable arrows and techniques. Both the Koshala and Lanka princely households could have mastered the technology of using copper and bronze, and would have had possession of or exclusive access to copper and tin ores. Rama, however, walked all through his exile and during the Lanka campaign, pointing to horses not being domesticated and yoked to chariots. Riding came much later, when horses were bred and improved upon to be strong enough to carry a man and his usual trappings.

Rama's achievements, especially his victory over the Lankan princes who were marauding all over and up to the Himalayas, would have reverberated across the civilization—in particular, among the princely households of the Indus-Saraswati region, who had led the subcontinent earlier during the time of the Shruti or Vedic compilations but ceded eminence to the Koshala region during the period of the Smritis and the organization of a formal state. The presence of Rama's brother Bharata in the northwest, and his descendants thereupon, would have directly exposed the regional kings to the advantages bestowed by bronze arrows and other equipment for warfare. An extensive process of diffusion and imitation of the innovation necessary for tools and techniques would have ensued, and also the search for the requisite ores.

The discovery of large copper ore deposits in northern Rajasthan, where Khetri still remains a major mine in India, and those of tin in Khyber-Pakhtunkhwa, would have endowed the northwestern region with a huge strategic advantage. This coincided with the rise of the Kurus in the late fifth millennium BCE. Almost simultaneously, the Iksvakus weakened. There were splits in the empire during the reign of the eighty-fifth ruler, Agnivarman, dated to around 4400 BCE, and thereafter the Iksvaku dynasty disappears from the genealogical records for nearly a millennium.

In northwest India and broadly along the Indus-Saraswati region, the genealogical records from the Puranas are available for the 35 rulers of the Kuru dynasty till the Mahabharata war in 3138 BCE. That is from the first ruler Puru to Yudhisthira, estimated to span 1,050 years, as per the yardstick of an average of 30 regnal years per ruler. The chain of evidence, from the Ramayana and the rise of the Kurus, points to the Bronze Age having begun in India from the early sixth millennium BCE, let's say around 5200 BCE. It would push the world chronology, which dates the Bronze Age from 3300 to 1200 BCE, by around two millennia. This is another consequence of our project of rediscovering and properly chronicling Indian antiquity, and this impacts the chronology and understanding of world civilization itself.

We do not have a map of the Kuru realm, let's say around 4200 BCE, when this dynasty would have been fully established and well known. Such maps are hard to obtain for anywhere in the world, and we need to work with whatever data is available. The Kuru capital was in Hastinapur, on the western bank of the Ganges and at the edge of the Gangetic Plains. It is geographically contiguous and a part of the socio-economy to the west, a territory covering, for instance, Kunal, Rakhigarhi and Khetri.

Moreover, Indraprastha, analogous to present-day Delhi and around 150 kilometres away, was certainly a part of the empire at the time of the Mahabharata. As was Kurukshetra, which was about the same distance away. The latter was pretty much within the core area of the Kuru empire, and the periphery which was directly ruled by them could conceivably have extended more than twice in radius or 300–500 kilometres. Thus, it brought the copper mines at Khetri and Rakhigarhi and several other Harappan sites within the empire's direct purview. The affiliates and allied kings could have extended the zone of influence another few hundred kilometres in radius, and even further, perhaps up to the seas.

Evidence after the third round of archaeological excavations at Rakhigarhi[6] dates the culture up to 6000 BCE. A couple of large houses with six bedrooms, with a courtyard and drainage system, have been found. Utensils made of gold and silver, ornaments of silver and copper, exquisitely finished clay pots and a dinner set, a colourful piece of worn cloth, skirts and shawls make for a very significant range of finds. These could be dated to several layers and periods in Rakhigarhi, but they set the record straight on several key aspects of the cultural and civilizational development in India.

Gold and silver occur in free form and do not need much processing, and were mostly procured from outside India and through trade. Utensils made of these imply their acquisition in substantial amounts, and the presence of very rich and elite socio-economic strata. Copper, on the other hand, needs high temperature furnaces—albeit much lower than that for iron—and smelting chemicals, to be extracted and refined from its ore. Copper processing technology, and the knowledge of alloying it with tin to make bronze, could thus be easily dated to many centuries prior to the late fifth millennium BCE, based on the available archaeological evidence itself.

The Kuru dynasty, the rising power in the northwest region, would have used its control of the huge copper resource far and wide. It was perhaps a superpower in India in the Bronze Age. Some of it could have been through warfare, which the greatly superior bronze arrows, armours and other equipment and the large resource base would have endowed them with. It would have led to the accumulation of economic resources and the projection of socio-political power. A lot of the latter was symbolically wrought through marriage alliances with important kingdoms, down the generations of the Kuru dynasty, and from the North-West Frontier Province to northern Bengal and eastern Maharashtra. This included Koshala too, and that would have meant that the Kurus had arrived as the new emperors of India's King-Emperor framework.

The entire northwest region where the Harappan sites have been found and the small and large kingdoms there that have been identified to have participated in the Mahabharata war were certainly an important part of the Kuru empire. The framework extended all the way to the kings of the coastal south and Lanka, and the rest of the Indian subcontinent, as noted in the fourth chapter—archaeological evidence from other regions is yet to be found, although that from the astronomy, calendars and textual and genealogical sources abound. The Kuru empire, however, had taken shape around a millennium prior to the Mahabharata war, by 4200 BCE.

The recalibration of the transition from the twenty-eighth Treta to the Dvapar Yuga would have broadly coincided with the rise of the Kurus to pre-eminence. The events of the Ramayana in 5100–5000 BCE are reckoned to be in the Treta Yuga and that of the Mahabharata from 3200 to 3102 BCE in the Dvapar Yuga. There was no defining or incontrovertible astronomical event, such as a major planetary conjunction, in between. And it is hard to date the transition firmly based either on the 1,200-year Yuga or the 12,000-year Chatur Yuga system.

The transition could have been guided by the political economy. A shift in India's centre of gravity was effected by around 4200 BCE, from the Iksvakus to the Kurus in the northwest. Linking the transition to the Dvapar Yuga with that of the pre-eminent dynasty could have heralded the trend of major rulers commemorating their ascension as the start of a new era or saka in India. The trend, remarkably, originated with the thirty-fifth ruler of the Kuru dynasty, and the start of the Yudhisthira saka in 3138 BCE. Many rulers named new eras, or tried to do so, after themselves subsequently.

The Mahabharata, akin to the Ramayana, was the result of turbulence in the pre-eminent dynasty of its time. Both were long-standing dynasties, having run into the thirty-fourth and sixty-third generations respectively, and had a guiding influence all over the Indian landmass. The ascension of the rightful successor is at the core of Indian state and society, enunciated by the *Manusmriti* and other Dharma-shastras. It ought to be smooth and well-planned from the birth of the eldest son. The situation was awfully muddled, much more so than in the case of Rama, which also meant a delay of 14 years, a series of unforeseen and painful events, but there was no fratricide or involvement of outsiders and lesser kings. Rama's claim to the throne was always beyond any kind of doubt or challenge.

The situation in the Mahabharata, known to every Indian since its occurrence in the late fourth millennium BCE, was at the foremost a question of dharma, to which the Shastras or the constitution and convention or precedent did not provide a clear answer. It was far more complex than what any modern state has reckoned to have faced in the last few hundred years. The debate, efforts and the erudition, the standing and diversity of the personalities involved exceed any other monarchic or democratic transfer of power in a state thereafter, and in the history of human civilization. Primogeniture was accepted, but does that mean that the eldest son of the younger brother who ruled briefly will succeed to the throne? Or will it be the eldest son of elder brother who was set aside earlier because of visual disability? Moreover, the latter, Duryodhana, is incapable of upholding a ruler's dharma and the other, Yudhisthira, is its shining, confirmed example.

As the next generation comes of age, the turbulence in the Kuru dynasty comes forth. A decade and a half of dramatic events, intrigue and manoeuvres eventually leads to a full-scale war. It pulls in kings from all over the Indian civilization, who took the side of one or the other cousin brother, with each king struggling with the dilemma himself. Krishna's advice and interventions, highly regarded by everyone, did not work either.

The war lasted 18 days, saw the deployment of the best of battle tactics, equipment and resources, and the valour and ethics of just war, but led to massive losses and the annihilation of most. Yudhisthira survived, as did his four siblings, and was crowned the thirty-fifth ruler of the Kuru dynasty. He reigned as per the highest standards of dharma, on the lines of Ram Rajya. Around 36 years later, in 3102 BCE, he handed over the reign to Parikshita—the grandson of his younger brother Arjuna, since all his own children, those of his four siblings as well as those of Duryodhana and his brothers were killed in the war.

THE VIGNETTES

A significant interlude in the Mahabharata is the dialogue between Krishna and Arjuna, which took place when the two armies were standing face to face just before the beginning of war. Arjuna was, by far, the greatest warrior and Krishna had agreed to be his charioteer. Arjuna was experiencing severe self-doubt about going ahead and was fearful about the mayhem that would ensue among his beloved, respected compatriots and family members.

The dialogue was composed as the *Bhagavad Gita*, the best-known ancient Indian text and a part of the Mahabharata, all of which was compiled by Ved Vyasa. It is a stand-alone text too, and comprises 700 verses organized into 18 chapters. The *Gita* is a fine exposition of philosophy; it elaborates on the definition of the self being separate from the body and being a microcosm of the all-encompassing eternal and supreme 'Brahman', on how the body can be elevated to the realization of the self through yoga and devotion, and how the soul is entangled and can be liberated. It is the distillation of Indian philosophy and is closely aligned to the Vedanta school.

Chronologically, the *Gita* can be put together with the Upanishads, and follow the Shruti and Smriti texts. The Mahabharata war raised a new set of fundamental questions, which the Shruti's Vedic Samhitas and their respective Brahmanas and Aranyakas and the Smriti's Dharma-shastras could not resolve. Arjuna's doubts and fears expressed these at the individual level. These questions of the state, society and individual needed to be addressed by elevating them to philosophy and by extending and integrating the Shruti and Smriti texts. The *Gita*'s answers are indeed cogent and arguably they are still unsurpassed, and they have been explored, evolved and enunciated repeatedly ever since their inception.

The dating of the beginning of the Bronze Age in India to the early sixth millennium puts the Mahabharata period towards the peak or the mature phase of the period characterised by the use of these metals. This is reflected in the range of sophisticated arrows, armour and other weapons. There is no riding on horses in the Mahabharata war but chariots abound, although used only by the leading warriors, of whom there are only a couple dozens.

The current understanding is that horses were domesticated in the Eurasian steppes around 5500–3500 BCE. The earliest evidence of horses interred with remains of chariots have been found in the 16 graves at Sintashta in Southern Russia, and dated to 2100–1700 BCE. The site is located straight up north from the North-West Frontier Province. The spread of horses was nothing short of explosive, and within 500 years, horse-drawn chariots were available in Mesopotamia and Egypt. The Sintashta evidence gathered from so many graves at one place implies that horse chariots were being widely used for at least a few hundred years prior to it and so they were sparingly used up to a millennium earlier. Archaeologists are conservatively inclined when it comes to dating these phenomena, and if we stretch the use of horses in chariots to the late fourth millennium and given the speed of its spread and India being closer, some horses would have been making their way here by the time of the Mahabharata.

The simultaneous and even prior domestication of horses within India and their use in chariots cannot be ruled out. This rhymes with the gross underestimation of Indian antiquity in almost every development and aspect, including the beginning of the Bronze Age, by up to a millennium or two. Moreover, the subsidiary and supportive materials and technology for the construction of war chariots were already present and had reached high levels of sophistication in India. For instance, the transportation by carts has been going on since the eighth millennium BCE. The use of copper and bronze had started during the Ramayana time and then led to the rise of the Kurus with major copper deposits nearby and tin transported from Khyber-Pakhtunkhwa.

Coming to the rest of the world, the Mesopotamian civilization started taking shape during the fifth millennium BCE. The Sumerians and Akkadians, including the Assyrians and

Babylonians, came into their own in Mesopotamia from 3100 BCE. The Egyptian civilization also started emerging along the Nile delta. Towards the Far East, the Chinese civilization appeared in the Yangtze River basin in the late fourth millennium BCE. They make for an interesting and comparative world order, along with the much older Indian civilization. This is one of our areas of exploration in the next chapter.

8

'POST-MAHABHARATA' PERIOD: 3102–325 BCE

The Mahabharata was a watershed event in the history and civilization of India. On ascribing the right place to it and dating it correctly as we go along, and by analysing its implications and the events it led to, the war can be seen as a pivotal event for world history itself. The web of evidence from multiple sources and their linkages will open up new vistas of understanding for us and enable us to attempt the corrections that have been long overdue. These will open up a new set of inquiries and the answers, whether definitive or tentative, would significantly realign the way we see India and the world.

There is a case for wholesale reconstruction. This is inevitably so, as the data from the oldest civilization is rightly identified, validated, put together and assessed. The onset of civilization in India in the mid-eighth millennium BCE, instead of Mesopotamia around 5000 BCE, pushes the world's civilizational antiquity by around two and a half millennia. It is not a minor or peripheral correction, but of the quantum kind and the front and central, as India is also located virtually at the epicentre of Eurasia—the zone of civilizational evolution of humankind post-Holocene, and India's huge landmass also juts towards the north and the deep south, which leads to it being intertwined with every development all around the world.

This correction by adding two and a half millennia to known history at the start of civilization will understandably push back the markers of its evolution in a similar way. They may appear startling at first, since we have all been conditioned, over the decades, to a particular worldview. Civilizational evolution is a long process passing through small and large steps, unless it is broken by some cataclysmic event that could lead to its extinction. This has not been so since the end of the last Ice Age, and certainly not for India, where we have found the continuity of civilization stretching over ten millennia.

The beginning of human civilization in the Stone Age is validated, but we have recalibrated its transition to the Bronze Age by about two millennia. That is to the late sixth millennium or around 5200 BCE, instead of the prevailing idea that posits that it began in 3200 BCE. The transition first happens obviously in India. The onset of the Bronze Age used to be associated with the Mesopotamian civilization, which had appeared much later. It was considered the oldest among all civilizations, without the Indian data being ascertained and taken into account. Similarly, the use of horses in war chariots is being taken back further to the mid-fourth millennium or around 3500 BCE. This too would have happened first in India. The tools and technologies using bronze would by far be in the most advanced stages in India, including, for instance, the design of a spoked or suitable wheel and other equipment, and suitable horses once available—from the Eurasian steppes or groomed domestically—would be quickly put to use and their potential exploited sophisticatedly.

The advances in the technology for waging war[1] were concluded upon as a key factor in the evolution of civilizations, in one place and relative to others. It ramped up the process and led to rapid improvements and innovations in allied technologies, which set in motion a range of politico-economic and socio-cultural shifts. Horses, gunpowder, rifles, tanks and so forth have been great advances in warfare technologies in the history of human civilization. The Mahabharata would have seen the first significant deployment of horses in a war in the world, albeit in chariots and not yet for riding. Access to horses seems to have been limited to the leading warriors, and chariot-driving would have been a rare skill too, thus granting those few warriors a pivotal influence in the war.

The Mahabharata war shook Indian civilization. It impacted the political sphere to start with and moved on to the socio-cultural one consequently. Most of the kings across its length and breadth participated in it. A recent study identified and counted them to be sixty-two in number.[2] Of these, 36 fought for Duryodhana and the Kaurava side and 26 for Yudhisthira and the Pandavas. They came with their armies and participated with their full might. The highest proportion was from the Indus-Saraswati region. Their large number, and with the next most represented figure being from the western part of the Gangetic Plains, indicate that this part of the Indian landmass was the most organized socio-politically, and perhaps the most advanced in the late fourth millennium BCE, and populated too.

The majority of the kings were killed in the war. This would have caused a political upheaval and those on the losing (Kaurava) side would have found their authority severely compromised. A small but indicative example is of Brihadbala, the last ruler of the erstwhile imperial Iksvaku dynasty, who was killed by Abhimanyu, Arjuna's son. The dynasty had been reset a few hundred years ago, after existing unrecognized for nearly a millennium since its dismemberment during the reign of the eighty-fifth ruler, Agnivarman, around 4400 BCE. Brihadbala participated as a minor king, and his death marked the formal end of the Iksvaku dynasty.

A vast majority of dynasties and kings would experience a similar fate, and that would have caused a political upheaval across Indian civilization at that time. The economies of virtually all the states would have weakened. Massive losses to armies on both sides would have caused deep social scars all over. These would have affected the authority of small and large states, although the pre-eminent position of the righteous Yudhisthira as the inheritor of India's King-Emperor framework would have been a source of strength. He and his brothers would have had to work earnestly for restoring order, and also for uplifting society's morale and its cohesion.

Reprisals against the defeated are a natural consequence of war. We do not hear anything further of Brihadbala and the remnant of the Iksvaku kingdom. It was possibly carved up or merged with one or more neighbouring states that supported the victorious Pandavas. The Kauravas had enjoyed greater support in the Indus-Saraswati region, particularly the kingdoms west of the Indus and further northwest, such as Gandhara and Kamboja. The consequent socio-political upheavals in these border areas of Indian civilization would have had major long-drawn implications in this Post-Mahabharata period.

There is a momentous beginning to the Post-Mahabharata period, in terms of the astrophysics and calendar-Yuga system and the contours of the unfolding Indian history. On 18 February 3102 BCE, there was a major conjunction of all the five planets and the sun and moon in the Aries constellation visible to the naked eye. This was a rare astronomical event, occurring once in a few millennia. It was conspicuous enough all over India to precipitate the final calibration of the Yugas and calendars. The twenty-eighth Dvapar Yuga was wrapped up with this, and the date and year were determined to be the beginning of the twenty-eighth Kali Yuga or era.

Simultaneously, the duration of this Kali Yuga was redefined to 432,000 years, a multiple of 12,000 in reference and continuance of the Jovian cycle and the system of 360 days per year upheld by Indian astronomy. The other sequential and earlier three Yugas of a Chatur Yuga continued to be in the ratio of four, three and two to the duration of the Kali Yuga. The system of reckoning of long cycles of time was hugely expanded, to a Manvantara comprising 71 Chatur Yugas, and so on to Kalpa, one day of Brahma, Pralaya, and Brahma's lifespan of 100 years.

This meant the continuation of the twenty-eighth Kali Yuga for all practical and civilizational purposes, forever. It stabilized the calendar for all time to come. The cycles of Manvantara–Kalpa–Pralaya–Brahma's life created a large space for conceiving a variety of narratives, particularly in the Puranas. These were used to explain and propagate the thoughts of earlier texts and also to build upon further, largely for the consumption of the masses.

Indian civilization moved to its next phase, in terms of the defining contours, in the year 3102 BCE. Krishna passed away and Yudhisthira relinquished the throne. He anointed Parikshita, and marched along with his brothers and Draupadi towards the Himalayas and into oblivion, marking the end of their era. They were civilizational giants, whose personalities and influence reverberated throughout India, and they came to shape it significantly and indelibly for all time. The events of 3102 BCE, though in the offing for some years, were rather sudden, and were hastened by Krishna's demise. It would have caused a vacuum socio-politically, thereby giving wind to several existing as well as new forces.

In the 3102–325 BCE period, a lot was happening elsewhere in the world too. The Mesopotamian and Egyptian civilizations were reaching maturity and the Chinese too, after a late start, were arriving there. Towards the latter half of the period, the two civilizations to India's west were converging in the middle space and leading to an explosion of cultures, of which the Greeks and Persians were the most significant in the beginning. Several new ones emerged, who took the shape of stand-alone civilizations in their own right. All of them would have been influenced by the much larger and many-millennia-older Indian civilization. There would have been an interesting and important flow of ideas, material and people among them. This exchange among civilizations adorns our rediscovery of the Indian chronology and history in this chapter.

DISAGGREGATION, RISE OF MAGADHA

The third millennium BCE opens with the Kuru dynasty at the peak of its glory. They were at the fulcrum of India's King-Emperor framework, and were regarded as the latter throughout the civilization. While Valmiki had described the geographical expanse of the civilization in the Ramayana, dated to around 5000 BCE, the term 'Bharat' or 'Bharatvarsh' for the civilization is best ascribed[3] to the nineteenth ruler of the Kuru dynasty. He is described in the Adi-Parva of Ved Vyasa's Mahabharata, and taking our yardstick of a thirty-year regnal period on an average for a ruler, he would have ascended to the throne around 3618 BCE. This aligns well with the establishment of the Kurus' pre-eminence in Indian civilization.

There is a record of two land grants made to temples by Janmajeya, son of Parikshita, dated to the twenty-ninth year of his reign, the year 89 in the Kali era or 3013 BCE.[4] The temples were at present-day Hampi, in Karnataka, where he is described as seated on the throne of Kiskindha, and at Ukhimath in Kedarkhanda-Uttarakhand, which puts him on his imperial throne in Indraprastha. Full and clear details of the grants are available, with each running into about two dozen lines.

The Hampi grant has been written about in an article published in the journal *Indian Antiquary* and the Ukhimath one is currently rendered into a copper plate and displayed prominently at the temple. The grants would have been originally recorded in Shruti, or verbally, and suitably proclaimed, executed and carried further as an imperial order. The description of Janmajeya being seated at Kiskindha is a mark of his recognition as the ruler all over the subcontinent, and illustrative of the prevalent King-Emperor framework in India.

In the first century of the third millennium, the Kurus suffered major reverses. The sixth post-Mahabharata ruler, Nichaksu, was defeated by the Salva tribe from the Trigarta kingdom located in the lower hills of Himachal Pradesh and Punjab. The tribe is described as non-Vedic and did not accept the supremacy of the Kurus. A major flood followed and the Kurus were forced to abandon Hastinapur and shift their capital to Kausambi, near Prayagraj in eastern Uttar Pradesh. The reverses would have dented the pre-eminent position of the dynasty as a military-economic power and socio-cultural centre. They set it on a path of slow decline, and the Kurus became one of the many rulers in India by the mid-third millennium BCE.

None of the next twenty-three rulers after Nichaksu could regain pre-eminence, and the Kuru dynasty shrank to insignificance by the end of the millennium. The decline was relative too, as several other kingdoms became stronger. The Kurus' defeat by the Trigarta tribe was possibly a sign of things to come. The Indus-Saraswati region was rising to its peak around 2500 BCE, in terms of socio-economic development, aided by trade with emerging civilizations to the west as well. Besides Trigarta, Sindhu-Sauvira was another prominent kingdom from the region.

Gandhara and Kamboja further up north, though not within the Indus-Saraswati region, would have gained immensely from the trade and transactions. Take, for instance, the supply of tin from Khyber-Pakhtunkhwa. All four of them had sided with the Kauravas in the Mahabharata war, and would have experienced distrust and discomfort with the Kurus thereafter. A consequence of conceiving the developments in the Indus-Saraswati region in a flawed fashion and thinking of them as exogenous to Indian civilization is that the well-developed states and kingdoms there have gone altogether missing or have been grossly undermined in the narratives. Thus the techno-economic and socio-political history of the Indus-Saraswati region and its links as a part of the evolution of Indian civilization need to be systematically unpacked and reassembled for the third millennium and further.

The unpacking-reassembling process will apply just as much to the Gangetic Plains and the rest of India. We need to unpack what we know, which fortunately grows as one comes forward in antiquity, but that has not been interpreted properly and wrongly assigned chronologically. The errors have been brought about as well as exacerbated by the limiting 1920 construct, and could range up to a couple of millennia. From our rediscovery of the Indian chronology, for example, a dozen or so major kingdoms akin to those termed *mahajanpada*s would be dated to around 2500 BCE, and not 600–300 BCE. This is a massive correction, and indicative of the magnitude of errors that have prevailed.

The third millennium BCE was a period of transition—from around 2800 BCE, when the Kurus started declining, at least relatively, to around 2200 BCE, when Magadha had risen to pre-eminence. The interregnum of 600 years was the time of disaggregation of the deep-seated and ingrained King-Emperor framework of Indian civilization. The Kurus, though, would have continued to be regarded as emperors, and looked up to by other rulers and people in the entire landmass, but only symbolically or just in name. They now lacked the social-cultural-moral leadership of Koshala or the Yudhisthira-period Kurus, as well as the dominance of its political economy.

The Mahabharata war had divided the Indian states and kings down the middle. Its consequent socio-cultural scars and fissures and the lack of a strong and guiding centre, within a few centuries, would have opened up new possibilities for the ambitious in particular. This would certainly be so in the Indus-Saraswati region, which was also undergoing rapid socio-economic development—and also for many other regions throughout India. For these, we do not have much archaeological data from the third millennium BCE. Thus, we shall use the Indus-Saraswati data to project trends for the wider Indian civilization.

Over 2,000 sites have been identified in the Indus-Saraswati region, and many more would have sprouted, and almost all of them would have reached maturity by the mid-third millennium BCE. The region would not be cartographically much different from present-day India; in fact, it would be more extensively inhabited, with the river Saraswati still in full flow. There would have been large urban centres such as Rakhigarhi in the area of the Saraswati-Drishadvati rivers, Mohenjo-Daro to the west of the Indus and the port cities Dholavira and Lothal, and plausibly, another few hundred cities and towns of various sizes and thousands of rural hamlets.

The living habitats were indeed fabulous, with large and small houses, often with more than one storey, lined neatly along the wide streets and with drainage systems. There was well-organized urban infrastructure, with the areas clearly marked out for dwellings of families from different socio-economic classes, factories for mass production and grain storage, and public amenities such as the great bath at Mohenjo-Daro. The material artefacts that were found point to a lifestyle not very different from present-day India, or, let's say, a century ago, in terms of the eating habits and ingredients for cooking, the fabric and apparel, the jewellery, the cooking and serving utensils, and the farm implements.

Transportation over the length of a thousand kilometres in the Indus-Saraswati region would have been largely led by cattle-carts, indicating the presence of navigable roads. There is no incontrovertible evidence of the presence of horses and their usage. It implies that they continued to be a rarity, and mostly imported over long distances from up north for the very elite and for highly critical war purposes, for instance during the Mahabharata war a few centuries earlier. The port city of Dholavira, planned over 54 acres, with an elaborate system for ferrying and storing fresh water from nearby streams, the division into a citadel, middle and lower towns, and trade-related infrastructure, point to the importance of coastal shipping within the region and beyond.

They had mastered the use of stone and baked bricks, and to an extent copper, for all possible purposes and to high sophistication.

The elaborate fortification, for example, at the centrally located Kalibangan and the planned town Dholavira imply the presence of serious external threats, whether from large armies or groups of miscreants. There were many kingdoms in the Indus-Saraswati region, around a dozen or so and as in the rest of India, from the time of the Mahabharata. These would have jostled for expansion, as the idea of a just war was deeply ingrained in the construct of the civilizational state, from the *Manusmriti* onwards.

Archaeological data and the civilizational reconstruction from the Indus-Saraswati region gives us an authentic, elaborate picture of Indian civilization at large. Such a reconstruction will broadly apply to the other regions in the mid-third millennium BCE. The level and the nature of the techno-economic and socio-cultural components of civilization would be similar. There were local differences and nuances, for instance, in the materials used for construction, which was mainly stone in coastal Dholavira and baked bricks in the bulk of the Indus-Saraswati region, but wood in the Gangetic Plains.

Sixteen great states, termed mahajanpadas, for the agglomeration of urban and rural settlements and with a ruling lineage are identified in the currently prevailing textbooks.[5] Each one of these is mentioned in the Mahabharata, and they were among the 62 kings who participated either on the Kaurava or the Pandava side. The war was in 3138 BCE. They would have existed and continued into the third millennium; but dating their 'rise' to 600–300 BCE in the textbooks is clearly wrong. The error is by a whopping three millennia, and needs to be promptly corrected. Such an error and its prevalence are hard to understand, and this is an example of the insidious effect of the faulty 1920 construct of the Indian chronology. It should have been done away with many decades ago. The textbook writers are no researchers, indeed.

Such blunders happen and persist when the textbook writers continue to reject any Indian history prior to 600 BCE as per the construct, in the teeth of all the data that was available by

1920 and has since been accumulated. They also do not refer to the voluminous ancient texts running into the thousands and dated over the continuum of the preceding eight millennia; the corpus is larger than it would be for all other civilizations put together for the BCE period. They instead rely on their later offshoots—Jainism and Buddhist texts, incidentally found to be wrongly dated by more than a millennium as mentioned in the fifth chapter. There too, greater emphasis and reliance is placed on foreign sources and the description of foreign visitors, who would have barely managed to find their feet here and are likely to have gained a superficial and much more inferior and inadequate understanding. This is appalling as a method of referencing, compiling and documenting data and conclusions for a textbook.

Moreover, there were not 'sixteen great states' but a larger number and they covered an area not only up to Central India but the entire landmass—up to Pandya in the extreme south and Sinhala or the Lankan island that was a part of civilization for millennia in the past and later. This is another error about something so obvious, but possible when the faulty 1920 construct is held to be true and our worldview and mindset are still colonized. The research lacks calibre and the methods to question, go beyond and get the phenomenon right. How the textbook writers of Indian antiquity got it so dramatically wrong and continued along for many decades is perhaps an interesting question for sociology and anthropology research. The damage and confusion they wrought on school and college students, among others, is another matter altogether.

The genealogies of rulers for most of the kingdoms—a better term since all the states were monarchies—are available, or easily traceable. We, however, are tracking the chronology of Indian antiquity, as per the King-Emperor framework and the reigning dynasty and its empire. For four centuries, from around 2600 to 2200 BCE, there was no pre-eminent dynasty. Among more than a couple of large kingdoms spread through India, the Panchala located east of Kuru gained a march over the others. The boost could be at the cost and result of the weakening Kurus. There was disaggregation, though, at the civilizational level, and perhaps a sense of drift too.

The equilibrium soon shifted eastwards, to Magadha. It was a large, significant kingdom, since Brihadritha established the dynasty there around 3500 BCE. He traced his descent from the Kurus. The tenth king, Jarasandha, was cornered by Krishna into a duel with Bhima and was killed. His son Sahadeva fought in the Mahabharata on the side of the Pandavas and died in the war. This is a representative case of the impact of the Mahabharata war on the kingdoms and dynasties spread around India, and the socio-political upheaval it would have caused.

The rise of Magadha, however, is related to the use of iron. The kingdom was particularly well endowed with iron ore and the metal was far superior to bronze for weaponry and most other purposes. The constraints were that it required a higher furnace temperature, almost twice, and the refining process was intricate for getting the right properties of the metal. The widespread use of iron is conventionally dated to 1200 BCE, which is regarded as the time of the transition from the Bronze Age to the Iron Age. This needs to be corrected and re-dated, taken back by a millennium or two given our construct and the rediscovery of the Indian chronology.

We reassigned the coming of the Bronze Age to two millennia earlier, around 5200 BCE, going by dating the advent of civilization to the eighth millennium and in India, instead of the fifth millennium in Mesopotamia, and the events and techniques described in the Ramayana. Thereafter, the Indian techno-economy progressed apace, and perhaps hastened, as is generally the case, due to a major war in the early fourth millennium BCE. The Iron Age would have started earlier too. It took two millennia to get from the Bronze Age to the Iron Age, when civilizational progress is conventionally based on Mesopotamia, and which is now shown to be preceded by Indian civilization that came three millennia earlier. Thus, iron use could have started one to two millennia earlier in India, or 2200–3200 BCE, although its widespread use and the coming of the Iron Age would be in the later third millennium or around 2250 BCE.

This is based on historical trend analysis. The relevant data is on the 'wootz', which is a spectacularly advanced steel used for making swords and daggers. It finds mention in the Greek records from Alexander's time[6] and the Lankans learned to make it from the Cheras in Tamil Nadu in the fifth century BCE. The three steps that are involved—the progress from producing rudimentary iron to steel, the advance to manufacturing sophisticated and special-purpose steel, and the acceptance, use and spread of technology from one end of India to the other—would have taken a few hundred years each. It would have amounted to iron being available in India prior to 1500 BCE and perhaps further back.

The advent of iron use apart, from textual and genealogical data and civilizational trends, we can see that Magadha was rising to its pre-eminent position in India by the end of the third millennium BCE. The Brihadritha dynasty oversaw that rise. Its last ruler, Ripunjaya, reigned for 50 years. He was killed by his minister, however, who put his son Pradyota on the throne in 2132 BCE.

BULK 'UNPACK–REASSEMBLY'

The rediscovery of the Indian chronology in the second millennium BCE is the most challenging, and thereby important. We know a good bit, but it is poorly interpreted and understood in terms of the flow and sequence of events, and thus wrongly dated. The errors range up to a millennium and more, and encompass virtually every event.

You may have noticed the shift in the type of task at hand. It was initially to find relevant data that has either come about in various disciplines since 1920 or that has been ignored and undermined earlier, and then to methodically put it all together for dating, in case of the first two periods of our construct. For the two later periods, the task is primarily to reassess the dating of major events and personalities from the 1920 construct, with respect to the updated, advanced and multidisciplinary Four Periods construct, and then to correct and align them suitably. This will involve a sharp, no-holds-barred reappraisal, which could lead to the falsification and thereupon the correction. But that is the way of scholarship and the quest of getting the phenomenon right, incrementally and gradually, or in major leaps and holistically.

We saw in the fifth chapter that the two pivotal events of Indian chronology—Buddha's nirvana in 1807 BCE and Ashoka's ascension in 1472 BCE—got re-dated to the second millennium. These were huge corrections but also significant and much needed for the right understanding of Indian antiquity. The re-dating was based on the massive data available from multiple sources spread over many time periods, for instance the genealogies, the Puranas, and Jain and Buddhist texts from India, Tibet, China, Burma, Sri Lanka and Persia. The two dates are linked, and much of this data was available in 1920 as well. But the colonial chroniclers tried to fit them to the faulty idea of the contemporaneity of Alexander's attack and Chandragupta Maurya. It is a fine case study on the ways and means usually deployed, involving a lot of convenient picking and choosing from Puranic and other data and the squeezing of periods, to arrive at and impose the wrong dates cavalierly.

This is also an apt demonstration of the worldview and mindset of colonial chroniclers around the time of the 1920 construct. The unscientific method and the unscholarly act have bedevilled the Indian chronology ever since, and also that of many Asian nations and civilizations around the world. Therefore, the dating of the events from the second millennium BCE needs to be further unpacked and reassembled en masse or in bulk.

Fortunately, not many dates from the 1920 construct are currently reiterated by the textbook writers who have followed in its wake. The 2021 edition of Thapar's *Early India,* as noted in the first chapter, lists just about a dozen dates or periods in half a page for the entire BCE period. The next 1,300 years occupy a page and a half. Unpacking and reassembling them, even across the two later periods of our construct, 3102–325 BCE and 325 BCE–CE 1192, is not much of a task. The understanding and its narrative, however, are considerably altered. We shall get into them, to the extent essential for our endeavour of rediscovering the Indian chronology and for the sake of cogency and continuity.

Getting back to the second millennium BCE, Magadha's rise to imperial status in India was established by the first couple of centuries. The dynasties, though, were short-lived, unlike the Iksvakus and the Kurus, with the Sisunaga replacing the Pradyota dynasty in 1994 BCE. The latter, during their 138 years of rule over five generations, did bring the large state of Avanti in Central India under the direct rule of Magadha. Sisunaga was the king of Kashi and managed to defeat the Magadha ruler and occupy its capital, Girivraja or Rajgriha.[7]

The fifth ruler of the Sisunaga dynasty was Vidhisara, wrongly called 'Bimbisara' by Vincent Smith, and he was a contemporary of Gautama Buddha. He annexed Anga, a large state covering the eastern part of Bihar and a good portion of Bengal, establishing the pre-eminence of Magadha in India. Vidhisara's son, Ajatshatru, became the ruler in 1814 BCE, in the eighth year of whose reign Buddha attained nirvana.[8] The eighth ruler Udayana—not Ajatshatru as incorrectly deciphered by Pargiter from the Puranas[9] and used by the textbook writer of the 1920 construct, Vincent Smith—built the city of Patliputra on the southern bank of the Ganges, in the fifth year of his reign, 1748 BCE.

In 1634 BCE, Mahanandin, the tenth and last ruler of the Sisunaga dynasty, was succeeded by his illegitimate son, Mahapadma. He took the surname 'Nanda'. By eliminating several ancient dynasties such as the Iksvaku, Panchala and Kalinga, he became the unitary ruler of India from the Himalayas to the Vindhyas. Mahapadma had a long reign and he hoarded a lot of wealth through extensive taxation and came to be known as 'Dhana-Nanda'. He had a run-in with Chanakya, who vowed to overthrow him.

Chandragupta Maurya was also an illegitimate son, of Mahapadma, and was guided by Chanakya to occupy the throne of Magadha in 1534 BCE. His task was eased by the nine sons of Mahapadma, who followed in quick succession in just over a dozen years, and ended up causing much transition, upheaval and disaffection in a short span of time. Thus, the correct date for Chanakya, which, in effect, started my quest and resulted in this endeavour of rediscovering the Indian chronology, was in the sixteenth century BCE—well over a millennium earlier than Alexander's attack and even before the Hellenic civilization had starting taking shape.

By the mid-second millennium BCE, the out-migration that would have set in after the sites in the Indus-Saraswati region started getting abandoned a few centuries previously, would be completed. A bulk of the migration would have been eastwards, plausibly towards the fast-rising region around Magadha. The people of port sites such as Dholavira, which had trade links with Mesopotamia and further with Egypt, would have brought along many new ideas and technologies. One of them could have been writing.

Just the mention of the idea and the writing tool and medium would have been good enough in the case of Indian civilization. An advanced language and learning system was already established, for the rest of the pieces of the script and techniques to be put in place, plausibly in a matter of weeks but well within a year or so. India did not need conceptual inputs either, as the symbols had existed and the techniques for engraving them on clay tablets, stone and other material were well developed for over two millennia and evidently from several Indus-Saraswati sites.

A script is essentially a set of well-organized symbols, linked to audible sounds and organized as alphabets and further on into words and sentences. The latter could not have been more developed with the Shruti system in place, perhaps even today, than it was in the mid-second millennium BCE in India. The Brahmi script would have evolved here, and in the process, would have advanced the technology of writing for the world itself. This is an example of how a much more advanced, bigger entity catches up with its contemporaries, and then goes past them quickly and by a huge margin; as the United States would do with any great information technology ideas germinated elsewhere.

Chandragupta Maurya's grandson Ashoka, who had been veering towards Buddha's teachings and becoming its champion, would have seen writing as another new thing to do. Its advantages of stealing a march over others and previous rulers and of preserving written material for posterity, particularly when carved on stone, would have greatly appealed to an enterprising person such as Ashoka. The language and teaching-learning system has been around since the early seventh millennium BCE, and the adoption of writing in India would not have been any more cumbersome than the switch from using pen and paper for centuries to the computer keyboards just over a couple of decades ago.

Thus the invention of the fairly sophisticated Brahmi script almost at one go in India and its use in the edicts by Ashoka was not out of the course for Indian civilization. This was an odd experiment though, not adopted by other rulers, and we do not find any more such edicts for over a millennium. The Shruti system would have been the mainstream all along and for long afterwards. Ashoka's reign of thirty-six years till 1436 BCE was followed by the nine rulers of the Maurya dynasty. The last one was murdered by his general and minister Pushyamitra Shunga in 1218 BCE.

There was out-migration to the west as well, from the Indus-Saraswati region, where most of the kings had sided with the defeated Kauravas in the Mahabharata war and consequently experienced greater socio-political turmoil. Many small and large groups, particularly from the Kshatriya (warrior) varna who were excommunicated, moved to the west of the Indus. They may have continued further, on to the Persian, Sumero-Akaddian and Greek regions. Their intermingling with the locals there created a degree of socio-political linkage with Indian civilization. The resulting alliances and combinations started to revert and attack the western fringes, as Yavanas from the time of the later Mauryas.

A lack of suitable attention being paid to the northwest borders by the last Mauryan ruler and his self-indulgent ways precipitated Pushyamitra's revolt. Attacks from that side were to form into a major trend and an influential factor. They would thenceforth and forever keep Indian civilization and its rulers on their toes and challenged. The chronology and account of the second millennium BCE, consequent to the bulk unpacking and reassembly of dates, does come across very consistently and cogently in the flow.

THE NORTHWEST LIVENS UP

The Shunga dynasty was established quickly, as Pushyamitra performed the 'Aswamedha' sacrifice soon after taking the reins. Aswamedha was a major Vedic ritual, performed by the emperor in the Indian political economy to subjugate any other claimant to the throne and demonstrate his supremacy in the realm. A horse was led over the various parts and borders of the empire, followed by the ruler's army, and all the kings and chiefs were to welcome them. Any resistance or reluctance on their part was countered and extinguished. The horse, on its return to the capital, was sacrificed after an elaborate ritual and the celebrations would last for more than a week.

The sacrifice was a historical and trendsetting event for the ruler and his dynasty in Indian civilization. Only the claimant to emperor status could perform the Aswamedha, and Yudhisthira did so after winning the Mahabharata war. Pushyamitra was the first thereafter. His grandson, Vasumitra, took over the reins in 1108 BCE and faced the first Yavana attack. The five kingdoms—Uttar Jyotisha, Divya Kataka and Simhapura in present-day Afghanistan, Urasa in the North-West Frontier Province and Abhisara in west Kashmir—that came together to challenge Vasumitra's authority were conquered and driven further west. These kingdoms were ruled by the excommunicated Indian Kshatriyas and located on the other side of the Indus.

They were not Greeks, or coming from thereabouts, as the kingdoms in that region were still in formative stages and yet to be connected to India in any way. The term 'Yavana' in the ancient texts is used in general for all renegade kingdoms and communities. Their westward migration on being defeated and dispossessed would have led to them coming across other small and large communities and kingdoms, forming alliances and coming back to attack as well. 'Yavana' was thus the generic term for communities and kingdoms located particularly to the west, as 'Saka' was largely used for such groups from the north. They kept coming here from the early first millennium BCE, as visitors or armed hordes.

The Shunga dynasty ruled Magadha for 300 years. Its tenth ruler, Devahuti, who had taken to easy, licentious ways and started living in Vidisha in Madhya Pradesh, was deposed by his Brahmin minister, Vasudeva, in 918 BCE. The latter's Kanva dynasty lasted eighty-five years, when Srimukha of Andhra-Satvahana lineage and employed as a minister, took over the reins in 833 BCE. The Andhra-Satvahana had a long and stable reign, with thirty-two rulers of the dynasty occupying the Magadha throne till 327 BCE.

The Magadha empire had started fraying with the reign of the last three rulers of the Andhra-Satvahanas. Many princes of the dynasty and other kings all over India had started acting independent and divided the empire. The second-last ruler at

Magadha was Chandrasri, also noted as Chandrabija, and the last one, a minor, was killed by his regent, Chandragupta, in 327 BCE. He set up the Gupta dynasty. Chandragupta's father Gatotkachchha had also served at Magadha as a minister, and he belonged to the Lichchhavi region of Nepal. The immediate task at hand for the Gupta dynasty was to regain control of the empire.

Much was happening to the west of India in the first millennium BCE.[10] Three civilizations took shape around 1200 BCE—the Hellenic one from the throes of the Aegean, the Syriac from the Sumero-Akkadian, Egyptian, Aegean and Hittite, and the Persian from the Sumero-Akkadian to start with, and then the Syriac. There was an influx of people into the Aegean basin in Greece, from the twelfth century BCE onwards, from the east and northwest, which reactivated the civilization. Interestingly, instead of unitary empires and monarchies, the Hellenic region got organized into sovereign city-states.

The Hellenic civilization adopted the Phoenician alphabet in the eighth century, which gave a fillip to writing and Homer's works followed soon afterwards. Subsequent to a population explosion, the Greeks set up colonial city-states in southern Italy, around the Black Sea and the French coast, and shifted to cash-crop farming and manufacturing for export in the seventh century. There was intense competition among the city-states, as well as warfare, which gave a push to the new ideas and innovations in science, technology and philosophy. The continued aggressive expansion triggered an attack by Achaemenian emperor Xerxes of Persia in 480 BCE, but he was defeated by a coalition of city-states led by Sparta and Athens.

The Greek states swung between hereditary rule, democratic city governments and being part of the Athens Empire. They saw intense artistic and intellectual activity and engaged in chronic inter-state warfare in 431–338 BCE. In Macedon, a state towards the northern periphery of the Hellenic civilization, Philip became the ruler of the hereditary monarchy in 359 BCE. He managed to unite all the Greek states, barring Sparta, into a confederacy by 338 BCE. Philip's son, Alexander, became the ruler in 336 BCE, and decided to go on an eastward campaign. Alexander overthrew Persia's Achaemenian Empire in 331 BCE, and that also opened up its dominions further east and north for Hellenic expansion. He reached India's northwestern periphery in 327 BCE, with the intent of carrying his campaign further.

Alexander absorbed Gandhara, which had become a vassal of the Persian Empire, along with its capital, Takshshila. He soon faced resistance from the clans in the Kunar, Swat and Buner valleys bordering present-day Afghanistan and Pakistan. The chiefs of Pushkalavati, or present-day Peshawar, particularly Asvaka, challenged Alexander for major battles. He got injured too from a spear thrown at his shoulder. The siege of a hill fort north of Attock in Pakistan took weeks to successfully complete in early 326 BCE and resulted in a massacre. Thereafter, he crossed the Indus into Punjab and lined up for a big battle on the banks of the Jhelum River in July.

The adversary was Porus, a regional king, who massed a comparable force on the other bank of the Jhelum. At the outset, Porus invited Alexander for a direct fight or duel, but the latter fell off his horse at the first charge and had to be rescued. Alexander then took a part of his force twenty-seven kilometres upstream for crossing the river more easily and opened another front. Porus's son confronted him with a contingent. In a fierce fight, Alexander lost his favourite horse and the son was killed. The main force that had faced Porus started crossing the river, and a huge two-pronged battle ensued. Towards the end of the day, Alexander sent a series of emissaries and Porus agreed to end the fight.

One could question Alexander's wisdom in mounting a campaign when the rainy season had started and the rivers were in full flow, but the battle with Porus sobered him. He got a sense of what awaited him further, up to the Magadha emperor. The troops revolted and he decided to end the campaign soon after this and go southwards along the Indus River and then turn back. He was harassed along the way and had to fight at least a couple of battles. There are no contemporary Indian accounts of Alexander's two-year campaign in India, as if it was nothing extraordinary and of no consequence or impact for the civilization.

All the above information comes from Greek accounts, and there would be a considerable degree of glorification and exaggeration. A few chroniclers accompanied Alexander during the campaign, and their writings and that of his naval commander are put together notably in Arran's text, *Anabasis*, but it was written 500 years later. Diodorus, Strabo and Plutarch, in that sequence in posterity and from 21 BCE to CE 119, have other accounts that are available. Alexander's campaign ending in 325 BCE and marking the close of the 'Post-Mahabharata' period, in hindsight, did have important consequences. And this is the topic of our next chapter.

An interesting question, at this point, relates to the fast rise of the Greek or Hellenic civilization from a tiny base. It was barely five centuries old when Alexander reached India, a civilization dating back to the eighth millennium BCE or nearly fifteen times older. The extraordinary energy, aggression and expansionist tendencies of the Greeks can be attributed to two factors. First, its organization into a dozen and increasing number of city-states, which fuelled competition, needed to be one up on others for survival, and thus had incessant and indecisive wars. Second, there was the population explosion in the seventh century, barely a hundred years after the civilization had formed, and this would have been due to migration of people from all around.

The organization into city-states would provide greater opportunities to the migrants in comparison to, let's say, a large empire. And when many states are in close proximity and constantly at war, migrants would be sought after too. They could come from far and wide, and would bring knowledge and ideas, and the intense rivalry would provide a fertile environment for putting them to use and to debate and develop further. These, however, would be copied soon and the advantage over others and particularly neighbours would be blunted, and the search for innovations would begin yet again.

Conditions to spur innovation are at the core of understanding the comparative advantage of political economies. It is well put together and articulated in *Competitive Advantage of Nations*[11] by the Harvard strategy professor Michael Porter. All the conditions were favourable for the rise of Greece, and the incessant wars would have intensified the urgency and speed of innovation. These would be in the areas of science, technology and economy, and also, just as importantly, in socio-political organizations and the philosophies of life and living.

Hellenic Greeks in the eighth century BCE were well placed in having some of their bearings from their Aegean past, and the close proximity of the Egyptian and Mesopotamian civilizations, though in the later stages, and of the Persian one evolving almost in parallel with it. The migrants and ideas would have come into the Greek cauldron from all over. And from India too, as the Persian civilization was in close and vigorous contact with it; for instance, Gandhara had become its vassal state. The post-Mahabharata turbulence in India, especially west of the Indus, would have provided a ready and willing source of migrants and collaborators. Philip's formation of the Greek confederacy and the ascension of the highly capable and ambitious Alexander would have added two important elements for its phenomenal outward surge in the mid-fourth century BCE.

India was a huge, advanced and well-settled civilization during the latter half of the first millennium BCE. Though divided into over two dozen large states with their subsidiary or loosely aligned states, most of them were individually several times bigger and more advanced than even the whole of the Greek confederacy. Most of the Indian states and kings still recognized the Magadha ruler as emperor, though its control was fraying, particularly at the edges and borders.

Alexander's campaign, thus, rightly pulled into India after the defeat of the Persian ruler, and then ended in the borderlands. It was fairly correctly reflective of the balance of military, economic and socio-cultural power, notwithstanding Alexander or Porus's valour, in the third century BCE. The campaign, however, was the first incursion into the Indian landmass and civilization from the west. The Eurasian regions to the north were sparsely populated and yet to organize into civilizations and states, and to the east, contact was yet to be made with the Chinese.

9

'GUPTA–RAJPUT' PERIOD: 325 BCE–1192 CE

The last of our Four Periods construct of the chronology of ancient India is relatively short, being half in terms of its duration, but just as eventful. Many new forces come into play. The contours of Indian civilization and history took on a different hue and a separate path while sustaining the continuity. In this period, the foundations and moorings of the civilization held forth. And its unfolding richness and complexity remain of much consequence even in present-day India.

There was a shift and a degree of cyclicality in the 'Post-Mahabharata' period. Indian civilization evolved and spread across its huge landmass during the first two periods of our construct, or for over 3,000 years, largely in isolation. It made major and, of course, pioneering strides in the techno-economic and socio-political domains, as needs came up along the evolutionary path, and acquired a comprehensive, integrated identity by the end of the fourth millennium BCE. There was no other civilization of any substance around the world at that time. The next earliest civilizations, the Mesopotamian and the Egyptian, started their march around 3000 BCE. The Mahabharata war shook India's socio-political structure and one of its consequences was out-migration and thus a shift away from its isolation.

While every kingdom was affected by the war, those to the west of the Indus were particularly vulnerable. They had mostly sided with the losing Kauravas. Many warrior jaatis were excommunicated and there was widespread disturbance and disenchantment in the north-west region. A response was to find areas that were less hostile and available, which could only be further to the west and the north. This out-migration would have taken Indian civilization to the empty and less populated, barely civilized areas, along all the four techno-economic and socio-political domains. Out-migrants would have intermingled with the local aborigines, and the areas would have undergone a civilizational surge.

Persia was geographically contiguous and would be the first destination for migration and thereby extending its influence there. The time-spaces would plausibly extend along the Hilly Flanks and all the way to Greece and the known world and beyond by then. The westward migration would have been relatively great, as the climatic and terrain conditions were tougher up north. Going by the migratory patterns usually observed, they would have moved away in small groups to start with, while maintaining contact back home, and subsequently larger groups and their entire communities would have followed suit—to form exclusive enclaves in the areas they migrated to and further on to encompassing and composite kingdoms, since they possessed the know-how for organizing a state. It would have started in the third millennium BCE and continued apace. The defeat of five northwestern kingdoms in the hands of the Magadha ruler Vasumitra in 1108 BCE would have given the out-migration a fillip.

The out-migrating Indians would have seeded and certainly accelerated the evolution of civilizations to the west of India. They had much to teach and impart, given the lead of many millennia and across domains and disciplines. The formation of the Persian, Syrian and Greek civilizations almost simultaneously, around the beginning of the first millennium BCE, would owe a lot to the

Indian out-migration and intermingling. Much of the Indian ideas on state and philosophies, astronomy and calendars, mathematics and metallurgy and so on would have been learned and debated. This, for instance, would have happened in the newly-formed Greek city-states that were experiencing a population explosion and were forever looking to go one up on the others, from the eighth to the sixth century BCE. Newer, younger civilizations tend to develop fast and catch up, especially when internal rivalry and the threat of external attacks and survival are propelling them forth.

Alexander's attack on the Indian periphery was in many ways the closure of the loop or the cycle of forces unleashed consequent to the Mahabharata war and the out-migration thereupon. The Eurasian civilizations, from India to Greece in the west, had got pervasively connected by 325 BCE. This would soon expand to include areas in the north too. Being many times bigger in population, economy and geographical area and also much older and more advanced, India would certainly be the fulcrum and mother lode of civilizations in the millennium leading to the Common Era and centuries thereafter.

Hordes from the north would soon start organizing themselves and also marching on to India. These hordes, similar to Alexander, would pose an external challenge that Indian civilization had not faced for over seven millennia of its evolution. Its isolation would be over and the dharma-based socio-political order would come under strain. The pace of events quickened, each setting in motion certain forces, and reactions and responses thereupon. We shall cover the fourth period of our construct in smaller bites of duration.

The exploration will be greatly enhanced by the availability of epigraphic data, virtually from the beginning of the period in 325 BCE. Most of the epigraphic inscriptions mention clear dates, often in more than one era, and some genealogies of the person commissioning it. The mention of the dates lends epigraphic data to sharper cross-validation. They are specific, precise and thus apt for the chronological purposes, far more than the archaeological data. More textual data is available not only from Indian sources, but also from Greeks who accompanied Alexander and visited subsequently; Chinese sources are available for the latter half of the period.

SAMUDRAGUPTA FIGHTS, UNITES

In chapters one, four and five, we ascertained the contemporaneity of Alexander with Chandragupta of the Gupta dynasty. It was based on philology and phonetics, genealogical data from multiple sources, calendars and eras, and inscriptions. He ascended to the throne of the Magadha Empire in 327 BCE. The Guptas were Kshatriya local chiefs and associated with the kings of Nepal, and were known as 'Parvatiyas' or 'from the mountains'. His grandfather joined the services of the Andhra-Satvahana rulers at Magadha, and his father, Gatotkachha, rose to be a minister in the empire.[1]

Chandragupta followed suit, won many battles for Magadha, and was appointed commander-in-chief by the ruler, Chandrasri. He married Kumaradevi, the daughter of the king of Nepal, while Chandrasri married her sister. Chandragupta, in effect, controlled the empire. Some cross-linkage with Chandrasri's queen led Chandragupta to kill the Magadha ruler and have himself appointed as regent to the minor, Puloman III. After seven years, Chandragupta deposed Puloman and proclaimed himself the Emperor of Magadha in 327 BCE. The empire during the rule of Chandrasri and a couple of his predecessors had started fraying at the edges and many kings in the Gangetic Plains were becoming independent. Chandragupta brought the region up to Prayagraj under control.

His son Samudragupta was deputed to tame the unruly communities in the northwest region and in this, he distinguished himself. Chandragupta, however, had other ideas and planned to put a son from his other wife on the throne. Samudragupta, on getting wind of it, marched back to Patliputra, killed his father and step-brother, and ascended the Magadha throne in 320 BCE. He immediately launched a major campaign and defeated eleven kings in South India, nine kings in North and Central India, Kamrupa in the east, and the Yavanas, Kshatrapas and Shahis in the northwest.

Samudragupta brought the area between Bengal and the Indus, the Himalayan foothills and the Narmada, under his direct rule. He formed vassal-type alliances with the kingdoms in the frontiers of Assam, Rajasthan and other defeated kingdoms, and all the kingdoms in South India accepted his might. With those further in the northwest and up to the Scythian kingdoms around the river Oxus in Central Asia, he maintained diplomatic relations. Samudragupta thus united the polity and established his authority over the entirety of the Indian landmass. There would have been areas which put up some resistance or displayed a grudging acceptance, particularly in Punjab and further northwest, but no king could pose an upfront challenge. To proclaim his sovereignty and authority, he performed the Ashvamedha sacrifice, probably between the fifth and the ninth year of his reign, let's say in 313 BCE. Much of the information on Samudragupta is validated by gold coins, grants and inscriptions, including on the Ashokan pillar erected a millennium earlier at Prayagraj.

Vincent Smith, who put together the 1920 chronology construct, called Samudragupta the 'Napoleon of India' and a ruler of exceptional capacity and varied gifts in his compilation of Indian history.[2] The unification of the polity would inevitably lead to economic stability and progress and to a flourishing of art and culture. Samudragupta himself was proficient in music and poetry. After ruling for fifty-one years, he ensured a planned and orderly transition of the reign to Chandragupta II in 269 BCE.

Another set of events was unfolding in India's west and further, after Alexander abandoned his India campaign in 325 BCE. He marched south along the Indus, and though he had a fleet of boats readied to travel along the sea coast, he decided to ride and walk with his troops across the desert towards Persia. Alexander spent the next couple of years restoring order in the Persian part of his empire, and suddenly died in Babylon in June 323 BCE, aged thirty-two. He did not designate a successor, and the empire was carved up into four kingdoms. Seleucus Nikator, a senior general, got the largest chunk, extending from Syria and Asia Minor or Turkey, up to the territories west of the Indus.

There was a massive struggle within and among the four post-Alexander kingdoms, and Seleucus was eventually crowned king in 312 BCE in Babylon. He came to the eastern fringes in 305 BCE, when Samudragupta's sovereignty and control all over India, including the northwest, was well established. Seleucus was vulnerable, and to secure the eastern border, he entered into a friendly understanding. His claim to areas in present-day Baluchistan and Afghanistan were ceded to Samudragupta, in exchange for 500 elephants.

Seleucus also sent an envoy, Megasthenes, to the Magadha court, who compiled a text on Indian geography, products and institutions of government during his long stay of many years. The text, *Indica*, though lost, was excerpted and referenced by several Greek writers later. Most of them have been heavily censored for reliability and accuracy, as there are lots of obvious errors. Perhaps Megasthenes himself, to start with, was ill-informed or misled by his sources. But the text was used as a credible and principal resource on Indian history in the run-up to the 1920 construct of the chronology.

The excerpts by themselves cannot add up to the whole text, by definition, and the errors do raise doubts on its credibility. It is hard to say clearly whether the Magadha ruler whom Megasthenes is referring to is Chandragupta Maurya as concluded in the 1920 construct. This single, error-prone, hearsay-based and splintered text cannot be considered authoritative. It falls far short, is not really needed either, when there are thousands of books on ancient India and dozens directly related to the chronology and genealogy of the period. These have since been methodically compiled for clarity of understanding and internal and external consistency across time and space. Megasthenes' *Indica* is of little use even as a source of occasional, corroborative data.

In another five decades, or around 250 BCE, Seleucus started losing control of the eastern fringes. The local Greek overlords in Parthia and Bactria, the northern parts of Persia and Afghanistan respectively, became independent. Samudragupta had decided on extending direct rule to the area east of the Indus, and would not have vigorously resisted emergence of similar Greek chieftains in Baluchistan and Afghanistan ceded by Seleucus in 305 BCE. Several such principalities were formed in the northwest and came to be known as the Indo-Greeks. They started making inroads to the east as well, and around 175 BCE, the Parthian king Methradates annexed western Punjab and the Kabul-based Menandar reached up to Awadh and faced the Magadha army.[3]

Chandragupta II, who took over from Samudragupta in 269 BCE, focused on eastern Madhya Pradesh and Gujarat and extended his empire till the Arabian Sea. He did carry out an expedition to Balkh in northern Afghanistan, across the Indo-Greek territories. Kumaragupta ruled from 233 to 191 BCE and Skandagupta from 191 to 166 BCE, as the fourth and the fifth rulers of the Gupta dynasty. Skandagupta's reign coincided with the severity of the Sakas' raids deep into India. The Sakas, also known as Huns or Scythians, were nomadic tribes from Central Asia, who, on facing a deterioration of their pastures, started moving south and overwhelmed the Indo-Greek kingdom of Bactria. They established themselves in the west of Kandahar by around 200 BCE, with the area coming to be known as Saka-Stan, and made inroads till Kathiawar in Gujarat and Mathura.

Another horde of nomads called Yuezhi, from the grasslands of western China, after losing a battle to another confederation of eastern nomads in 176 BCE, started migrating west and south and into India through Bactria and Kabul. They, like the Sakas, were ace archers and horsemen and also tribes, and yet had not evolved into citizens of a state. One of the major Yuezhi tribes, the Kushanas, brought together the other tribes in the latter half of the first century BCE. Their chief, Kujula Kadphises, conquered many Indo-Greek kingdoms and came to control the bulk of northwest India, just after the turn of the millennium.

The Scythians—the preferred term as 'Saka' tends to gets mistaken with the Sanskrit word for 'era'—would have intermingled with the Yuezhis, and got dominated and subsumed under the Kushanas. On the other side, the Gupta dynasty was greatly harassed by the Scythian inroads into India and persistent attacks. By the time of Skandagupta's death in 166 BCE, the empire had considerably weakened, with the treasury emasculated and coinage debased. Moreover, Skandagupta did not have any offspring and appointed Narsimhagupta, the minor son of his step-brother, as heir. The nephew came of age five years later, and ruled till 128 BCE, but the Guptas' imperial authority was truly over by that time. The last ruler of the dynasty, Kumaragupta II, was defeated in 82 BCE by a contemporary king as per the Aphsad inscription of Adityasena, and died the same year.

While Alexander's campaign was till the northwestern periphery and was that of an established civilizational state, the Scythians were an entirely different matter. They raided deep into the Indian territory and up to its heart, the Gangetic Plains. It was not like the army of an organized state ranged against another, and far from the construct and procedures of a 'just war' that had prevailed since the seventh millennium under Indian civilization. Alexander, who broke the isolation of the Indian state, was not aware of and did not adhere strictly to the procedures of 'just war', but at the construct or concept level, there was some consistency—with the armies of opposing rulers ranged face to face and if one king was defeated or killed, his state would be acquired by the winner, else some kind of deal or treaty was reached, as was the case with Porus.

Scythian raids were a transient and fast-moving operation and the tribes could strike anywhere. They could disassemble and regroup anytime on facing threats or losses. The armies of the Indian kings and the Magadha emperor, organized to fight as per a plan in well-defined spaces and times, and through intricate manoeuvres and duels, had no definitive answer for this. But the loss of life and valuables was significant. A sense of panic would have spread and reverberated across the civilization, given the unpredictability of an impending attack. The inability to counter and eliminate the hordes effectively for many decades after, let's say 200 BCE, would have led to the weakening of the authority of the Magadha emperor and other Indian kings and the demoralization of people at large.

There was a deficiency in the technology for war, either to match or to counter, on the Indian side. The Scythians had superior horses and access to the much larger base of supply for replenishment and enhancement from Central Asia. Their skills in riding and archery while moving were hard to match too. Indian texts frequently describe the Scythians as people who came as a swarm of locusts that utterly destroyed the Gupta empire.[4] Such raids have been hard to defend against and eliminate till even the present times, and flat open spaces make it tougher.

The Chinese civilization faced similar threats, although of comparative severity, about half a millennium later. Incidentally, these were from the Xiognu confederation, which defeated the Yuezhis in 176 BCE and forced their migration towards and into India. The Xiognu set up an empire centred at Mongolia and indulged in similar raids and war with the Chinese empire. Its answer was to build a wall, which started in the seventh century BCE and continued till the seventeenth century CE, for over two millennia. Such a wall was inconceivable in India given the terrain. The Indian response was forts and ramparts and a counteroffensive group of troops. But this left swathes of its territory and the bulk of the population exposed to the raids and to harm.

VIKRAMA, SALIVAHANA

You may have noticed the coherence in the dating of the origin, flow, severity and impact of the Scythian-Yuezhi raids and the travails of the Magadha rulers from Kumaragupta's time, and the weakening of the empire from the time of Skandagupta—who spent his life waging wars against the Scythians and died fighting on the bank of the Sutlej. Dates and descriptions for the Scythian part and also the Indo-Greeks are as per the 1920 construct and specifically from the books of Vincent Smith. Those for the Gupta dynasty are based on Indian sources.

On the other hand, such coherence does not exist at all for the Maurya empire and its rulers. The northwest region was not a concern till Ashoka, who ruled till the ninetieth year of his dynasty, and there is no mention of Scythian raids for the next and remaining six rulers who continued for another forty-eight years. Such raids are non-existent in all descriptions, either by Vincent Smith or Indian sources, and not put forth as a cause of the decline of the Maurya dynasty. Thus, the contemporaneity of Alexander's attack and the resultant Indo-Greeks and further with Chandragupta Maurya and his dynasty is misplaced and wrong.

The two-sided evidence, on the existence of coherence and the lack of it, is a robust proof for the much-needed correction. Alexander's contemporaneity with the Gupta dynasty is valid. And the confusion wrought by the 1920 construct should be finally laid to rest. The consequent damage done to teaching, learning and research for a century is substantive, but we need to take it in stride and try to make up for it. The correction and clarity and the absence of error and confusion in a vital part of the ancient Indian chronology will certainly bring about renewed vigour and spurt in the efforts for the requisite cleaning-up and updating and the discoveries further on.

Barring the founder Chandragupta, all six rulers of the Gupta dynasty had long reigns, ranging from twenty-five to fifty-one years. All of them were dedicated and capable rulers. They led from the front whether in the unification and expansion of the empire by Samudragupta and Chandragupta II, or the fight against the Scythians from Kumaragupta and Skandagupta to the latter three rulers. In 82 BCE when the last Gupta ruler Kumaragupta II was defeated, and also died, the Scythians were running riot through the country. They had set up a kingdom in the northwest around Takshshila, with two satrapies at Mathura and Saurashtra in Gujarat.

This was a period of shock for Indian civilization, and its King-Emperor framework had come unstuck. The emperor was the principal protector and guiding pin of the civilization, from the Surya-Vansha Iksvakus and Chandra-Vansha Kurus to the Magadha rulers of various dynasties. No new obvious and credible claimant was on the horizon. A confluence of factors led to the four lineages being consecrated as 'Agni-Vanshas', or the lineages of fire, in a ceremony at Mount Abu in southern Rajasthan. The legends related to their origin were discovered and intertwined, and these—Paramaras, Pratiharas, Chalukyas and Chahmanas—were together styled as inheritors of emperor status. The most significant were the Paramaras, who already had a long-standing kingdom based around Ujjain.

The four lineages were intended to rule the bulk of India, and the styling gave them an aura and a sense of responsibility, and for the then demoralized masses an imperial entity to look up to. It also meant institutional continuity and unity when the bedrock of civilization was indeed shaken and appeared under threat. Thus, Vikramaditya of the Paramara dynasty, with its capital at Ujjain, was crowned in 82 BCE. So, there was no gap at the imperial level of even a year after the end of the Gupta dynasty. The lineage of the Paramara dynasty had extended over 300 years to 392 BCE, and Vikrama's father Gandharva-sena was the seventh king. They ruled a good part of Malwa, around present-day Indore, and the Deccan up to Andhra. Gandharva-sena, who had won back his capital, Ujjain, from the Scythians, made way for his highly promising second son after ruling for a couple of decades.

Vikrama's coronation was an elaborate affair, with the blessings and lessons on statecraft or the Dharma pouring in from far and wide. He got down to work with vigour and launched a campaign against the Scythians. The campaign largely succeeded in taming and driving them west of the Indus. His general, Vikramshakti, is reputed to have won many battles and installed a compatriot, for instance, as the ruler of Kashmir. Tranquillity was restored, and Vikramaditya could concentrate on establishing his recognition and prominence over the kings spread throughout the Indian landmass. He also took a wife each from the Pratihara, Chalukya and Chahmana dynasties to unify the four Agni-Vansha Rajput lineages.

A significant move was to adorn his court with nine accomplished individuals or the 'Nav-ratnas'. Of these, Kalidasa specialized in literature, Varamihira in astronomy, Dhanvantari in medicine, and they were exceptional in the annals of Indian civilization. Vikramaditya travelled across the Gangetic Plains to visit Nepal, where the empire 'Sindhu in the west, Rameshwaram Setu in the south, Badrinath in the north and Kapila in coastal Bengal' was proclaimed. And a new era or saka was defined after his name, starting from 57 BCE. The 'Vikrama Era' gained widespread recognition and remains the most referenced in West and North India till today. Vikramaditya established a degree of sovereignty all across Indian civilization, but after the end of his long reign in 19 CE, its 18 parts became independent kingdoms.

Unlike the Iksvakus and Kurus, the King-Emperor type of relationship did not extend to Vikramaditya's successors. His son, Devbhakta, had a short reign of 10 years. The Scythian raids restarted and when Salivahana, Vikrama's great-grandson, took over the reins, the situation had become as precarious as over a century and a half ago. The Scythians had not been eliminated by Vikramaditya, as they retained control in the northwest beyond the Indus and their presence and that of the satrapies in Mathura and Kathiawar would have continued. The latter would have quickly reactivated given the weakness of Vikrama's successors, and linked up again with their compatriots. Moreover, the Kushana rule under Kujula Kadphises had started stabilizing just after the turn of the millennium or, let's say, from year zero to 25 CE.

The Kushanas had a ready source for the construct of a state and the trained manpower for administration from the Indo-Greek kingdoms they had deposed. While retaining access to China, they sent armies—still raiding hordes, largely—up north towards Central Asia and further to the west. This enhanced their resource base and depth, and their inroads to the east of the Indus became bigger and wider in the second half of first century CE. These set the stage for a strong rebuttal from Salivahana, on taking the Paramara throne at Ujjain.

Salivahana's counter-charge was relatively more definitive. He not only cleared the Scythians till the Indus, but also defined the river as the dividing line, with land to the east being 'Sindhu-sthana' and to the west 'Maleecha-sthana'. The Scythians were 'barred' from crossing the Indus and he made arrangements for preventing them from doing so.[5] Another era or saka was proclaimed from 78 CE, when Salivahana took over the reins. This indicated a degree of rivalry with Vikrama, and marked a division in the dating and calendars through the civilization, as the Salivahana era or saka became popular in southern and eastern India.

The Vikrama saka starting 57 BCE, and the Salivahana saka or simply 'Saka' starting 78 CE, besides the Kali saka or era beginning 3102 BCE, are the standard across all inscriptions and other dating ever since. Often the event dates are recorded as per more than one era but always so in one of the three. Sometimes, other less prevalent and local eras are also mentioned.

Salivahana also had a long reign, of 50 years and up to 138 CE. His 'division' and border arrangements started fraying towards the end. In the west of the Indus, Kujula Kadphises, the founder of the Kushana kingdom, was followed by Vima Kadphises. Kanishka, the third king, was not a direct descendant of the founder but from another Kushana tribe, and occupied the throne in 127 CE. Kanishka established his capital at Purushpura in Gandhara, or present-day Peshawar in the Khyber-Pakhtunkhwa province of Pakistan. His empire would have reached its peak around 140 CE, during his 23-year reign till 150 CE, and extended well into the east of the Indus and up to the Gangetic Plains. It also included Sindh, Bactria, eastern Persia and the Xinjiang region in China.

Kanishka left a rich repository of statues, coins and inscriptions. The empire had moved beyond the early Indo-Greek orientation during Kadphises, to include Persian-Zoroastrian and Buddhist influences. He did encourage Buddhism and played a role in its spread to China through the road across Karakorum. Mathura was certainly a stronghold, where a large statue of Kanishka with Brahmi inscriptions has been located. Kanishka's successors, Huvishka, 150–180 CE, and Vasudeva, 180–230 CE, who consolidated and continued to rule the vast empire, got gradually assimilated into Indian culture and practices. Huvishka, in particular, focused on his base in Mathura; Vasudeva's loss of his western territories to the Persian Sassanid empire in his later years marked the beginning of the decline of the Kushanas.

They started losing territories in the east too. In a couple of decades, the Kushanas were reduced to ruling parts of Punjab with their capital at Takshshila, and by 300 CE, they were indistinguishable from the several kingdoms dotting the Indian landscape. The Paramaras were not doing too well either. The emperor-like presence of Salivahana started waning in the last decade of his reign and he died in 138 CE. The next few rulers quickly lost their territory and standing. Among other Agni-

Vanshas, Pratihara established his dynasty in Bengal. He was a scholar of the Atharva Veda and led the revival of Vedic practices in the region. Pratihara's son, Gaurvarma, extended the kingdom to Gauda-Desha, present-day Odisha.

The Chalukya-Vansha remains in formative stages during the early centuries of the Common Era, as *Bhavishya Purana* genealogies do not identify it with a specific region or kingdom. Chahmanas, however, found their feet at Ajmer in Rajasthan. Vayahani is identified as the originator of the dynasty, whose elder son Tomara went to rule at Indraprastha, the area in and around Delhi. It is hard to date the reign of the Agni-Vanshas other than the Paramaras. The Puranas give a fairly clear, sequential list of kings in a genealogy, but hardly any details on dating and only for a few, and one has to try finding them in other texts and sources.

In 300 CE, the age of empires and large kingdoms that traversed the Indian geography was truly ebbing. Vikrama did create the semblance of a civilization-wide empire, which was resurrected to a degree and for a couple of decades by Salivahana. The Kushanas who rose from the northwest and ruled far beyond and further to the north and west of India, besides a large territory in the mainland and Gangetic Plains, had shrunk to little more than a principality in Punjab by 250 CE. The civilizational threat posed by the Scythians-Yuezhis, however, got neutralized through cultural and religious co-option and amalgamation.

THE RAJPUT SPREAD

In the latter half of the fourth period of the Indian chronology from 325 BCE to 1192 BCE, ours and the 1920 construct start converging. For instance, the dating of Harsha, king of the Paramara dynasty with its capital at Kannauj in the heart of the Gangetic Plains, is almost identical and in the mid-seventh century CE. This is primarily due to the records of Chinese traveller Hiuen Tsang, who visited during Harsha's reign.

The convergence of the dates and the fairly well-aligned Indian dating thereafter illustrate the limitation of the 1920 construct, and that of largely relying on non-Indian sources and data and its consequences. It is the Greek and Persian sources, created by those who travelled to India or those who did not and wrote many centuries later, for the before the Common Era period. And also the Chinese sources for the Common Era afterwards. Any Indian data was either ignored or deemed false or not deciphered correctly and properly. Preparing the chronology and history of a huge civilization based only on external data is a recipe for disaster.

This was strange, as Indian textual data extends into many millennia BCE and is more than all other ancient civilizations put together. And it was already compiled by the late nineteenth century, and reckoned to be larger than the Greek and Latin corpus combined. Depending on the accounts by foreign travellers who faced many handicaps in getting to the facts and their right proportionality and sequentiality, is hazardous and limiting to start with.

The two-sided error in the research method, precipitated by altogether ignoring or undermining Indian data in the teeth of the basic tenets of scholarship, is not an oversight or an act of incompetence. But it is assuredly the result of the prevailing colonial mindset and worldview and the agenda of subjugating India, which permitted them to ride roughshod all over it. The lack of scholarly checks and balances back in 1920 or any corrections subsequently is evidence of continuance of that mindset and its hold over us.

For over a couple of centuries after 300 CE, the King-Emperor framework that we have used for tracking the Indian chronology since the seventh millennium BCE becomes a poor guide. The Agni-Vansha lineages that were styled to inherit the emperor mantle in 82 BCE, after a promising start with Vikrama and Salivahana, were nowhere near pre-eminence now. There was no external threat to Indian civilization as a whole, from 300 to

600 CE. It was a period of peace and well-being, and saw much progress in the fine arts, literature and temple architecture. There were a dozen or so major kingdoms, and many smaller ones, who often engaged in conflicts and battles for conquest and expansion.

These battles were mostly and strictly between the armies of kings. They were often guided by the need of a newly appointed king to prove himself or the surge of ambition in a ruler who also perceived some weakness in the neighbouring kingdoms. The battles usually ended with payment of a recompense and acceptance of superiority, even seniority. The bulk of the population was unaffected. There has been evidence of farmers quietly tilling their fields while a battle raged shouting distance away.

One of such ambitious kings was Harsha. He was the younger son of the king of Thanesar, who had greatly expanded the kingdom towards the northwest and to Gujarat in the west. A family feud, which involved the kings of Kannauj and Gauda and led to the death of his elder brother, brought Harsha to the throne of Thanesar and Kannauj in 606 CE. He aggressively built a large empire, covering most of the Gangetic Plains as well as Punjab, Gujarat and up to Assam. His capital was Kannauj, where Hiuen Tsang visited him and became a friend and admirer.

Harsha's southward expansion was stalled by his defeat in the hands of the Chalukya king Pulkeshin II on the bank of the Narmada. He ruled with finesse and oversaw a period of socio-cultural advancement, with Harsha himself writing three acclaimed Sanskrit plays. His long reign lasted till 647 CE, but he died without a successor. From Harsha's empire, three major kingdoms arose—the Gurjar-Pratihara in the west, the Pala in the east and the Rashtrakutas in Central India. The title 'Gurjar-Pratihara' could indicate a link with Agni-Vansha Pratihara who had set up his dynasty in Bengal, which his son extended to Gauda or Orissa. The Gurjar-Pratihara outlines the Agni-Vansha lineage and continuity.

Bhoja of the Parmara dynasty is reckoned by Puranic

genealogies as the tenth king after Salivahana. The 10 kings ruled for 556 years, which, with Salivahana's death in 138 CE, would let one estimate Bhoja's reign as ending in 693 CE. His regnal duration was fifty-five years, so the period is 638–693 CE. Bhoja was as celebrated a king as Harsha in the first millennium CE, for his valour and the expansion of his kingdom and for scholarly pursuits and patronage of art and culture. Bhoja's capital was at Dhar in southwestern Madhya Pradesh. And the kingdom extended from Chittor in Rajasthan to the Konkan, and from the banks of the Sabarmati to Vidisha, northeast of Bhopal.

Unlike Harsha, Bhoja barely finds a mention by textbook writers. Even so, Bhoja's regnal period is erroneously dated to '1010–1055 CE', which was much later. Vincent Smith did not bother, as there was no account about Bhoja written by foreign visitors; the post-Independence writers, as in the case of Harsha too, gave the narrative a spin and branded him a Buddhism sympathizer, as the 'other great' Ashoka, although he was a devout Shaivite. This is another illustration of the poor and the deviant methods that have been at play in deciding the Indian chronology and history, giving the scholarship a bad name and making the discipline prone to faulty teaching and learning and ultimate confusion.

For the third Agni-Vansha lineage, the Chalukyas, we need to pick the thread from the victory of Pulkeshin II that thwarted the southern expansion of Harsha, beyond the Narmada. It happened in the early part of Harsha's reign from 606 to 648 CE, so it can be dated to around 620. Pulkeshin II was the great-grandson of the founder of the Chalukya kingdom, Pulkeshin I, in Badami in 543 CE. The dynasty ruled the bulk of the Deccan, from the Narmada in the north up to the borders of the Pallavas in Tamil Nadu, though the extent of the kingdom kept waxing and waning. They were defeated by the Rashtrakutas in 753 CE.

A branch thereof, the Eastern Chalukyas, had set itself up in the coastal districts of Andhra Pradesh in 624 CE and continued to rule the area till the eleventh century. There was a revival too, with the coming of the Western Chalukyas in 753 CE and their capital in Kalyana in Karnataka, and the dynasty continued up to the end of the twelfth century. The Chalukyas recognized their linkage with the Solanki dynasty, who ruled a good part of Gujarat and some of Rajasthan, from 940 to 1240 CE. The latter, termed 'Chalukya-Solanki', facilitated the tying of the Chalukyas together and the continuity from the Agni-Vansha lineage founded in Mount Abu in Rajasthan, certainly to the level of a testable hypothesis.

Of the fourth Agni-Vansha, the Chahmanas, we know little between the third and seventh century—as is the case for the other three. The Puranic genealogies are patchy in this interregnum and become even more so afterwards. In the absence of a thorough alternative, one has to consider the dating that has been based on, built around and aligned to the flawed 1920 construct. Although it is currently not possible to outline the specific genealogies and chronology for these centuries, the Chahmanas did exist. From the seventh century, we have adequate data and records of the Chahmanas as a major ruling lineage in and around Rajasthan. This date, however, needs to be tested for consistency and coherence during the first millennium CE, internally and externally with the Four Periods construct.

Taking a leaf from what we seem to know, the Chahmana lineage spread into nearly two dozen dynasties and states. They formed, diverged and converged every few decades till the twelfth century CE, with cooperation and conflict within the lineage and those around. Taking in the overall scenario along the time of the first millennium CE and the spaces of Indian civilization, the four Agni-Vansha lineages together had been and remain the largest factor to reckon with. With their primary bases in Dhar in Madhya Pradesh for the Paramaras, in Kannauj in central Uttar Pradesh for the Pratiharas, Badami and Kalyana for the Chalukyas, and across Rajasthan and further for the Chahmanas, the Agni-Vanshas covered the bulk of India and did so far more than any other lineage.

They also had a close affiliation with several Surya-Vansha and Chandra-Vansha dynasties dotting the length and breadth of Indian civilization, for instance from the Himalayas to the seas along the north–south axis. The Agni-Vanshas together represented the integration not less than or inferior to that achieved at the peak of the Gupta and Maurya dynasties, and even to that of the Kuru and Iksvaku dynasties. The experiment and initiative to provide continuity to the King-Emperor framework of India at Mount Abu in 82 BCE had succeeded after all. It had not been a straight path and the final outcome too was not as envisaged, of having a single emperor-like dynasty regarded throughout India as of yore. But the end result was substantive and the initiative worthwhile.

RAIDS FROM THE WEST AND NORTH

To India's west, the first millennium CE was very eventful. After Alexander's death in 323 BCE, the huge territory divided among his generals fell into chronic warfare. Much of it melted away; for instance, as independent Indo-Greek kingdoms in India's northwest borderlands. In the Mediterranean basin, the long-standing state of Rome quickly expanded and took control, also of mainland Greece between 148 and 146 BCE. The rise of the Roman Empire and Christianity followed from the turn of the Common Era.

The Roman Empire started declining from around 300 CE, which is very short-lived by Indian standards and also those of other empires of the East at that time, such as Persia and China. It was as much due to internal strife as the attacks of tribes including Huns and Scythians—who ascertainably took 300 years or so to reach there after India, and possibly on being blocked here. Europe slowly turned to the inward-looking precepts of

Puritanism, and slid into the proverbial 'thousand years' of the Dark Ages.

In Persia, the Zoroastrian Sassanid Empire took root in the early third century, and came to occupy present-day Iran and Iraq, and at times extended till the eastern Mediterranean and India. It lasted till the mid-seventh century, and left an imprint on the art, literature and architecture in the wider world for long. A development, though apparently minor at that time, was the assertions of Mohammad, a trader in Mecca in the thinly populated deserts of Arabia. He was disenchanted with the prevailing state of morality, polytheism and idolatry, and sought solitude in a cave. He is stated to have received revelations from the angel Gabriel in 610 CE—who conveyed the will of God across Abrahamic religions.

The revelations continued, Mohammad started preaching, but faced resistance from the higher classes at Mecca. He shifted to Medina in 622 CE and was able to bring all the tribes around together, and got them to sign a 'Constitution of Medina'. Under his political and religious authority, the tribes, now united and termed 'Muslims', repulsed attacks from Mecca and then took control of it. All tribes of peninsular Arabia were brought together and integrated into a single political-religious entity at the time of Mohammad's death in 632 CE. The political unity and the religious zeal, their belief in being superior in comparison to the infirmities of all other faiths and societies, set them on a course of conquest.

The four Caliphs, as the first political successors of Mohammad, overran Iraq in 633–37 CE, Syria including Palestine in 633–41 CE, Egypt in 639–41 CE, Iran in 642–51 CE, Northwest Africa in 647–98 CE, and most of the Iberian Peninsula in 710–12 CE.[6] They attacked Constantinople and French Gaul too, but failed to conquer them. The speed and scale of their spread across settled civilizations was breathtaking. It was primarily a political or Arabian conquest, as religious conversion to Islam was focused upon only when the Caliphate states were well established. An Arab general named Mohammad 'bin' or 'son' of Qasim crossed the Makaran desert in 711 CE to attack Sind.

While the kings all over India were Rajputs,[7] Sind was a rare exception. The reigning Brahmin king was slain and Muslim rule was established in 712 CE. Although the de facto boundary of the Indus was breached, the Sind kingdom just stayed put. It did not much disturb the civilizational continuity within and was a non-event beyond. It was a one-off event, as no Muslim attack or expansion happened for nearly three centuries.

The Arabs made inroads into the heartland of the Abrahamic religions and conquered huge swathes of the land around at great speed. It relates to the 'nomad' advantage against settled civilizations, of having been organized and acquiring a sense of purpose. We saw this for the Scythians-Huns-Yuezhis against Indian and European civilizations around five centuries ago. The nomadic tribes have little to lose and they are hard to track and confront. The advantage turns into win-ability when backed by new and superior war technology; for instance, the horses and the riding and archery skills. The latter imparts speed and thus facilitates rapid inroads, as nomads are not constrained by the norms and the ways of settled civilizations.

Arab nomadic tribes also possessed superior horses. They could have made up for their disadvantages in terms of fighting skills in comparison to the Scythians with much better knowledge of the opposition by being closely affiliated for a long time. The novel religious precepts, besides providing the necessary zeal or sense of purpose, would have imparted a newfound confidence and a sense of superiority, or at least a lack of any inferiority. This conceptual preparedness would have been critical as the Arabs, unlike other nomads earlier, often tended to stay put after raids in settled civilizations and had their task cut out for them to restore order. Their ability to establish state-like caliphates, by extending Muslim precepts into policies, procedures and norms of the administration and societal conduct, enabled the transition of conquests into long-run victories.

For over three centuries, Indian civilization remained undisturbed and the states continued along the pattern established by the eighth century CE. There were over a dozen large kingdoms and their affiliates, who used to be in a protracted game of one-upmanship and conflicts, but these did not affect much of the population and civilization. There were personality and regime changes, sometimes involving some mergers of states and territories. The battles too followed a code of conduct and well-defined rules, and any deviation was scoffed at. This was feasible and enforced, since the kings came from the Agni-Vansha and other affiliated Rajput lineages, with the exception of the Muslim enclave in Sind.

In 977 CE, Sabuktigin became the chief of Ghazni in southwest Afghanistan. As governor under the Muslim Samanid Empire of Persia, Sabuktigin had led a successful campaign to overrun other small principalities in the region. He subsequently received the title 'Nasiruddin' from the Caliph. His territory was unruly and impoverished, and Sabuktigin embarked upon raids into the much wealthier Punjab region to the south. The first raid was in 986 CE, to which the Punjab king Jaipal retaliated with an attack on Ghazni a year later. Skirmishes continued, and Jaipal pooled together other princes to mount another attack, but that was not successful either.

On Sabuktigin's death, his elder son Mahmud was initially denied governorship, and had to mount a march on Ghazni to acquire the position in 997 CE. Mahmud launched into the business of raids soon after. His first raid was in 1001 CE, and he planned for one every year. Sticking mostly to the plan, he conducted seventeen raids till his death twenty-nine years later in 1030 CE. The loot was enormous, and his reign is called the 'Golden Period' of the Ghaznavids. The raids were on the lines of those carried out by Scythian and Arabian tribes in the past, but he relied much more on the precept of a Muslim 'Holy War' against the idolaters of India, to raise the zeal of his troops. This raised the level of plunder and destruction, particularly of temples, which were major repositories of wealth anyway.

The raids became bigger and went deeper into India, all the way to Mathura and Kannauj towards the southeast and to the Somnath temple in the southwest in 1023 CE. The latter was particularly gruesome and also the most rewarding to Mahmud, in the form of the temple booty he carried off and its pieces he evocatively displayed and put to use in Ghazni. The raid had a sobering effect on the Indian kings and princes, who used to take pride in their valour, and elicited strong disapproval from the masses at large. They had not experienced such venom and sustained attacks on their temples and ways of worship anytime in their long memory and history. The emotional and social impact of Mahmud's raids was large, though the bulk of India remained untouched and its wealth was barely dented.

Mahmud did not take any territory, barring an outpost at Lahore in Punjab, so the rulers and Indian states that came under attack remained largely undisturbed. The defence and counterattacks by Indian kings were, however, weak and wanting, and resulted in a series of adverse outcomes. They were perhaps too deeply entrenched in the Indian rules of battle and conduct, which also emphasized duels and individual valour. Mahmud's raids, especially the latter ones, involved large contingents. Arabic horses provided the lead and enabled penetration, but there usually was a large retinue of foot soldiers and elaborate paraphernalia which could have been a slow-moving and soft target.

The supplies would stretch or become dependent locally, as the campaign moved deeper into India, and could have been exploited to turn the balance. The returning contingent, slow-moving and more elaborate after the loot, would be very vulnerable, but perhaps the Indian rules of engaging only in frontal, well-announced battles would have come in the way. After Mahmud's death, the Ghaznavids started weakening, and all the Persian and

Central Asian territories were lost within a decade. It became more dependent on the raids into India for sustenance, but those faced stiffer resistance, and ended altogether by 1070 CE. The dynasty pulled along for a few ascensions of the chiefs, and was defeated by the Ghorids in 1170 CE.

Hailing from Ghor in central Afghanistan, the Ghorids were vassals of the Ghaznavids. After the defeat and destruction of Ghazni and the death of its purveyor soon after and the assassination of the heir, Ghiyasuddin was elevated to be the chief in 1173 CE. He ruled with his younger brother Muhammad. The latter trained his attention on India by attacking Multan and acquiring a part of Sind. In 1178 CE, Muhammad tried penetrating into Gujarat but was badly defeated. He deposed the Ghaznavid prince from the Lahore outpost in 1186 CE, and came to rule substantial parts of Punjab and Sind.

Muhammad set up a normal state, in a departure from the earlier Afghans, in the fertile and prosperous territory. He also amassed a regular army to go deeper into India for greater wealth and sovereignty. In 1191 CE, Muhammad faced Prithviraj Chauhan of the Chahmana dynasty, supported by a confederacy of Rajputs at Thanesar, and was routed and wounded in the arm. He quickly recouped and returned better prepared in 1192 CE, and was victorious this time. Prithviraj was killed, and Muhammad went on to sack Delhi and Ajmer. This started a new phase in Indian history and civilization, which is the medieval one, and marks the end of the ancient phase, the time and space of our exploration.

10

THE BIG PICTURE

In the 'Exhibit' after this chapter, the rediscovered chronology of Indian antiquity is presented. It is organized around the frame of the Four Periods construct. Dating specific events and their sequence from around 9000 BCE to 1192 CE, gives the chronology its body and continuity. The dating runs into just under a dozen book-length pages, and make for the largest compilation prepared and integrated together on India's deep past. They are thus the most comprehensive till date.

The rediscovered chronology is a vital and much-needed advance on the understanding of Indian history and civilization. It supplants the 1920 construct, which suffered from major errors in the design or the basic conception of Indian antiquity and the detail or the dates of pivotal events. These infirmities existed in 1920 when a whole lot of data on Indian eras available from ancient texts was not taken into account. Instead, reliance was placed on half-baked conjectures and theories, which were aligned with the colonial agenda of undermining and subjugating India. And only the data that fitted was selected, some squeezed and force-fitted and the rest all ignored. This was deviant and amateurish, and as noted several times in the earlier chapters, was neither science nor scholarship.

Moreover, a huge body of data on Indian antiquity from multiple sources has become available in the past century. Archaeological data is rich and diverse, extending up to the eighth millennium BCE, and that from astronomy is mathematically precise and most of it verifiable by anyone, now or later. The Yuga system, on proper analysis, leads to extraordinary, accurate insights into the long time cycles over millennia, and the genealogical data for shorter cycles of decades and centuries retains continuity and goes all the way to the early seventh millennium and covers many lineages and regions. It is truly exceptional for the case of Indian civilization. This wealth of data is a researcher's delight.

In addition to this, the data used in the rediscovered chronology is put to the test of validity and reliability as per the best of the scientific method. The data is mostly verifiable at the source and within a discipline, and it is nonetheless cross-validated with other sources and disciplines. In some instances, only a part of the data or observation that has been definitively validated and distilled upon is taken. Thereafter, the multidisciplinary research comes into play for putting together the data and the analysis and for drawing conclusions. The construct is tested for validity and internal and external consistencies across periods, in Chapter Five particularly, and within a period in the subsequent chapters.

Therefore, there is an overwhelming case for adopting the rediscovered Indian chronology. The 'push' of the flawed 1920 construct and the 'pull' of the updated data of the past century and the world-class scientific and multidisciplinary method render the switchover inevitable. This brings the Indian chronology on a par with that of the very best of Europe and West Asia, and this is certainly deserving of the world's oldest civilization. It adds over four millennia to the antiquity of civilizations in the world, and provides a new window into the exploration and understanding of human evolution.

Any research output, however, is open to scrutiny and falsification. The scrutiny could happen soon or any time later, in India or elsewhere. The falsification of a date or a series of dating, and even the construct itself, is the way of science and inquiry. A new question leads to newer findings and conclusions, and better hypotheses and theorizing, as part of the never-ending quest for better understanding of a phenomenon. In case of the Indian chronology, there are three sets of avenues for further exploration and research. First, the findings of one or more disciplines need to appear in all the other relevant disciplines as well. For instance, the conclusions based on astronomy, the Yuga system and genealogical data for the Gangetic Plains during the seventh to the second millennium BCE should appear with archaeological data as well. The lack of such data presently does not disprove the conclusion, but opens an important vista for archaeological explorations in this time and space.

Second, some of the conclusions based on trend and logical analysis, but lacking in empirical evidence currently, are still in the hypothesis stage. They stand till proven otherwise and are replaced by a superior explanation. In the Indian chronology, such conclusions are presented in quotes, for example the beginning of the 'Copper Age' in the late sixth millennium and the 'Iron Age' in the last couple of centuries of the third millennium BCE. Direct empirical evidence is likely to come from archaeological explorations, and also possibly from the discovery of some new data in ancient texts and better analysis and dating of inscriptions and references.

Third, all ancient texts carry some legendary and allegorical parts. This is so for the texts from India as well as elsewhere. One has to carefully cull the data that is relevant for the research questions and then suitably validate it. For research on the chronology and dating, which is a mathematical and ordinal fact, the standards and preciseness for validity are indeed exacting. A reference in an Indian epic or the Purana needs to be tested for internal consistency and the sequentiality of the dating of other events within the source text and also for external consistency with other relevant texts and the Puranas, and then supported by astronomy and as many more observations.

On the other hand, research on the narrative part will cull different sets of references and test them for validity in the requisite ways. Ancient texts are a source of relevant and valid data, just like archaeological sites and the finds therein. It is up to the ingenuity and skill of the researcher to make the most of an available source. We must note that the texts, whether Indian or Christian or Islamic that came much later, were compiled to serve a variety of purposes and they are not made to order for scientific research and questions thereupon. They are, however, all that we have and are invaluable sources of data on the antiquity.

There is still a lot to be discovered from the Indian texts. It is a huge corpus, more than that available from all the other civilizations combined, particularly for the antiquity. The extraordinary Shruti-Gurukul system of India ensures completeness and precision for a bulk of them. Ongoing projects of digitization have greatly enhanced clarity and access, also through ever-improving translation software, to a wider range of researchers. The rediscovered chronology will provide a facilitative frame and a backbone for much vigorous and productive research on the Indian texts.

This applies as much to archaeology, which has hitherto been stunted by the flawed 1920 construct, and will see the rightful time and spaces opening up. A useful first step will be to initiate a re-examination of the existing findings and conclusions, in light of the rediscovered Indian chronology. There will be plenty in the archives that was set aside as not fitting or force-fitted to the earlier construct, to be reassessed. Archaeology has proven to be the weak link in our rediscovery endeavour. It needs to be invigorated to a great degree, not only in the temporal dimension and till the Holocene, but more importantly, in the spaces of the Gangetic Plains and coastal regions. The rediscovery endeavour has shifted several of these time-spaces from 'we don't know that we don't know' to the 'we know that we don't know', and the discipline of archaeology needs to measure up to it and do its part.

By way of summing up, we take a look at the evolution of civilizations in the world. It is a comparison and contrast between the time-spaces as understood presently with those emerging from the rediscovered Indian chronology. This will make for a major correction and an advance in the understanding of history and the world with respect to the antiquity, the sequencing and the likely flow of ideas, developments and people, in the evolution of world civilization as a whole and its constituent parts. The civilizational re-look builds a case for assessment of the discipline of history itself, and the application of the scientific method therein. It is about where they stand currently, and the beginning, progress, failings and gaps of the discipline of history, and also recent trends and initiatives.

The re-look and assessment will show us the way forward for the subject of chronology and the discipline of history as a whole. A variety of important pointers emanate from our rediscovery endeavour, on the whats and hows of going further, for research, teaching and learning in India. Much of these are important and useful for the world at large too.

ON CIVILIZATIONS

Arnold Toynbee, in *A Study of History*,[1] mapped the civilizations of the world. His analysis and conclusions on the rise and fall of civilizations have faced much criticism and have fallen out of fashion. But the study remains about the most comprehensive and cogent compilation of data on the civilizations, particularly their comparative periods and inter-linkages.

The beginning of civilizations in the world is dated to 3300 BCE, with the Sumero-Akkadian or Mesopotamian civilization, closely followed by that of the Egyptian in 3100 BCE. Toynbee identified three other independent civilizations—the Aegean Greek, beginning in 2900 BCE, the Indus in 2600 BCE and the Sinic in 1200 BCE. These dates have since been refined by a century or two, although the evidence on the Aegean is thin and uncertain. All other and subsequent civilizations in Eurasia are considered either 'affiliated', such as the Indic to the Indus, the Hellenic to the Aegean, the Syriac to the Mesopotamian, Egyptian and Aegean. Or 'satellite' civilizations, for instance Persian to the Mesopotamian and Syriac, and the Korean and Japanese to the Sinic.

Our dating the beginning of Indian civilization to the mid-eighth millennium or around 7500 BCE is a huge leap of over four millennia, in terms of the longevity and antiquity of world civilizations. This could appear inconceivable, but the evidence is incontrovertible and robust, and the conclusion is beyond any doubt or confusion. There is a continuous chain of evidence, and from more than one discipline and multiple sources, which are not only independent but also mutually consistent. The astronomy, the calendars and the Yuga system, and the texts and genealogies, make for an entirely separate set of sources and disciplines. Their data, in its origin, nature, presentation and preservation, is different and diverse. In addition, the hard or material evidence from archaeology, for instance the Hakra Wares culture from Bhirrana in the Indus-Saraswati region, is dated up to the eighth millennium or 7500 BCE.

A civilization is a techno-economic and a socio-cultural entity. It displays substantive development along each of the four dimensions, which are closely inter-linked and mutually supportive, to give the civilization a distinctive identity, cohesion and thus solidity and longevity. All of these had emerged in the Indian civilization by the mid-eighth millennium BCE, give or take a couple of centuries. This beginning is also consistent, from the longer time and wider spaces. The hunter-gatherers had come to dominate the bulk of Eurasia by 25,000 BCE, and were living all over the biggest landmass on earth. Its cooling thereafter, to the 'Last Glacial Maximum' in 20,000 BCE, and a round of heating-cooling and then heating of 'Younger Dryas' till 9000 BCE, brought an end to Ice Ages and the earth's temperature rose to the present levels and marked the advent of Holocene.

The Lucky Latitudes saw the earliest year-round occupation of sites and settling by hunter-gatherers, in which India offered the largest space. The Hilly Flanks in West Asia, which also saw an early settling soon after the Holocene, was at a comparative disadvantage for evolving into a civilization. It was hilly and the settlements were mostly unconnected nooks, whereas India offered flat, open lands served by monsoonal rains and perennial snow-fed river valleys. The Hakra Wares culture and the Lahurdeva–Bhirrana–Mehrgarh nodes, each a thousand kilometres apart, and dated to the mid-eighth millennium BCE, imply a wide civilizational spread. India had the technological, economic, social and cultural building blocks of a civilization in place by 7500 BCE and that led to rapid development thereupon.

The evolution of a politico-administrative state, generally taken as the most advanced and final piece in the emergence of a civilization, is dated to the early seventh millennium BCE, with the Iksvaku dynasty. It meant establishment of the institution of a king or monarchy in a state, and importantly, with a formal constitution—in the form of the *Manusmriti*, which outlined the role and responsibilities of a ruler, the checks and balances, and the laws and mechanisms of their enforcement. The text, moreover, extended into the stratification and organization of society into a cohesive whole and defined the skills and contribution of every member and their living routine from a day to various phases of life. This was a two-way institutionalization of the king and his state, to and from the society.

The *Manusmriti* was a toolkit for the spread and continuance of a state as well. The varna-jaati system of stratification defined and facilitated the transition of pre-existing social groupings and the development of the required skills and attitudes towards an ever-better economy and society. An institutionalized state provided the needed political order. The *Manusmriti* was followed by more Smriti and related texts, which elaborated on the state and society, and they became the code of Indian civilization. The Iksvaku dynasty, within a few generations, but certainly by the mid-seventh millennium BCE, came to be looked upon as the ideal and emulated by social groups spread over the geography of India. The dynasty was the rule-provider, and over generations, would have become the guide for kings and social conduct and got recognized as the thought-leader and pre-eminent king or emperor throughout Indian civilization.

The resulting King-Emperor framework remains unique to India. It provided cohesion and a distinctive identity to the civilization, and continued as the model of Indian statehood and polity till the early second millennium CE. This was for over eight millennia. The socio-cultural and the thematic and philosophical components continue and are alive in present-day India too, making it a ten-millennia-long civilization. To start with, the King-Emperor framework was only conceptual and principle-based, from, let's say, the early-seventh millennium to the weakening of the Iksvaku dynasty in the mid-fifth millennium BCE. It was strong though and could be coercive if and when needed, not only for the kings but every member of Indian society.

The Iksvaku dynasty lasted for two and a half millennia and eighty-five generations, making it the longest-ruling lineage in the world till date and by a long distance. The Kuru dynasty replaced the Iksvakus in pre-eminence and as 'emperor' around 4200 BCE. The standing of the Kurus too was almost entirely civilizational, as we saw during the Mahabharata war. The power of the King-Emperor framework, however, was underlined by the participation of 66 kings with their full might in the war in 3138 BCE, from the length and breadth of the Indian geography and civilization.

Indirect or direct rule over territory, from large spaces to the entire Indian subcontinent, came still later, with the rise to pre-eminence of the Magadha dynasties from around 2000 BCE.

Such territorial rule was made feasible, or at the least facilitated, by the technologies for faster movement, with the coming of horses and chariots. Alexander's campaign to India, which ended in 325 BCE, was indeed a watershed in the deployment of technology for fast movement, in order to attack, occupy and rule far-off territories.

Our rediscovery of ancient India's chronology would imply an overhaul of the timelines of civilizations in the world. Toynbee's chart prepared a few decades ago still prevails broadly and the correction will be by a stupefying four millennia. The update will be chart-busting, in a way, with the Indian and world civilization beginning from 7500 BCE. His distinction between 'Indus' and 'Indic' is incorrect too, and needs to be merged and replaced by the 'Indian' civilization—looming overwhelmingly large for nearly ten millennia to the present and dwarfing every other world civilization in terms of its antiquity and longevity. An early overhaul and correction of civilizational timelines will be apt.

A similar correction is needed in the timelines and understanding of the formation of state in the world. Political scientists such as Francis Fukuyama[2] date the first such state to around 770 BCE with the Eastern Zhou dynasty in China. This is exceptionally wrong too, as the Iksvaku dynasty, with its conception and institutionalization of the ruler 'king' and of the constitution, the *Manusmriti* and other texts, happened in India by the mid-seventh millennium BCE. A degree of coherence, however, is in the duration of the run-up from the coming of civilization to the establishment of its final piece, the state. It was 500 years in the case of China from 1200 BCE, and under 1,000 years for the Indian civilization from 7500 BCE.

The recalibration of civilization and the state by around four millennia into antiquity, and to India, would open a thoroughly new perspective on human evolution in the world. A variety of interesting and fundamental questions would open up, not only in the disciplines of political science and history, but also in sociology, anthropology, economics, management and so forth. We shall be able to make major corrections in our understanding, which will certainly give a fillip to the social sciences and scholarship in the world. An area of direct relevance is the inter-linkage among civilizations on the flow of people, ideas and developments, over millennia and centuries.

Indian civilization, besides being the earliest by far, was also huge in its expanse and presumably population too. Settlements in the Hilly Flanks were sort of contemporaneous with those in India, but took much longer and finally fructified into the Mesopotamian civilization in the Tigris-Euphrates deltaic region. There could conceivably have been some interactions and outflows from India at that antiquity itself, given the proximity and contiguity and the much advanced socio-economic development in the similar Indus-Saraswati region. This would have continued, particularly due to the practice of excommunicating groups and kings who used to fall foul of the dharma or lose battles in India, and westward migration was often the most viable option.

A lot of such migration was precipitated by the Mahabharata war of 3138 BCE, especially among the kingdoms in the Indus-Saraswati region who had mostly sided with the losing Kauravas. India would have certainly contributed a great deal to the rise of Persian, Hellenic and Chinese civilizations in the late second millennium BCE. That would have continued with the Roman, Christian and Islamic ones, which came later, and their inter-linkages in evolution within. The re-conception and exploration of the civilizational linkages and their evolution, in light of the rediscovered Indian chronology, will make for great scholarship, findings, and corrections too.

THE 'SCIENCE' OF HISTORY

History is indeed a hoary subject for study and writing, but it is relatively young as a social science discipline. The earliest compilations are travelogues and documentations—for instance, of Greeks who accompanied Alexander's campaign around 325 BCE or their later compatriots, and of Chinese monks during the first millennium of the Common Era. These are much referred to and relied upon, while being very error-prone and impressionistic and at best a slice of history, as we noted in previous chapters. In addition, there are hagiographies of rulers around the world, who had a lot of interest in over-projecting their success and virtues and were mostly written by their courtiers, and therefore lack in accuracy.

In India's case, there is in addition a huge corpus of ancient texts, which were largely religious but also covered various vocations such as medicine, astronomy, and Arthashastra, and the myriad literature of poetry, epics, drama and more. They also carried data on the events, socio-economic-cultural developments and genealogies. These were referred to by British officials and intellectuals from the late eighteenth century to make sense of the huge subcontinent at hand, and for suitably administrating and gaining the most out of it. The texts were complex and very different or alien and dumbfounding in their range and apparent antiquity, but the task of imposing order was urgent and a large pool of officials needed to be quickly trained and equipped.

British officials were indeed constrained in the language and understanding of the Indian context and were steeped in the agenda of colonization and subjugation, and the early ones in their Christian worldview too. Several first-cut, hurried and even fanciful conjectures were put forth and gained currency, as noted especially in the second chapter. All of this came together, though hastily and haughtily, in the 1920 construct of chronology and books of Vincent Smith. These became the 'authoritative history' of India, and were used for teaching, training and all official references and purposes throughout the empire.

The scientific method, which evolved in the natural sciences such as chemistry and biology from the seventeenth century, started being applied in the social sciences nearly a couple of centuries later. The earliest applications were in economics, for example by Adam Smith, and the discipline came to be aligned with the scientific method in the second half of the nineteenth century. Psychology, anthropology and sociology followed in a few decades. The discipline of archaeology is a combination of the natural and social sciences and began at the turn of the twentieth century, and provided the first set of outcomes of the scientific method in history and initiated its reorientation.

History and its chronological backbone, however, carried the legacies and excesses of the various imperial and colonial regimes. The bulk of it was regional or civilization-based, and was not global, and the respective local histories did not integrate into a consistent whole and there were wide-ranging and significant inconsistencies. A wrong turn certainly was the rise of communist or leftist ideology in the world and the creation of a few regimes in the early twentieth century. These regimes avowedly believed in rewriting the past and in aggressively using the doctrine-suffused narratives for advancing their cause. This was activism, and neither scholarship nor truthful application of the scientific method, and anything inconvenient was done away with or reinterpreted.

European colonizers wrote the history for the rest of the world, and imprinted it with their constraints and agendas, at the overall and region-civilization-specific levels. Most of the time, the colonizers believed and engaged in the 'civilizing mission' of Christianity and some of the writers of history were devout Christians. Though rarely stated overtly, the biblical '4004 BCE as the date of creation' did influence their thinking and work. Thus, there was a tendency to fit everything in other civilizations after the date of the 'biblical creation', force-fit some more, and ignore anything dated earlier or declare it as mythical. This is also evident in Toynbee's mapping of civilizations in the world from 3300 BCE. The Indian chronology and history, being the oldest, naturally suffered the most from colonial distortions.

Another remarkable deviation was to attribute most of the significant civilizational developments and inventions to the Greeks, to whom the European colonizers somehow found affiliation. The evidence on the origin and existence of Aegean Greek civilization from 2900 BCE is feeble and the Hellenic Greek is a later and short one, in effect post 800 BCE and till around 200 BCE. In any case, the Hellenic civilization was a derivative one and largely formed with the in-migration from others around the world. A bulk of the inventions, for instance, in mathematics, astronomy and philosophy was brought to Europe during the Renaissance in the fourteenth century. Bulk of whatever was European had been destroyed and emasculated during the preceding ten centuries of the Christian Dark Ages, and the source was mostly Islamic material,[3] which in turn could have originated in Persia and India. Much of this, though, was quickly attributed to the Greeks.

Getting back to Indian 'history' as a case, the findings from inscriptions and numismatics were carefully studied in the nineteenth century, and included the breakthrough of deciphering the Brahmi script. Towards the end of the century, archaeological excavation started, leading to the discovery in the 1920s of the Harappa and Mohenjo-Daro sites in the Indus-Saraswati region. These, going by the trend, were deemed exogenous to Indian civilization, and the 1920 chronology construct was retained as such, in the face of mounting evidence in subsequent decades. It remains largely so till date, and thus the scientific method has yet to find proper application in the writing of Indian history, particularly with respect to its backbone, the chronology.

After Independence in 1947 and for most of the time, India had a socialist dispensation, having its moorings towards leftist ideology. It imported their beliefs and approaches of aligning and using the historical narratives, for the cause and their form of 'nation building'. The dispassionate study of history through the scientific method remained a non-starter. The socialist-leftist orientation, which dominated the intellectual and academic superstructure, got to work on the narratives and had a field day. The chronology was not updated, despite the burgeoning archaeological and other data that we have deployed, and we are left with the unscientific and further distorted narrative part.

Indian history, therefore, needs to see the full and proper application of the scientific method. We have covered a significant part though, by addressing the chronological backbone of ancient India's history, which was the weakest link. For the later period, that is after 1192 CE, the correction will largely relate to the scientifically validated and dispassionate narratives and understanding, as the chronology part is broadly in place. These are still early days, as 'we know that we know' is only a small fraction of ancient India, over its vast geography and timelines. This knowledge and understanding will have to be properly aligned with the continuum of the later period. It will raise a variety of interesting and challenging questions and anomalies and will spur the requisite explorations, leading to great insights and superior reconstructions of India's past.

The rediscovery of the Indian chronology, and consequently the correct understanding of its history from the scientific method, would call for similar endeavours in the rest of the world. It would be particularly needed for non-European civilizations and nations. They will have also suffered from the colonial distortions, and most having come under the spell of leftist activism, an overlay of the latter too.

Since the 1990s, there have been attempts to research and write 'global-institutional' histories. This helps address the problem of individual civilizational and regional histories not being consistent, and not adding up to a whole. The study of a phenomenon, in its full institutional context and across the entire geographical expanse, generates less error-prone and more robust conclusions. They can be highly insightful and fully explanatory as a theory too, for example Acemoglu and Robinson in *Why Nations Fail*[4] and

Sven Beckert's *Empire of Cotton*.[5] In the rediscovery of the Indian chronology, we have deployed the best of the multidisciplinary scientific method, and related it to the evolving techno-economic and socio-cultural context of India and the timelines of other contemporary civilizations globally.

WAY FORWARD: THE 'THREE-PRONGED' STRATEGY

The rediscovery of the Indian chronology is indeed a large and complex research endeavour. It comprises a huge number of components or dates, with the dating of every individual event potentially a topic of intensive research. The strings of dates need to make for an internally and externally consistent continuum, arranged along the ordinal scale of years, decades, centuries and millennia, in order to be called a chronology. Dating of each individual event is based on several data points and sources, which need to be validated separately, and then linked to the data of all related events. The multitude and range of linkages among events and their dates make the research enormously complex too.

The sources of our data fall into the domains of natural as well as social sciences, and cover many disciplines. A chronology researcher needs to have the capability and comfort level in each of these scientific disciplines, and also the felicity to move across disciplines and draw balanced conclusions. Astronomy and astrophysics ground the data on the calendars and Yugas, physics on the isotope-based dating and technologies, economics and sociology on other archaeological finds, and language and content analysis on ancient texts and genealogies. Thus the multidisciplinary research method had to be mounted with the requisite rigour, as the events and dates are many millennia into the deep past and had rarely been explored scientifically.

Such a research, therefore, can only be the beginning of a long journey. Our conclusions on the Indian chronology and history thereupon mark a major shift in its time and space, and will lead to a reconstruction of the understanding. They extend the world civilization itself, by around four thousand years into the eighth millennium BCE, engendering major implications downstream and in a range of disciplines.

The conclusions are paradigm-shifting, as conceived by Thomas Kuhn in his 1962 classic *The Structure of Scientific Revolutions*.[6] They will call for an unpacking of a huge bulk of existing knowledge and understanding and then building an equally extensive knowledge base anew, not only at the scholarly level but also in all the relevant areas and up to the masses—where the outdated and falsified 1920 construct of Indian chronology had percolated. This will mean rewriting school and college textbooks, in line with the rediscovered chronology, and segregating the research findings, materials and books that are now rendered obsolete.

The journey ahead, thus, is complex and challenging. A new paradigm tends to face resistance initially, from the superstructure that had been created and from the myriad constituencies and stakeholders that have accumulated during the prevalence of the earlier paradigm. This resistance needs to be faced and overcome, and a constituency for the shift needs to be developed, activated and invigorated. Here, I draw upon my expertise and experience of handling strategic shifts in large corporations and government institutions to evolve a 'three-pronged' strategy as the way forward:

Scholarly thrust: While this book is a comprehensive, stand-alone and robust treatise on the chronology, it puts forth a whole lot of consequent anomalies and gaps. The historical narrative built around the 1920 construct needs to be unpacked, for what is falsified and what remains, and the suitable corrections thereupon in the specifics and themes. This will open up a variety of research questions and their explorations along one or more disciplines.

An all-round scholarly thrust, through a range of qualitative and quantitative methodologies and theoretical and empirical studies, will build the new knowledge base around the shift. Several research programmes within the history discipline and in related multi-disciplines can be designed and launched around the anomalies and gaps, which are apparent presently and will appear along the way. The rediscovered chronology will certainly spur research at the individual level, by way of the interesting questions it throws up, and will catalyze the establishment of large research programmes at the institutional level.

Mass re-learning: Indian history is a topic of much interest and debate among the educated and in most spheres of life. This is welcome, but when the discipline is suffused with a plethora of anomalies and gaps, the outcome is more confusion. It descends into partisanship, prejudices and polemics, and plays into the civilizational faultiness, often exacerbating them. This book is intended for the general audience, and brings about a sober, authoritative resolution to one of the most volatile and contentious parts as well as the backbone of Indian history and antiquity.

The book will engender unlearning, and knowing anew the corrected and updated chronology among the huge mass of the interested. As awareness of the right chronology spreads and the consequent scholarly work accumulates, the debates will cross a tipping point, towards being educative and a positive. These are always the objectives of scientific inquiry and scholarship, and Indian history should see the full force and light of it, soon.

Indian campaign: The construct-level shift in chronology and history clears the confusion and distortions of centuries, and provides the rightful moorings to Indian civilization and nationhood. It will certainly lead to a stronger sense of Indian identity and confidence by being rooted in the most ancient and pioneering civilization in the world. Thus, the Indian state should actively welcome and support the shift and adopt the rediscovered chronology as the official one.

The support could take the form of a well-orchestrated campaign, in India and overseas. Domestically, the state could undertake a prompt revision of history and other relevant textbooks, push through their adoption in school and college teaching, and support concomitant and wide-ranging research programmes. A redesign and revamp of archaeology, museums, archives and other related departments is needed too. Internationally, the campaign could initiate the realignment of world, regional and national chronologies and the history thereupon. The previously colonized and non-European countries will be fertile ground, and that will help bring around the rest too.

The three prongs of the way-forward strategy are mutually reinforcing, and suitably address the time and spaces. 'Mass re-learning' will be initiated with this book itself, and could soon reach most of those actively interested and engaged in the debates on Indian history. The awareness will expand to the next and further layers of the public, and will in turn catalyze early thinking and activities with respect to the 'scholarly thrust.' This will prepare the ground for the consideration of the 'Indian campaign' and discussion at the right levels, followed by a few significant steps forward, then on to the larger and concerted initiatives.

The output of the 'scholarly thrust' could start accumulating in a few months, in the form of articles and comments in mass publications, although the output from research studies and explorations will take longer. This will reinforce 'mass re-learning' and invigorate the 'Indian campaign.' The three-pronged flywheel will start spinning in progressively wider domestic and international spaces and in more impactful ways over the next months and years. The needle will thereby tip towards the rediscovered Indian chronology and history, in order to quickly take hold and institutionalize the shift.

EXHIBIT

INDIAN CHRONOLOGY
c. 9000 BCE—1192 CE

I. 'Early Settling' Period [*c.* 9000–6777 BCE]

c. 9000	End of last Ice Age or Holocene in India
c. 8500	Stabilization of the south-west monsoon and flow of Himalayan and other rivers in the Indian geography
c. 8500	Year-round occupation of sites in the Gangetic Plains—from evidence at Lahurdeva in eastern Uttar Pradesh of rice cultivation, animal domestication, handmade red-ware pottery—part of the 'Lucky Latitudes' and in parallel to the Hilly Flanks in West Asia
c. 8000–7500	Earliest settlements in the Indus-Saraswati region, with round-sunken dwellings at Bhirrana and wheat, barley cultivation and pit burials at Mehrgarh
c. 7500	Makings of a civilization, in an arc, around the known Lahurdeva, Bhirrana, Mehrgarh nodes, each nearly a thousand kilometres apart
	Hakra Wares culture
	Technologies to construct dwellings, manufacture pottery and jewellery, and process stones

	Travel, transportation and trade, to procure raw materials, for instance lapus lazuli from hundreds of kilometres away, and mechanisms for communication, exchange
	Emergence of a language
	Techno-economic and socio-cultural building blocks of a civilization in place
c. 7250	The need to accurately predict the onset of monsoons in India
	Linkage between the passing and recurrence of seasons and the movement of the sun and moon along constellations
	Techniques to take note of astronomical observations and make projections for the year
	Invention of numbers and mathematics, to prepare calendars
	Development of the Sanskrit language, albeit without a script, and the Shruti ecosystem, including the Gurukul learning tradition
c. 7250–7000	Compilation of the Rig-Veda in the still-evolving chhanda Sanskrit, in the Indus-Saraswati region
	Conception of the five-year Yuga, twenty-year Chatur Yuga cycles, and the techniques of recalibrating annual calendars
c. 7000	Conception of the state and organized society with the *Manusmriti*
	Manu, the first ruler, and the beginning of India's first dynasty, Iksvaku of Koshala, in present-day central Uttar Pradesh
	Emergence of the King-Emperor framework of Indian civilization, and the advent and availability of dynastic genealogies
	Initiation of the organization of society along the 'varna-jaati' system

c. 6800	Recalibration of the Indian calendars and Yugas to the Jovian cycle or that of Jupiter, proportionate to 12 earth-years Re-casting of the Yugas to 1,200-year cycles Invention of the zero, place value of numbers, and arithmetic
6777	Commencement of twenty-eighth Treta Yuga 27 Chatur Yugas and twenty-eighth Krita Yuga in the previous conception thus extend up to 7322 BCE

'Ramayana–Mahabharata' Period [6777–3102 BCE]

c. 6777–6000	Rapid civilizational advance in the Indus-Saraswati region, evidently, and plausibly in some other regions of India
c. 6700–6500	Significant advances in mathematics, from arithmetic to geometry and trigonometry, and its applications in economic measurements and transactions, religious practices, architecture and others
c. 6500	Fully evolved Sanskrit language, with grammar, etymology and phonetics, which meet the requirements of the Shruti-Gurukul system
6500–5500	Compilation of the Sam-Veda and Yajur-Veda, the Brahmanas and Aranyakas texts of the respective Vedas, mostly in the Indus-Saraswati region
c. 6250–5500	Compilation of Vedangas and other Smriti Dharma-shastra texts, in the Gangetic Plains Spread of the states, institutionalization of the king and dharma-based constitutional code, and the establishment of the varna-jaati socio-economic-political order, through India's geography, including coastal regions, with the efforts of Sage Agastya

	Sprouting of pilgrimage centres and the practice of Kumbh Mela every 12 years at four pivotal locations
c. 6000	Iksvaku, the pre-eminent and model dynasty and the ideal state, looked up to as the civilizational 'Emperor' by kings all over
6000–5250	Shift in the centre of gravity of Indian civilization, from the Indus-Saraswati region to the Gangetic Plains
5200–5000	Copper-bronze technology in a few kingdoms, and its usage for superior arrows, lending, for instance, Koshala and Lanka princes a key advantage
5114	Birth of Rama, sixty-fourth in the lineage of the Iksvaku dynasty
5075	Defeat of Lanka king Ravana, and crowning of Rama as ruler
5075–5025	Early indications of the direct and affiliate rule in the empire, with the brothers Bharata in Gandhara, Laxmana in Bengal and Shatrugana at Mathura, and the sons Lava in the northern part of Koshala and Kusha up to the Vindhyas
5250–4500	Archaeological evidence for the emerging large urban centres at Rakhigarhi, Mohenjo-Daro, Kalibangan, and ports at Lothal and Dholavira in the Indus-Saraswati region
c. 4750	Finds of large copper deposits at Khetri in northern Rajasthan and tin in Khyber-Pakhtunkhwa, propelling the rise of the Kurus in the Indus-Saraswati region
4400	Weakening of the Iksvaku dynasty, during the reign of the eighty-fifth ruler, Agnivarman
4200	Establishment of the Kurus as the pre-eminent dynasty or 'Emperor' in India, with their capital at Hastinapur

	Kurus, a 'Bronze Age' power, within 500 km of Rakhigarhi and Kunal, where copper smelters have been found, and Khetri mines
c. 4200	Transition to the twenty-eighth Dvapar Yuga, coinciding with the rise of the Kurus to preeminence, and setting the trend of major rulers and dynasties commemorating their ascension with the start of an era
c. 4500–3100	Archaeological evidence from over 2,000 sites in the Indus-Saraswati region—with a network of large-small urban and adjoining rural settlements, large dwellings and sophisticated public infrastructure and planning, and extensive domestic trade and international too, through ports—by far the largest, most advanced civilization of its time
	Indicative of the civilizational developments in the rest of the Indian landmass as well and to largely similar levels and kinds
c. 3180	Turbulence in the Kuru dynasty on the question of the ascension of the thirty-fourth ruler, when the elder brother is blind and the other infirm
c. 3155	The question comes to a head when the next generation comes of age, with the Dharma Shastras failing to provide a solution
3138	The Mahabharata war between the Kauravas and the Pandavas, and kings from all over the Indian civilization aligning with one or the other side and participating with full might
	The Pandavas emerge victorious and Yudhisthira is crowned the thirty-fifth ruler of the Kuru dynasty
	The *Bhagavad Gita*, the renowned text of philosophy, takes up fundamental questions in

	a dialogue between the ace warrior Arjuna and his guide and charioteer Krishna; the text is chronologically concomitant to the Upanishads—the third set of ancient Indian texts, after Shruti and Smriti
	Chariots and horses used in the Mahabharata war, then a rarity, and the horses were plausibly imported in small numbers from central Asia, for the use of lead warriors
3102	Death of Krishna, Yudhisthira relinquishes the throne and anoints Parikshita, Arjuna's grandson, as the next Kuru emperor

'Post-Mahabharata' Period [3102 BCE–325 CE]

c. 3102	Aftermath of the Mahabharata war reverberates through India's political-economy, as a huge number of kings and warriors were killed, causing upheaval in many states and forcing succession
	Krishna-Yudhisthira work towards smooth succession and healing social scars, particularly in the 26 states that supported the Pandavas
	Destabilization and social disenchantment much higher in the 36 states that aligned with the Kauravas, especially in the north-western region
	Beginning of the twenty-eighth Kali Yuga was proclaimed
	Duration of Kali Yuga is redefined to 432,000 years, a multiple of 360 days in Indian lunisolar calendar and 1,200 years in hundred Jovian cycles
	Perfection in the calendars and long-run timekeeping and the calibration techniques and procedures—in comparison, Europe achieves the latter with the proclamation of the Gregorian calendar in 1582 CE

c. 3000	Ved Vyasa, the compiler of the Mahabharata text, uses the term 'Bharat' or 'Bharatvarsh', ascribing it to the nineteenth ruler of the Kuru dynasty, who gained 'Emperor' status around half a millennium earlier; Valmiki's Ramayana had earlier described the geographical expanse of Indian civilization
c. 2900	The sixth post-Mahabharata or forty-first Kuru ruler, Nichaksu, loses in battle to the Salva tribe from the Trigarta kingdom to the west, and Hastinapur is flooded, forcing the shift of the capital to Kausambi near Prayagraj
c. 2700	Kingdoms in the Indus-Saraswati region and further north-west near the peak of socio-economic development, including trade
	Stabilization of the Mesopotamian civilization to the west
2800–2200	Period of disaggregation in Indian civilization, with weakening Kurus among a couple of dozen major kingdoms, ranging up to Pandya in the extreme south
	Panchala, located east of the Kurus, gains a march over others
c. 2500	Saraswati ceases to be a snow-fed river, becoming non-perennial and monsoonal
c. 2300	Rise of the Brihadritha dynasty of Magadha to pre-eminence
	Invention of iron furnace and processing technology, leading to wide-ranging usage in the last quarter of the third millennium
	Magadha an 'Iron Age' power
2132	Ripunjaya of the Brihadritha dynasty of Magadha is killed by his minister, who starts the Pradyota dynasty

1994 Fifth ruler of the Pradyota dynasty, which had brought Avanti in Central India under the direct rule of Magadha, is defeated by the king of Kashi, Sisunaga, who makes Girivraja its capital

c. 1900 Most of the Indus-Saraswati sites abandoned, consequent to gradual drying up of the Saraswati and the weakening of its core, setting in out-migration, the bulk of it towards the east and flourishing Magadha and some to the west

1814 Ajatshatru becomes the sixth ruler of the Sisunaga dynasty; his father Vidhisara or 'Bimbisara' had annexed the Anga kingdom to Magadha and was a contemporary of Gautama Buddha

1807 Buddha's nirvana

1748 The eighth ruler, Udayana, not Ajatshatru, builds the city of Patliputra on the southern banks of the Ganges

1634 Mahapadma, an illegitimate son of the tenth Sisunaga ruler Mahanandin, ascends the Magadha throne and starts the Nanda dynasty

1534 Chandragupta, an illegitimate son of Mahapadma, deposes the inheritor with the guidance of Chanakya, and starts the Maurya dynasty

1472–1436 Ashoka's reign at Magadha

Adapts the writing technology, with possible inputs from the out-migrants of the Indus-Saraswati region who were aware of writing due to the trade with Mesopotamia, to commission edicts on rocks and stone pillars—while the Shruti system remains mainstream and no such writing is found for over a millennium

1218 Pushyamitra Shunga, the general and minister of the Mauryas, deposes the dynasty, triggered largely due to the neglect by later rulers of the

	north-west region that had turned restive; quickly brings the empire under control and performs the Ashwamedha sacrifice—the first ruler of India to do so after Yudhisthira
c. 1200–600	Rise of three civilizations to India's west—Persian, Syrian and Greek
	Population explosion in Greece, which gets organized into sovereign city states, engaging in intense rivalry and wars, which spurs rapid techno-social-philosophical advance
1108	Vasumitra, grandson of Pushyamitra, defeats a 'Yavana' alliance of five kingdoms—the term used for renegade kingdoms and communities mostly west of the Indus—and drives them further away
918–327	Kanwa replaces Shunga dynasty at Magadha, and its four rulers reign for eighty-five years
	Replaced by the Andhra-Satvahana dynasty
	Then after 506 years by Chandragupta, founder of the Gupta dynasty
340–327	Philip from Macedon in northern Greece organizes city-states into a confederation
	Philip's son, Alexander, marches on an eastwards campaign and defeats the Persian Achaemenian empire, to reach India's periphery
327–325	Alexander takes control of Gandhara, a Persian vassal kingdom
	Overcomes resistance from the border tribes and engages in battles with the Pushkalavati or Peshawar chief and the Asmaka kingdom
	Faces Porus, a regional king on the banks of River Jhelum, sends emissaries towards end of the day and the battle ends
	Alexander's troops revolt and refuse to march further

He travels south along the Indus, and then back west through the desert

'Gupta–Rajput' Period [325 BCE–1192 CE]

320 Samudragupta ascends to the Magadha throne, deposing his father

Immediately launches an all-round campaign, defeating:

Nine kings in North and Central India

Eleven kings in the south

Kamrupa or Assam in the east

Yavanas, Shatrapas and Shahis in the north-west

Establishes direct rule from the Himalayas to the Narmada and Bengal to the Indus, vassal-type alliances with frontier states of Assam, Rajasthan and the south, and diplomatic relations with states north-west and up to River Oxus

c. 313–269 Samudragupta performs Aswamedha sacrifice to proclaim his authority all over the Indian landmass

Unification of the polity leads to economic progress and flourishing of art and culture

After fifty-one years of reign, Samudragupta ensures orderly succession by Chandragupta II

323–c. 250 Alexander suddenly dies in Persia, without naming a successor

Empire is carved up into four kingdoms, with his senior general Seleucus Nikator getting the largest and eastern chunk up to the Indus

Seleucus reaches a friendly understanding with the Magadha emperor, ceding control of Baluchistan and Afghanistan in exchange for 500 elephants

c.250–c. 175 Greek overlords in Parthia, Bactria and west of the Indus become independent, and several such principalities known as Indo-Greeks emerge along India's periphery

Indo-Greeks make inroads east of the Indus too, as Methradates of Parthian principality annexes Punjab and the Kabul-based Menandar reaches up to Awadh and faces the Magadha army

c. 225–c. 175 Scythian nomadic tribes from central Asia, also known as Sakas or Huns, start making raids deep into Indian territory

Kumaragupta, third ruler of the Gupta dynasty, launches a counter-expedition to Balkh, and the reign of the fourth ruler Skandgupta coincides with severe Scythian raids

Scythians overwhelm most of the Indo-Greek principalities in the north-west and establish a base west of Kandahar

175-c. 25 Yuezhis, another set of nomads from western China, start migrating west and south, on losing battle to a confederation of eastern tribes

Intermingling with other Scythian tribes, Yuezhis join forces, and the raids into India become bigger and deeper

Chief of a Yuezhi tribe Kushanas, Kujula Kadphises, brings various tribes together and conquers the rest of the Indo-Greeks, and comes to control the bulk of north-west India

166–c. 82 Death of Skandagupta, when the Magadha empire had considerably weakened

The next two rulers fail to stem the slide of the Guptas, with Scythians running riot all over its territory

82 End of the Gupta dynasty, when the last ruler, Kumaragupta II, loses to a contemporary king and dies in the same year

	Consecration of four lineages—Paramaras, Pratiharas, Chalukyas and Chahmanas—as Agni-Vansha Rajputs and inheritors of India's emperor status, in a ceremony at Mount Abu
	Coronation of Vikramaditya of the Paramara dynasty with its capital at Ujjain
82–c. 57	Vikramaditya launches a campaign to tame and drive away Scythians, and largely succeeds
	Restoration of tranquillity and Vikramaditya concentrates on establishing his sovereignty over kings throughout the Indian geography
	Adorns his court with 'Nava-Ratnas', including Kalidasa
57	Vikramaditya's empire from 'Sindhu to Rameshwaram setu and Badrinath to Bengal' is proclaimed, and a new Vikrama-Era or saka is started
c. 19	After Vikramaditya's demise, the next two rulers have short, ineffective reigns, and Scythians raids restart
CE	
78–138	Salivahana, Vikramaditya's great-grandson, on being crowned, launches a massive, definitive counter-charge
	Defines east of Paramaras Indus as 'Sindhu-sthana' and to the west 'Maleecha-sthana', bars Scythians from crossing the river and makes preventive arrangements
	Proclaims a new era or 'saka' from the year of his coronation
127–150	Kanishka follows Kujula and Vima Kadphises as chief of Kushanas, establishes his capital at Purushpura or Peshawar, with satrapies at Mathura and Gujarat

	Extends the empire up to the Gangetic Plains and Sindh and also Bactria, eastern Persia and Xinjiang region in China
150–600	Kanishka's successors, Huvishka and Vasudeva, start losing territories to the north, west and east, reduced to ruling parts of Punjab with their capital at Takshshila, and get assimilated as one of the many kings in the Indian milieu
	No external threat and the Indian landmass has dozen or so major kingdoms and many smaller affiliates
600–c. 1150	Harsha, with his capital at Kannauj, rises to prominence and controls vast swathes of area around, but on his death without a successor, the large kingdom is split into Gurjar-Pratihara in the west, Pala in the east, and Rashtrakutas in Central India
	Bhoja of Paramara lineage, with his capital at Dhar, asserts himself and extends his domain
	Chalukyas establish a large kingdom, with their capital at Badami in Karnataka, and rule a bulk of the Deccan, and later, the eastern branch rules coastal Andhra Pradesh and the western branch resurrects at Kalyana in Karnataka
	Chahmanas, the fourth Agni-Vansha lineage, spread into a couple of dozen states in Rajasthan and the rest of north India
	Rajpuṭ dynasties, including Agni-Vanshas, rule in all Indian kingdoms barring an exception or so
c. 622–711	Mohammad, a trader at Mecca, while meditating in a cave, receives revelations, then moves to Medina and starts preaching
	Brings Arab nomadic tribes in the peninsula to his view, gets them to sign a 'Constitution of

	Medina' as a single political-religious entity of the Muslims
	Muslim tribes raid and overrun kingdoms from Persia to north-west Africa and Iberian peninsula at spectacular speed
	An Arab general, Mohammad bin Qasim, after the conquest of Persia, crosses the Makaran desert to attack Sind in India, and establishes a kingdom
977–997	Sabuktigin becomes chief of Ghazni in south-west Afghanistan, as governor under the Persian Samanids
	Overruns other small, unruly and impoverished principalities, and decides on raids into Punjab to support his domain
	After the first raid, King Jaipal retaliates with an attack on Ghazni, but is not able to uproot Sabuktigin
997–1030	Mahmud, the elder son, on Sabuktigin's death, becomes chief after some struggle and a march on to Ghazni
	Quickly gets down to the business of raids and plans one every year, also relying on the precept of 'Holy War' against idolaters
	Conducts seventeen raids, and the loot makes for the 'Golden Period' of Ghaznavids, while not making a dent in Indian wealth
	Sobering effect on Rajput princes, but no loss of any states and rule, and much disdain among the masses on destruction of temples
1173	Ghiyasuddin, hailing from Ghor and a vassal of the Ghaznavids, destroys Ghazni and slays heir to become the chief
	Rules with his younger brother Muhammad

1178–1191	Muhammad decides to expand, not raid, into India and with planned attacks
	Acquires Multan, part of Sind and deposes the prince of Ghaznavid outpost at Lahore, to create a substantial domain
	Attacks Gujarat but is badly defeated
	Faces Prithviraj Chauhan, supported by a confederacy of Rajputs, in a major battle and is routed and injured
1192	Returns better prepared a year later, and turns victorious

NOTES

Chapter 1: Introduction

1 Toynbee, Arnold, *A Study of History*, Oxford University Press, Oxford, 1972.

2 Smith, Vincent A., *History of India: From Sixth Century B.C. to Mohammedan Conquest*, Grolier Society, London, 1906; Smith, Vincent A., *The Oxford School History of India,* Clarendon Press, Oxford, 1915.

3 Duff, Mabel C., *The Chronology of Indian History: From the Earliest Times to the Beginning of the Sixteenth Century,* Archibald Constable & Co., London, 1899, pp. 1–4.

4 Thapar, Romila, *Early India: From the Origins to AD 1300*, Penguin Books, London, 2021, pp. xiii–xv.

5 Morris, Ian, *War! What Is It Good For: Conflict and the Progress of Civilization from Primates to Robots,* Profile Books, London, 2014, pp. 70–72.

6 Thapar, Romila, *Early India: From the Origins to AD 1300*, Penguin Books, London, 2021.

7 Smith, Vincent A., *History of India: From Sixth Century B.C. to Mohammedan Conquest*, Grolier Society, London, 1906.

8 Cunningham, Alexander, *Book of Indian Eras, with Tables for Calculating Dates,* Thacker Spink, Calcutta, 1883.

9 Müller, Max, *A History of Sanskrit Literature: So Far As It Illustrates the Primitive Religion of the Brahmans,* Williams & Norgate, London, 1860.

10 Müller, Max, *A History of Sanskrit Literature: So Far As It Illustrates the Primitive Religion of the Brahmans,* Williams & Norgate, London, 1860, pp. 275–280;

Müller, Max, 'The Date of Chhandas Period', *A History of Sanskrit Literature: So Far As It Illustrates the Primitive Religion of the Brahmans,* Williams & Norgate, London, 1860, pp. 570–572; Jones, William, *The Collected Works of Sir William Jones, Volume 1-6,* Anna Marie Jones (ed.), London, 1799.

11 Müller, Max, *India: What It Can Teach Us?*, Funk & Wagnalls, New York, 1883.

12 Smith, Vincent A., *History of India: From Sixth Century B.C. to Mohammedan Conquest*, Grolier Society, London, 1906, pp. 1–5, 9.

13 Duff, Mabel C., *The Chronology of Indian History: From the Earliest Times to the Beginning of the Sixteenth Century*, Archibald Constable & Co., London, 1899.

14 Venkatachala, Kota, *Chronology of Ancient Hindu History Vol. 1 and 2*, Bharat Charitra Bhaskara, Vijayawada, 1957.

15 Karki, Rajnish, *Competing with the Best: Strategic Management of Indian Companies in a Globalizing Arena*, Penguin India, New Delhi, 2008.

16 Karki, Rajnish, 'Re-Discovering Indian Chronology', *Karki Associates*, February 2022, https://tinyurl.com/5n94pdyk. Accessed on 13 February 2024.

17 The description is distilled from the information available and easily accessible on Wikipedia: 'Lahuradewa', *Wikipedia*, https://tinyurl.com/bddpuyzt. Accessed on 13 February 2024; 'Mehrgarh', *Wikipedia*, https://tinyurl.com/bd6ss8bx. Accessed on 13 February 2024.

Chapter 2: Ways and Means of Indian Chronology

1 That is William Jones, born 1746 CE, died 1794 CE. The description is distilled from the information available and easily accessible on Britannica and *Wikipedia*: 'Sir William Jones', *Britannica*, https://tinyurl.com/bdzmb8t9. Accessed on 13 February 2024; 'William Jones (philologist)', Wikipedia, https://tinyurl.com/36t6jn47. Accessed on 13 February 2024.

2 Jones, William, *Discourses Delivered before the Asiatic Society: And Miscellaneous Papers, on the Religion, Poetry, Literature, Etc., of the Nations of India*, C.S. Arnold, London, 1824, p. 28.

3 Jones, William, 'The Tenth Anniversary Discourse', *Asiatick Researches or Transactions of the Society Instituted in Bengal*, Vol. 4, 1793, pp. xii–xiv.

4 Venkatachala, Kota, *Chronology of Ancient Hindu History Vol. 1 and 2*, Bharat Charitra Bhaskara, Vijayawada, 1957, pp. 56–57.

5 The description is distilled from the information available and easily accessible on Britannica and Wikipedia: 'Sir Alexander Cunningham', *Britannica*, https://tinyurl.com/yc5b9eeb. Accessed on 13 February 2024; 'Alexander Cunningham', *Wikipedia*, https://tinyurl.com/3zwuzzrz. Accessed on 13 February 2024.

6 Cunningham, Alexander, *Book of Indian Eras, with Tables for Calculating*

Dates, Thacker Spink, Calcutta, 1883, pp. v–vi.

7 Warren, John, *Kala Sankalita: A Collection of Memoirs on the Various Modes According to which the Nations of the Southern Parts of India Divide Time*, College Press, Madras, 1825.

8 Princep, James, *Useful Tables: Forming an Appendix to the Journal of Asiatic Society–Coins, Weights and Measures of British India – Part I*, Baptist Mission Press, Calcutta, 1834.

9 Cunningham, Alexander, *Book of Indian Eras, with Tables for Calculating Dates*, Thacker Spink, Calcutta, 1883, pp. vii–viii.

10 Ghosh, Amitabha, *Descriptive Archaeoastronomy and Ancient Indian Chronology*, Springer, Singapore, 2020, pp. 57–60.

11 Cunningham, Alexander, *Book of Indian Eras, with Tables for Calculating Dates*, Thacker Spink, Calcutta, 1883, pp. 110–115.

12 Ibid., pp. 53–54.

13 Ibid., pp. 4–5.

14 Ibid., pp. 11–15.

15 The description is distilled from the information available and easily accessible on Britannica and Wikipedia: 'Max Muller', *Britannica*, https://tinyurl.com/yvk3es8r. Accessed on 13 February 2024; 'Max Müller', *Wikipedia*, https://tinyurl.com/y6yyavs5. Accessed on 13 February 2024.

16 Müller, Max, *Sacred Books of the East: Set in 50 Volumes*, Motilal Banarsidass, Delhi, 1923.

17 Müller, Max, 'Origin and Progress of Sanskrit Philology', *A History of Sanskrit Literature: So Far As It Illustrates the Primitive Religion of the Brahmans*, Williams & Norgate, London, 1860, pp. 1–7.

18 Müller, Max, 'The Date of Chhandas Period', *A History of Sanskrit Literature: So Far As It Illustrates the Primitive Religion of the Brahmans*, Williams & Norgate, London, 1860, pp. 570–572.

19 The description is distilled from the information available and easily accessible on Dictionary of Irish Biography and Wikipedia: Murphy, David, 'Smith, Vincent Arthur', *Dictionary of Irish Biography*, https://tinyurl.com/4ztfwew4. Accessed on 13 February 2024; 'Vincent Arthur Smith', Wikipedia, https://tinyurl.com/5n7mcjaj. Accessed on 13 February 2024.

20 Smith, Vincent A., *History of India: From Sixth Century B.C. to Mohammedan Conquest*, Grolier Society, London, 1906, p. 4.

21 Ibid., pp. 19–20.

22 Ibid., 11.

23 Fleet, John F., *Inscription of Early Gupta Kings and their Successors,* Vol. III, Corpus Inscriptionum Indicarum, Calcutta, 1889.

24 Smith, Vincent A., *History of India: From Sixth Century B.C. to Mohammedan Conquest,* Grolier Society, London, 1906, pp. 42–74.

25 Smith, Vincent A., *The Oxford School History of India*, Clarendon Press, Oxford, 1915.

26 Singh, Upinder, *A History of Ancient and Early Medieval India: From the Stone Age to the 12th Century*, Pearson Education, Delhi, 2021.

27 Thapar, Romila, *Early India: From the Origins to AD 1300*, Penguin Books, London, 2021, pp. xiii–xiv.

28 Singh, Upinder, *A History of Ancient and Early Medieval India: From the Stone Age to the 12th Century*, Pearson Education, Delhi, 2021, pp. vii–ix.

29 Ibid., pp. 102–115.

30 Thapar, Romila, *Early India: From the Origins to AD 1300*, Penguin Books, London, 2021, p. 157.

31 Singh, Upinder, *A History of Ancient and Early Medieval India: From the Stone Age to the 12th Century*, Pearson Education, Delhi, 2021, p. 274.

Chapter 3: Findings—Advances: Archaeology, Astronomy and More

1 All the data has been validated, but what is easily and widely available on a web search is not referenced. Ascertaining some information by searching for relevant keywords and exploring further, albeit critically, for example on Britannica and Wikipedia, can be beneficially deployed with easy internet connectivity available everywhere these days, while writing and reading a book such as this in the current times.

2 Vronsky, I.M., 'History of Gold', *Gold Eagle*, 1 January 1997, https://tinyurl.com/5c8hh8vh. Accessed on 13 February 2024.

3 The description is distilled from the information available and easily accessible on Britannica and Wikipedia: 'Indus Civilization', *Britannica*, https://tinyurl.com/4wty52me. Accessed on 13 February 2024; 'Indus Valley Civilisation', *Wikipedia*, https://tinyurl.com/2p84zpn4. Accessed on 13 February 2024.

4 Siyajkak, 'The "Ten Indus Scripts" Discovered Near the Northern Gateway of the Dholavira Citadel', *Wikimedia Commons*, 2007, https://tinyurl.com/3zfwcbaz. Accessed on 13 February 2024.

5 Müller, Max, *India: What It Can Teach Us?*, Funk & Wagnalls, New York, 1883, p. 227.

6 Chatterjee, A., et al., 'On the Existence of a Perennial River in the Harappan Heartland', *Scientific Reports*, Vol. 9, No. 17221, 2019.

7 'About Scientific Reports', *Nature*, https://tinyurl.com/mrye4nme. Accessed on 13 February 2024.

8 Chatterjee, A., et al., 'On the Existence of a Perennial River in the Harappan Heartland', *Scientific Reports*, Vol. 9, No. 17221, 2019, p. 1.

9 The full explanation will take us long and well into advanced astrophysics, and those interested can refer to the extensive material available on web search. For those with a grounding in astrophysics and mathematics: Ghosh, Amitabha, *Descriptive Archaeoastronomy and Ancient Indian Chronology*, Springer, Singapore, 2020, pp. 61–71.

10 Reich, D., et al., 'Reconstructing Indian Population History', *Nature*, Vol. 461, No. 7263, 2009, pp. 489–494.

11 Shinde, V., et al., 'An Ancient Harappan Genome Lacks Ancestry from Steppe Pastoralists or Iranian Farmers', *Cell*, Vol. 179, 2019, pp. 729–735.

Chapter 4: Findings—Advances: Genealogies and Yugas

1 Arya, Vedveer, *The Chronology of India: From Manu to Mahabharata, From Mahabharata to Medieval Era, Volume I and II*, Aryabhata Publications, Hyderabad, 2019.

2 Bala, Saroj, Ramayana *Retold with Scientific Evidences,* Prabhat Prakashan, New Delhi, 2019. It is about the latest of several publications focused on dating the Ramayana and is based on the dialogue among their authors and cross-verification of findings.

3 The genealogy of the Iksvaku dynasty, easily available on web search and now suitably corroborated and validated, is: 1. Manu 2. Iksvaku 3. Vikuksi-Sasada 4. Kakutstha 5. Anenas 6. Prithu 7. Vistarasva 8. Ardra 9. Yuvanasva 10. Sravasta 11. Brihadasva 12. Kuvalasva 13. Drdhasva 14. Pramoda 15. Haryasva 16. Nikumba 17. Samhatasva 18. Akrsasva 19. Prasenajit 20. Yuvanasva 21. Mandhata 22. Purukutsa 23. Trasadsyu 24. Sambhuta 25. Anaranya 26. Trasadsva 27. Haryasva II 28. Vasumata 29. Tridhanvan 30. Trayyaruna 31. Trishanku 32. Satyavrata 33. Hariscandra 34. Rohita 35. Harita, Cancu 36. Vijaya 37. Ruruka 38. Vrka 39. Bahu (Asita) 40. Sagara 41. Asamanjas 42. Amsumant 43. Dilipa I 44. Bhagiratha 45. Sruta 46. Nabhaga 47. Amabarisa 48. Sindhudvipa 49. Ayutayus 50. Rtuparna 51. Sarvakama 52. Sudasa 53. Mitrasaha 54. Asmaka 55. Mulaka 56. Sataratha 57. Aidavida 58. Visvasaha I 59. Dilipa II 60. Dirghabahu 61. Raghu 62. Aja

63. Dasaratha 64. Rama 65. Kusa 66. Atithi 67. Nisadha 68. Nala 69. Nabhas 70. Pundarika 71. Ksemadhanvan 72. Devanika 73. Ahinagu 74. Paripatra 75. Bala 76. Uktha 77. Vajranabha 78. Sankhan 79. Vyusitasva 80. Visvasaha II 81. Hiranyabha 82. Pusya 83. Dhruvasandhi 84. Sudarsana 85. Agnivarna 86. Sighra 87. Maru 88. Prasusruta 89. Susandhi 90. Amarsa 91. Mahashwat 92. Visrutavant 93. Brihadbala 94. Brihatksaya.

4 Arya, Vedveer, *The Chronology of India: From Manu to Mahabharata, From Mahabharata to Medieval Era, Volume I and II*, Aryabhata Publications, Hyderabad, 2019, pp. 347–349.

5 Prabhakar, C.L., 'Veda in Ramayana', *Wisdom Library*, October–December 1975, https://tinyurl.com/mu7syppx. Accessed on 13 February 2024.

6 Arya, Vedveer, *The Chronology of India: From Manu to Mahabharata, From Mahabharata to Medieval Era, Volume I and II*, Aryabhata Publications, Hyderabad, 2019, pp. 381–383. He puts together the genealogy of the Kuru dynasty after ascertaining various sources, as: 1. Puru 2. Janamejaya 3. Prachinvan 4. Samyati 5. Ahamyati 6. Sarvabhauma 7. Jayatsena 8. Arachina 9. Mahabhauma 10. Ayutanayi 11. Akrodhana 12. Devatithi 13. Richah 14. Riksha 15. Matinara 16. Tansu 17. Ilina 18. Duhsanta 19. Bharata 20. Bhumanyu 21. Suhotra 22. Hasti II 23. Vikunthina 24. Ajamidha II 25. Samvarana IV 26. Kuru III 27. Viduratha 28. Arugvan 29. Parikshit 30. Bhimasena 31. Paryashravas 32. Shantanu 33. Vichitravirya 34. Dhritarashtra 35. Yudhisthira.

7 Pargiter, Frederick E., *The Purana Text of the Dynasties of Kali Age*, Oxford University Press, London, 1913; and the long riposte to his readings and assertions by: Arya, Vedveer, *The Chronology of India: From Manu to Mahabharata*, Aryabhata Publications, Hyderabad, 2019, pp. 440–450.

8 Venkatachela, Kota, *Chronology of Ancient Hindu History Vol. 1 and 2*, Bharat Charitra Bhaskara, Vijaywada, 1957.

9 Arya, Vedveer, *The Chronology of India: From Manu to Mahabharata, From Mahabharata to Medieval Era, Volume I and II*, Aryabhata Publications, Hyderabad, 2019, pp. 685–687.

Chapter 5: The Rediscovered Construct

1 Smith, Vincent A., *The Oxford School History of India*, Clarendon Press, Oxford, 1915, p. 88.

2 Ibid.

3 Fleet, John F., 'Mandsaur stone inscription of Yashodharman-

Vishnuvardhana', *Corpus Inscriptionum Indicarum: Inscriptions of the Early Guptas*, Vol. III, 1886, pp. 150–155.

4 Arya, Vedveer, 'The Epoch of Gupta Era (334 BCE) and Valabhi Era (319 CE)', *The Chronology of India: From Manu to Mahabharata, From Mahabharata to Medieval Era, Volume I and II*, Aryabhata Publications, Hyderabad, 2019, pp. 105–115.

5 Venkatachala, Kota, *Chronology of Ancient Hindu History Vol. 1 and 2*, Bharat Charitra Bhaskara, Vijayawada, 1957, pp. 87–99.

6 Ibid., pp. 19–22; pp. 38–43.

7 Pargiter, Frederick E., *The Purana Text of the Dynasties of Kali Age*, Oxford University Press, London, 1913.

Chapter 6: 'Early Settling' Period: c. 9000–6777 BCE

1 Morris, Ian, *Why the West Rules for Now: The Patterns of History and What They Reveal About the Future Profile Books*, London, 2010, pp. 67–73.

2 Diamond, Jared, *Guns, Germs & Steel: A Short History of Everybody for the Last 13,000 years*, Vintage Books, London, 1997, pp. 42–44.

3 Morris, Ian, *Why the West Rules for Now: The Patterns of History and What They Reveal About the Future Profile Books*, London, 2010, pp. 75–77; pp. 81–91.

Chapter 7: 'Ramayana–Mahabharata' period: 6777–3102 BCE

1 Huntington, Samuel P., *The Clash of Civilizations and the Remaking of World Order,* Simon & Schuster, New York, 1996.

2 Toynbee, Arnold, *A Study of History*, Oxford University Press, Oxford, 1972, pp. 73–85.

3 Morris, Ian, *Why the West Rules for Now: The Patterns of History and What They Reveal About the Future Profile Books*, London, 2010, pp. 175–181.

4 Fukuyama, Francis, *The Origins of Political Order: From Pre-Human Times to the French Revolution*, Profile Books, London, 2011.

5 Centre of Excellence for Indian Knowledge Systems, *IKS Calendar of 2024*, Indian Institute of Technology Kharagpur, Kharagpur, 2023, p. 12.

6 Bengrut, Dheeraj, 'New evidence suggests Harappan civilization is 7,000 to 8,000 years old', *Hindustan Times*, 22 December 2023, https://tinyurl.com/2wbb8vvx. Accessed on 13 February 2024.

Chapter 8: 'Post-Mahabharata' Period: 3102–325 BCE

1 Morris, Ian, *War! What Is It Good For: Conflict and the Progress of Civilization from Primates to Robots*, Profile Books, London, 2014.

2 Bala, Saroj, 'Abstract of Mahabharata Retold with Stellarium Views', *Archive*, 2019, https://tinyurl.com/yeyjf42x. Accessed on 13 February 2024.

3 'Where Did "Bharat" Come From? Tracing Origin of Bharatvarsh & Story of King Bharat | Explained', *News 18*, 6 September 2023, https://tinyurl.com/zzffyzru. Accessed on 13 February 2024.

4 Venkatachelum, Kota, *Age of the* Mahabharata *War*, ADRIPS, Vijayawada, 1991, pp. 47–51.

5 Singh, Upinder, *A History of Ancient and Early Medieval India: From the Stone Age to the 12th Century*, Pearson Education, Delhi, 2021, pp. 260–265.

6 Srinivasan, S., and S. Ranganathan, 'Wootz Steel: An Advanced Material of the Ancient World', *University of Illinois Urbana-Champaign*, https://tinyurl.com/26cwxep6. Accessed on 13 February 2024.

7 Much of this description and the data sources therein is based on: Venkatachala, Kota, *Chronology of Ancient Hindu History Vol. 1 and 2*, Bharat Charitra Bhaskara, Vijayawada, 1957, pp. 20–120.

8 Buddha's nirvana is dated to 1807 BCE and the eighth year of Ajatshatru's reign, and such a difference in the count of years in the chronology occurs due to the month or date of respective events, being early or late in the year.

9 Pargiter, Frederick E., *The Purana Text of the Dynasties of Kali Age*, Oxford University Press, London, 1913, pp. 20–22.

10 Toynbee, Arnold, *A Study of History*, Oxford University Press, Oxford, 1972, p. 72; pp. 530–538.

11 Porter, Michael E., *The Competitive Advantage of Nations*, Free Press, New York, 1990.

Chapter 9: 'Gupta–Rajput' Period: 325 BCE–1192 CE

1 Based, assessed and distilled, among others, from: Venkatachala, Kota, *Chronology of Ancient Hindu History Vol. 1 and 2*, Bharat Charitra Bhaskara, 'Vijayawada', 1957, pp. 212–228. See also: Arya, Vedveer, *The Chronology of India: From Manu to Mahabharata, From Mahabharata to Medieval Era, Volume I and II*, Aryabhata Publications, Hyderabad, 2019, pp. 238–246.

2 Smith, Vincent A., *History of India: From Sixth Century B.C. to Mohammedan Conquest*, Grolier Society, London, 1906, pp. 251–260.

3 Smith, Vincent A., *The Oxford School History of India*, Clarendon Press, Oxford, 1915, pp. 72–73.

4 Venkatachala, Kota, *Chronology of Ancient Hindu History Vol. 1 and 2*, Bharat Charitra Bhaskara, Vijayawada, 1957, p. 223.

5 Venkatachela, Kota, 'The Historicity of Vikramaditya and Salivahana',

Archive, 1951, https://tinyurl.com/3d4hx6as. Accessed on 13 February 2024.

6 Toynbee, Arnold, *A Study of History*, Oxford University Press, Oxford, 1972, pp. 537–38.

7 Smith, Vincent A., *The Oxford School History of India*, Clarendon Press, Oxford, 1915, p. 90.

Chapter 10: The Big Picture

1 Toynbee, Arnold, 'Civilizations of the World, 3100 BC to AD 2000', *A Study of History*, Oxford University Press, Oxford, 1972, p. 72.

2 Fukuyama, Francis, *The Origins of Political Order: From Pre-Human Times to the French Revolution*, Profile Books, London, 2011, pp. 110–16.

3 Strathern, Paul, *The Medici: Power, Money, and Ambition in the Italian Renaissance*, Picador Books, New York, 2016, pp. 81–89.

4 Acemoglu, Daren, and James A. Robinson, *Why Nations Fail: The Origins of Power, Prosperity, and Poverty*, Profile Books, London, 2012.

5 Beckert, Sven, *Empire of Cotton: A History of Cotton*, Penguin, London, 2015.

6 Kuhn, Thomas S., *The Structure of Scientific Revolutions*, University of Chicago Press, Chicago, 1962.

INDEX